China's Developmental Experience

China's Developmental Experience

Proceedings of
The Academy of
Political Science

Volume 31
Number 1

March 1973

Edited by Michel Oksenberg

The Academy of Political Science
Columbia University
New York

Copyright © 1973 by The Academy of Political Science
All rights reserved

Library of Congress Catalog Card Number: 72-97447

Cover design by Kenneth Sofer

Printed by Capital City Press, Montpelier, Vermont

Contents

Contributors

ALBERT FEUERWERKER, professor of history at the University of Michigan, is the author of *China's Early Industrialization: Sheng Hsuan-huai, 1844-1916, and Mandarin Enterprise*, and he edited *History in Communist China*. He has written numerous articles on historiography in contemporary China and on Chinese economic history.

VICTOR LI teaches law at Stanford University and taught previously at the University of Michigan and Columbia University. He is the author of a forthcoming study of the public security system in a Chinese county and the editor of a volume on Chinese foreign trade.

DONALD J. MUNRO, a philosopher, is an associate at the Center for Chinese Studies at the University of Michigan. The author of *The Concept of Man in Early China*, he is now writing an accompanying volume, *The Concept of Man in Contemporary China*.

MICHEL OKSENBERG, associate of the East Asian Institute, teaches Chinese politics at Columbia University. He has written on the policy-making process, local government, and elites in the People's Republic.

C.H.G. OLDHAM is deputy director of the Science Policy Research Unit at the University of Sussex in England. He is also associate director for science and technology policy of the International Development Research Center in Ottawa.

DWIGHT H. PERKINS, professor of economics, is also associate at the East Asian Research Center at Harvard University. He is the author of *Agricultural Development in China, 1368-1968, Market Control and Planning in Communist China*, and other works.

RICHARD M. PFEFFER, associate professor of political science at Johns Hopkins University, is the editor of *No More Vietnams?* He has written a forthcoming book on *Understanding Business Contracts in China and America.*

BENJAMIN SCHWARTZ is professor of history and government as well as a member of the executive committee of the East Asian Research Institute at Harvard University. He is the author of *Chinese Communism and the Rise of Mao, In Search of Wealth and Power: Yen Fu and the West*, and *Ideology in Flux.*

HENRY G. SCHWARZ, director of the Program in East Asian Studies at Western Washington State College, specializes in Chinese minorities policies. He is the author of several monographs and articles in learned journals on this topic as well as on contemporary Chinese politics.

VICTOR W. SIDEL, chief of the Department of Social Medicine at Montefiore Hospital and Medical Center, Bronx, New York, is also a professor in the Department of Community Health at the Albert Einstein College of Medicine and chairman of the department on its Montefiore campus. A recent visitor to China, he has written and lectured widely on the current health-care system in China.

JON SIGURDSON is a visiting research fellow at the Science Policy Research Unit, University of Sussex, in England. He was cultural attaché at the Swedish embassy in Peking from 1964 to 1967 and is now with the Swedish Ministry of Industry but on leave of absence with a grant from the Bank of Sweden Tercentiary Fund to study the internal transfer of technology in China.

TANG TSOU is professor of political science at the University of Chicago. He is the author of *America's Failure in China: 1941-50*, the coeditor of *China in Crisis*, and the writer of numerous articles on Chinese politics.

FREDERIC WAKEMAN, JR., professor of history at the University of California at Berkeley, is the author of *Strangers at the Gate: Social Disorder in China*. The editor of the works of the late Joseph Levenson, he is engaged in a study of Mao Tsetung, as well as in research on Ming-Ch'ing history.

J.B.R. WHITNEY is associate professor of geography at the University of Toronto. He is the author of *China: Area, Administration, and Nation-Building* and articles on environmental management in China.

MARTIN KING WHYTE is assistant professor of sociology at the University of Michigan. He is the author of "Red and Expert in China: The Cultural Revolution and Beyond" in *Problems of Communism* and of a forthcoming book on small groups in China.

Preface

This book is a unique contribution to American-Chinese understanding. Unlike other publications, it does not focus on Chinese foreign policy or the impact that an emerging China might have on international relations. Rather, it explores the lessons, both positive and negative, that may be learned from China's developmental experience which might have a bearing on Western societies and on other developing nations. The papers were discussed at a series of meetings sponsored by the Academy of Political Science and the National Committee on United States-China Relations at the Center for Continuing Education at Columbia University from October 26 to October 28, 1972. Wm. Theodore de Bary, Amitai W. Etzioni, Demetrios Caraley, Harvey Picker, and James W. Morley presided at these meetings. A number of others—Barbara Tuchman, William V. Farr, B. Preston Schoyer, Benedict Stavis, and Richard Sorich—made distinctive contributions to the conference proceedings and to the production of this volume. The project was supported in part by grants from the Henry Luce Foundation and the Rockefeller Brothers Fund.

The Academy's publications present information that may be useful in forming public policy, but they do not make recommendations regarding political issues. The contributors' views are their own and do not necessarily reflect those of organizations with which they are affiliated.

The Academy wishes to express its appreciation to Professor Michel Oksenberg of the East Asian Institute, Columbia University, for directing the conference and editing this book. The cooperation of the National Committee in using its good offices to enlist the authors and of the Center for Continuing Education in making its facilities available for the conference are also gratefully acknowledged.

ROBERT H. CONNERY
President of the Academy

On Learning from China

MICHEL OKSENBERG

At present, Americans are searching for innovative solutions to a dreary list of domestic problems: racism, bureaucratism,
urban decay, pollution of the environment, depletion of natural resources, inflation and unemployment, inadequate medical care for the
poor, the increasing use of narcotics, and the accompanying rise in
crime. These problems are interrelated, and none is the root problem
from which the others stem. Failure to grapple comprehensively with
all jeopardizes any gains that temporarily can be made. For example, urban renewal and government reforms will not solve the problems of the ghetto without increased employment opportunities for
blacks and reduction of the narcotics supply.

Although sometimes social ills have been cured without the reformers' understanding the true source of the disease, these particular
problems seem unlikely to be alleviated without accurate analysis
of their causes. Are these interrelated problems essentially the inevitable imperfections of a generally healthy system? Or, are they
manifestations of a system in serious trouble? That is, are these ills
the real disease, or are they the symptoms of a deeper disease? Will
marginal reforms provide a cure? Or do we require another period of
sweeping but essentially conservative reform, similar to the earlier
reform eras in the United States, such as the Progressivist era and the
New Deal? Or, is America doomed to decay until radical, even revolutionary, change fundamentally alters the institutions and values?

Facing such fundamental issues, Americans seem increasingly

willing to borrow ideas and solutions from abroad. Gone is the self-confidence of the preceding era, when the national myth was not only that the United States could handle any internal difficulty but that Americans had the insight to solve the problems of others as well. The nation, now awakening, has made discoveries: England has cleaned the Thames and eliminated the suffocating London fog; Japan is building the finest mass transit in the world; life expectancy is higher and infant mortality rates are lower in Western Europe; and peoples in many lands appear more relaxed, secure, and foresighted.

Of all the nations from which we might borrow, one is particularly intriguing—China. After all, that nation faced a seemingly insurmountable set of problems twenty-three years ago: civil war, hyperinflation, foreign domination, periodic famine, illiteracy, and superstition. Within a generation, most of these obstacles to development have been removed. The nation appears to have regenerated itself and to be making economic and social progress. Moreover, the Chinese have undertaken bold experiments in a number of areas that are of direct concern to us, such as bureaucratic practice, education, the patterns of urbanization, penology, public health, factory management, and civil-military relations.

With that in mind, a distinguished group of scholars interested in contemporary China recently met to evaluate the Chinese experience in national development, primarily in terms of its usefulness to the United States but also to other developed and developing countries. The results of the conference are assembled in this volume.

Differences in the Evaluations

Partly because the authors examine different spheres of Chinese achievements, their conclusions diverge. In the realm of science and economic development, the article on agricultural performance by Dwight H. Perkins portrays the enormous differences between the American and Chinese rural scenes. He demonstrates that the United States has little to learn in this area, but suggests that perhaps developing areas—such as India—might profit from the impressive Chinese experience. C. H. G. Oldham reaches similar conclusions in his survey of science and technology in the People's Republic: innovative, appropriate for other developing countries, but of lesser applicability to the technologically advanced world. On the other hand, J. B. R. Whitney's analysis of environmental control and Victor Sidel's description of public health conclude that the United States could profitably adopt Chinese attitudes and perhaps specific practices.

In the political and social realms, while pessimistic about America's willingness to borrow, Richard M. Pfeffer believes the Chinese have begun to find answers applicable to a problem that he feels plagues the United States: the unbridled expansion of unresponsive bureaucracy. Pfeffer does not believe the phenomenon is technologically determined. On the other hand, Martin Whyte argues that in China as elsewhere the structure and role of the family are affected greatly by the level of urbanization, technology, and economic development. As a result, Whyte suggests, in the realm of the family the Chinese are roughly following patterns which evolved in the West at an earlier stage. Both the Donald J. Munro analysis of Chinese educational philosophy and the Victor H. Li study of Chinese views on penology discover virtues neglected by the American policies in the same realms. Henry G. Schwarz, however, concludes that Peking's approach to national minorities opens no new vistas in considering our own minority problems.

Even empirical differences exist among the authors. Jon Sigurdson's capable summary of the decision-making pattern in the economy, for example, appears to leave less room for democratic participation by the masses than Richard M. Pfeffer suggests. At a more abstract level, in response to specific assignments, Albert Feuerwerker stresses the nationalistic dimension of the Chinese Revolution—the search for wealth and power—while Tang Tsou focuses upon the visionary dimension—the quest for a new moral order.

That the authors are not unanimous in their conclusions is not surprising. The judgments are colored by values and assumptions of the scholars concerning not only China but the United States. In many ways, as Frederic Wakeman stresses, China is in the eyes of the beholder. The vast, varied land enables the explorer to discover almost any form he wishes. The visitor finds and perhaps is guided to the China he hopes to discover. Moreover, to ask "What can we learn from China?" involves beliefs not only about what China offers but what America needs. Here, our authors reflect a wide spectrum, from radical to conservative. To a large extent, in fact, their distinctive tones arise not from their assessment of China but from their different feelings of urgency about America's problems.

There are other reasons for the differences. For one thing, as Benjamin Schwartz underlines, policies in China have evolved over time, varying enormously since 1949. In this preeminently innovative society, the Chinese have long abandoned or modified many interesting experiments. An irony exists: admirers may seize upon innovations which the Chinese have long since discarded. For example, the Chinese currently appear to be revising several Cultural Revolution innovations that many Westerners found so appealing. For example, Richard M. Pfeffer fastens upon the revolutionary committees and the May 7 cadre schools as innovative means for controlling bureaucratic imperiousness; but to judge from the official press, the Chinese themselves appear to be losing interest in these devices. Evaluating China's developmental experience for *our* purposes, in other words, is not the same as evaluating it for *their* purposes. What they reject may still have validity, although the failure of their social experiments (such as efforts to abolish private profit incentives) should at least serve as a warning to those who advocate similar measures elsewhere.

Moreover, some authors focus upon what the Chinese hope their experience will be, others stress what the Chinese think it has been, and yet others report the empirical evidence. What is China's developmental experience? Is it the hard reality—what actually has been achieved—or is it the direction of change and the aspirations? Should the stated theory and ideals, the unstated code that governs behavior, or the actual accomplishments command our attention? These are crucial questions, for although the achievements are impressive, the goals and processes pose some of the most fundamental challenges to American assumptions about man—for example, Mao's attempt to minimize social stratification in the course of industrialization and his search for nonbureaucratic methods of administration. The facet which one emphasizes, in a sense, helps determine the evaluation.

A complicating factor is that the Chinese themselves do not agree on these matters, as the intense political strife of the past six years demonstrates. Some Chinese leaders clearly think their achievements have been steady and substantial; others argue that, while Liu Shao-ch'i was in the top administration (1959-66), the record was highly unsatisfactory; others disown most policies pursued while Lin Piao had major responsibility for setting the nation's course (1966-71). Many previous interpreters of Mao's theories, most significantly Ch'en Po-ta, are now called swindlers who distorted Mao's true principles for careerist purposes.

Given the nature of the available evidence—the lack of firm statistics, the limitations of a short visit, the complexity of the subject, and the lack of clear guidance from the Chinese—research on China rarely overturns the hypotheses which guided the inquiry. Rather, it tends to refine and confirm the prior hunches. In sum, the differences among the authors reflect both the substantive differences among their specific topics and their divergent values.

Nonetheless, almost all the authors agree that in one way or another China's developmental experience offers valuable lessons. This in itself is noteworthy. The two world wars and the end of the missionary era signaled the end of the West's claim to ideological superiority. Perhaps Vietnam marks the end of any Western nation's claim to political superiority. (To be sure, Japan's defeat of Russia in 1895 and its showing in World War II are important here.)

This volume suggests that the economically developed world is now beginning to surrender its claim of a monopoly upon social and economic wisdom. Such a conclusion has both foreign-policy consequences and implications for the likely flow of ideas among nations in the years ahead. But before turning to the more specific essays, however, it pays to ask exactly why the change has occurred and why China specifically has emerged as the country which attracts such attention. Further, it seems appropriate for this essay to provide an overall assessment of the conference topic. This requires both a summary of China's developmental theory and of America's underlying conditions. For there to be any potentiality of transfer, this essay must identify some commonality in the situations of the two countries. To anticipate the conclusion, the situations are so different that only the spirit of the Chinese Revolution, in the broadest sense, seems applicable. Beyond this, the problems of transferring specific Chinese programs, admirably suited to a different context, seem vast.

Challenge of a Revolutionary Society

China appears as an influence and a source of ideas in the world today primarily because a revolution has occurred in that land. Let us recall that man's intellectual history from 1776 to 1949 can only be understood against the backdrop of six great revolutions: the American, the French, the European revolutions of 1848, the Paris Commune, the Russian, and the Nazi revolutions. Not all of these revolutions succeeded. But each was a bold attempt by revolutionaries to reshape the lives of their countrymen. The revolutionaries discovered new, dramatic ways to obtain political power, and they also raised profound questions about the nature and potentialities of man. As revolutionaries rather than reformers, they challenged the accepted order. That is why both the Meiji Restoration of Japan and Japan's postwar recovery, for all their success, have not had an intellectual impact upon the world. Japan's spectacular reforms posed no real threat to accepted values and institutions.

Moreover, subsequent revolution and reformist efforts have been affected by their forerunners, particularly their immediate predecessors. Can one understand the Bolshevik revolution without reference to the Paris Commune? Can one grasp Germany of the 1920s without considering the traumatic impact of events in Russia in 1917? Can one evaluate America's capacity to regenerate itself in the 1930s and 1940s without reference to the spur provided by developments in Russia and Germany? And consider the consequences of the October Revolution for China!

The learning process, then, is a complex one, and the lessons are not always positive. Both revolutionaries and antirevolutionaries study the failures as well as the successes of their predecessors in hopes of avoiding similar errors. Consider the Russian concern after 1917 to avoid Bonapartism, Mao's efforts to avoid Stalinism and de-Stalinization, and Regis de Bray's search for a route to power that would not yield centralized bureaucracy. Similarly, antirevolutionaries secure support by drawing dubious analogies with past appeasement of revolutionaries: Thiers's mobilization of France against the Paris Commune to avoid repetition of Jacobin Paris, 1793-95, and America's post-World War II vigilance against totalitarianism to avoid another Munich.

In a profound way, I suggest, ours has become, to a degree we do not yet understand, the post-Chinese revolutionary era. To be sure, with the worldwide diffusion of intellectual activity away from Europe and the United States, with the rapid global technological transformation, and with the tentativeness of the Chinese Revolution, it has not been as influential as the earlier revolutions. Nonetheless, the world is just beginning to come to grips with its significance. (One assumes here, of course, that the revolution and its institutions will survive the passing of Mao and that the validity of China's experience will not be brought into question after his death.) Our question, therefore, should be rephrased: What is the significance of the Chinese

Revolution? If the history of intellectual thought is any guide, this is the formulation which really shapes analysis about the lessons to be derived from China. The presence of *revolutionary change*, in short, conditions the approach and establishes the framework for thinking about what the Chinese experience offers.

The Chinese Revolution poses four basic challenges to widely accepted beliefs about the modern world. First, most Westerners accept society as necessarily imperfect; certain desirable values can be attained only at the price of other desirable goals. Second is the tendency to believe social change is best achieved through institutions, in a planned and gradual way. Third is the confidence that the modern state with all its power is the most effective means for furthering the interests of man; suitable means can be devised to minimize the harm which a state can do to its citizens. Finally, most Westerners believe that complex organizations and stratification inevitably accompany industrialization. Let us examine the Chinese disagreement with these views more fully.

Mao and his associates do not have a well-defined vision of the society they seek to build. Rather, theirs is a quest, a desire to reconcile the seemingly irreconcilables. In an oft-quoted 1957 statement, Mao succinctly summarized the quest: a society that is both democratic and centralized, both disciplined and free, both endowed with a general will and yet with each individual's heart at ease. Each of these seeming opposites has its definite intrinsic value. The predominant view in Western societies, of course, is that a society cannot be both democratic and highly centralized. Democracy entails the diffusion of power and authority; centralization, their concentration. In the West, the free, liberal society is generally considered the antithesis of the disciplined, highly ordered one. Discipline requires that individuals surrender the right of choice—the essence of freedom. To be sure, freedom requires structure and predictability, so that one's choices have predictable consequences. Freedom, in short, exists in a situation of structured choice; the wider the range of choice, the greater the freedom. Discipline involves placing restraints upon choice and creating a sense of obligation to choose a particular course; the greater the obligation for a particular choice, the more the discipline. Yet, Mao advocates both maximum freedom and maximum discipline—a seeming contradiction.

Mao believes in the dialectical process: what appears to be irreconcilable today may be reconcilable tomorrow. Given the current level of productivity and man's current level of consciousness, centralization and decentralization of freedom and discipline indeed seem contradictory objectives. But with further technological advance, greater abundance, and changes in man's consciousness, a synthesis can be achieved which man, in his currently more primitive state, can not envision. This demands both economic and ideological development. The task is to make sure man persists in his search for the higher stage of development. The Chinese Revolution makes a more optimistic statement about the potential of society than the predominant Western assessment: inevitable conflicts exist between various desirable social goals—such as between freedom and security—and each society simply must choose what mix it deems optimal.

The second challenge posed by the Chinese Revolution concerns the process of change. The basic Western assumption today is that meaningful progress can only be achieved in steady, measured, ordered ways. Great leaps and stops; the launching of such sweeping experimental programs as cultural revolutions before they have been tested in more limited ways; seeking noninstitutional means for achieving objectives; deliberate fostering of social tensions to arouse the populace; intensive attempts to change people's attitudes as an essential ingredient for securing maximum acceptance and commitment—these are not widely accepted as the most effective ways of securing change. Yet that is Mao's approach; although some of his colleagues disagree with the utility of all its aspects, the theory has yielded noticeable results.

Rather than using direct means to attain their goals, the Chinese leaders have adopted an indirect, deliberately zigzag course. They alternate between periods of mobilization, with an emphasis upon social change, unleashed advance, and conflict and periods of consolidation, with an emphasis upon developing institutions, planned advance, and reconciliation. This zigzag course is seen as the only way to maintain the quest for the irreconcilables, alternating the emphasis from freedom to discipline to freedom, democracy to centralization to democracy, struggle to unity to struggle. The development is a dialectical one, with the rulers confident that each stage represents a closer approximation of the ultimate synthesis they seek. Such a process of change obviously requires a high degree of consciousness among the leaders and of willingness to risk turmoil during the mobilization phase. It assumes that the process of social change can be the object of grand strategy. Those who adopt the American capitalist, the Western European socialist, and the Soviet socialist approaches, however, are less confident of this possibility. They believe the human limitations of leaders must be recognized; leaders simply cannot be intelligent or powerful enough to pursue a coordinated development strategy. Further, technological change is in essence unpredictable. So, at best, social change can only be a series of intelligent, politically coordinated, incremental responses to unforeseen circumstances.

Relatedly, the third challenge concerns the efficacy of the modern state. While recognizing the tactical superiority of the power of a modern state and hence the need to respect it, Mao and his associates apparently scorn the strategic advantages that most people today attribute to the modern state: its complex organizations, its well-defined modes of conflict resolution, and its extractive capabilities. They apparently believe that in any context, *over the long run*, the poor and disadvantaged can create or seize political power. Proper organization; effective, determined leadership; an intelligent strategy for forming alliances; and protracted struggle through the development of an independent military power—these are the essential and sufficient ingredients for a revolutionary group to seize power, providing it truly represents the interests of the majority of the populace. The Chinese Revolution has spurred thinking, in short, about the seizure of power. In this regard, its consequences are similar to those of earlier, successful revolutions. The unique contribution centers on Mao's emphasis on the potentialities of guerrilla warfare and on the capacity of a revolutionary group to sustain its cause among the populace, acquiring support if its cause is just. Oppressive governments, no matter what their military might, are vulnerable in the long run.

Many would argue, of course, that although in rhetoric the Chinese stress the vulnerability of the state, in fact they seek to build a modern state, with all its financial and military power. Although true, this is beside the point. Mao believes that if the Chinese people come to feel his regime is oppressive, it too will be vulnerable. As a source of doctrine for the seizure of power, then, the Chinese Revolution is an appealing reminder of the vulnerability of state power when that power is misused. It challenges the widely shared despair over the perceived worldwide trend toward statism.

The Chinese Communists argue that governments usually do become increasingly divorced from the concerns of their citizens. Ordinarily governments in *both* socialist and capitalist societies increasingly act on behalf of those who are part of the governmental structure and seek to suppress demands arising from elsewhere. Only the strongest measures can prevent the growing gap. Into this gap steps the guerrilla to organize the aroused populace against the bureaucracy. Here are the fundamental lessons which the Chinese, at least, believe this experience offers: to those with power, the strategy for maintaining a government responsive to the needs of the people; to those without power, the strategy for overthrowing an oppressive regime.

Finally, the Chinese Revolution challenges prevalent Western assumptions about the inevitable consequences of the industrialization process. To most observers, economic development requires increased specialization or an increased division of labor, urbanization, and the development of complex organizations to coordinate the productive process. Moreover, unequal distribution of rewards and the resulting social stratification are considered necessary mechanisms in society for recruiting and rewarding competent people for the performance of important tasks. Many of China's top leaders reject these beliefs. Under Mao's particular initiative, the Chinese have attempted to simplify organizations, to minimize stratification, to limit urbanization, and to avoid the parochial views that accompany specialization.

Chinese efforts, discussed in the essays below, have not been fully successful. Although the extremes of the very rich and the destitute no longer exist, the society remains highly stratified. For example, salaries in factories range from 18 yuan per month for factory apprentices to over 200 yuan for the leading technicians. Shoes vary in price from 3 to over 30 yuan, hats from 3 to over 300 yuan. There are considerable differences in income, in the styling and quality of clothing, and so on. Similarly, the extent of bureaucratic streamlining can be exaggerated. As to the struggle against bureaucracy, one need only see the vast number of clerks working in a Shanghai bank or explore the planning process to conclude that many complex organizations still survive. Concerning the division of labor, the highly skilled, highly paid jugglers, tumblers, and unicycle riders in the nation's several acrobatic troops (such as the Shenyang Troupe which toured the United States in 1972-73) dramatically reveal that certain kinds of specialization are highly esteemed. The overcrowded buses with commuters packed like sardines and the dark smoke spewing from hundreds of chimneys in the smog-filled cities testify that urban concentrations with their attendant transportation and pollution problems also exist in China. China is not yet an egalitarian, deurbanized, debureaucratized society, to say the least!

But the commitment to the goals is there. The aspirations as well as the reality and the progress to date as well as the distance yet to be covered merit attention. Indeed, the Chinese themselves recognized the obstacles and limited achievements to date. As a result of the commitment, however, China's pattern of industrialization is distinctive. The large coastal cities, such as Shanghai, have experienced basically a planned growth. Expansion of many urban services, such as public health or housing, has kept pace with industrial growth. Urban slums, which scar cities around the world, have been largely avoided in China. Urban population increases basically have been controlled, and a large influx of peasants into cities has been avoided. Indeed, the population in the urban core of Shanghai has been reduced. Privilege may remain, but those who are privileged feel under constant pressure to exhibit an egalitarian spirit and a willingness to serve their society unselfishly. High-status planners and engineers are encouraged to take the social consequences of their designs into account. While bureaucracy remains, repeated efforts have been made to reduce its size. The articles by Sigurdson, Sidel, Whitney, Pfeffer, and Munro all dwell on aspects of the total program. As all of the authors conclude, the Chinese experience challenges the assumption that America's current problems are, in part, the inevitable consequence of industrialization.

America and China Compared

The ideas that emerge from the Chinese Revolution, to repeat, challenge currently dominant beliefs in the West, particularly in the United States. But stimulating and provocative ideas are not necessarily applicable ones. They may simply jar us into thinking new thoughts. For the possibility of transfer, some similarity or comparability must exist, a theme eloquently developed in Frederic Wakeman's concluding essay.

At an earlier stage, until the development of Mao's ideology, Chinese intellectuals underestimated the difficulty of borrowing ideas from abroad. They paid insufficient attention to the search for indigenous ideas and domestic support for the doctrines they sought to import. Mao's particular genius was his understanding of his own society, not his knowledge of the ideas he borrowed and shaped for China's purpose.

A similar danger may now exist in the West. Indeed, many recent articles on China, if anything, have been overenthusiastic about the possibilities of borrowing. They suggest that we have much to learn, even specific lessons, if only we will, but they do not give thought to the problems of adaptation. (I hasten to add that most of the following essays, such as those by Munro, Li, and Sidel, explicitly recognize the difficulty.)

It pays, therefore, to recall the situation in which Chinese ideas and programs emerged and to draw a contrast with the United States. Since this topic is so complex, however, I wish merely to focus on a few limited, important, but often neglected differences between the two societies, while not repeating the many insights on the same subject in the articles by Tsou, Wakeman, Li, and Munro.

First, the Chinese Revolution is rooted in an assessment of the proper relationship between state and society *for the Chinese situation*. To oversimplify, from the erosion of Ch'ing state power in the mid-nineteenth century to 1949, Chinese society proved remarkably durable despite the political turmoil. The task was to create more effective political institutions and to use political power to transform the society. Indeed, the major obstacle to earlier reforms and revolutions was the resistance of the social order. In thinking of transforming his nation, Mao could take the underlying continuity of Chinese society for granted. In this regard, its long history under several regimes, its deeply rooted traditions, the common racial bonds of its Han people—all contrast sharply with the United States. In a fundamental sense, I suggest, American society is much more fragile. A nation of immigrants divided by both latent and manifest ethnic and value cleavages, the society is united less through a common past than through its present institutions and the sense of a common future. Further, China in 1949 was still basically a peasant society, while America as an industrialized society is more vulnerable to disruptions caused by a few. On the other hand, the immediate power of the American political system—its capacity to tax, its military might, and its penetration to the grass roots—is infinitely greater than that of pre-1949 China.

The implications of this difference for a strategy of change in America are profound. Mao's approach was first to create and seize political power; during this period, from 1935 to 1951, he deliberately minimized his challenge to the social order through his United Front alliance. After attaining political power he launched his major efforts to transform society. The Maoist strategy, then, at its most abstract level was to seize and strengthen the weaker of the political and social systems, and force the stronger system to change. The same underlying strategy in American society, that is, to confront the strongest institutions last, paradoxically entails working within the political system and creating new social institutions. The final challenge to the United States political system would come only after a new social order has been developed. The women's liberation movement pursues exactly such a strategy change today, as the labor movement did in the 1930s. Interestingly, the one area where the social system may be more resistant to change than United States political institutions (on matters dealing with race relations) is precisely where politically induced change is observable and where the guerrilla concept wins adherents (among urban blacks) as a method for attaining goals.

The strength of America's existing political system also means some of China's more specific solutions may be inappropriate to similar American problems. That is, without underestimating the power of the traditional Chinese state, it nonetheless did not possess the might of the Communist regime. The Communists have extended direct control of the state from the county into the rural village; they have increased manyfold the state's taxing power in terms of the percentage of the gross national product falling within the government domain. The greatly expanded Chinese state is the instrument through which the problems of 1949 have been solved. The prevention of urban ghettoes has been the result of the national government's control over population movement, for example. Full employment has been secured through a state-run unified system of assigning labor. Given the weakness of the state before 1949, the creation of powerful governmental institutions seemed like a reasonable solution at the time. But how about the United States? Given the current balance between state and society, would it be wise to search for solutions that demand an even stronger political system?

Another difference between China and the United States is the level of wealth and degree of equity already attained. The enormous wealth of the United States and its productive capacity enable it to contemplate solutions to its problems that the Chinese cannot yet consider. One major purpose of the Chinese Revolution is to build a prosperous and strong country. Economic development is a major aim of any program undertaken in China. Indeed, its importance in this volume is the major reason why the articles on economic develoment precede those on values. The quest for continued advance depends on both economic and political change. Neither leads the other; they are dialectically linked. Let there be no mistake: the Chinese see no intrinsic virtue in poverty. They hope their labors provide the foundations for a more prosperous, technologically advanced nation. Western students of China frequently neglect the utilitarianism of Chinese policies. In fact, the Chinese defend most of their policies not in terms of their intrinsic merit, but in terms of their suitability to their present economic and political conditions. It is a moot point whether at some future stage of development they will judge that large metropolitan areas or a high degree of specialization would be appropriate. Theory and practice must be joined in a specific context, they stress.

Further, it can well be argued that the abundance of America now extends to the majority of our populace. The struggle now is to include the remainder of the population. In China, however, due to the poverty and inequities of the past, the task is to extend benefits to 90 percent of the populace. The difference is significant. The Chinese can undertake solutions unthinkable in the United States. For example, rural communes today can purchase rather primitive dental chairs for $100 and crude dental drills for $100, and they can obtain a dental clinician with only one to two years training beyond high school. Dental care then becomes available to commune members at a level as good as or better than that available to perhaps 80 percent of the population. This is a step forward. But to use such inexpensive methods to extend dental care to black ghetto children would be considered an insult, and rightly so. The dental care made available to these children ought to be as good as that provided privileged, suburban white children. Inexpensive shortcuts will not be equitable. In short, providing equal opportunity to the minority of a population may prove to be as complicated as extending it to the majority.

Another crucial difference between the two is in the ideological or value realm. In his *Revolutionary Change*, Chalmers Johnson cogently notes that in a well-regulated society, the productive system and the accompanying division of labor must be synchronized with the society's value system. Put simply, the predominant beliefs must support and be supported by the existing economic system. Revolutionary situations develop, he argues, when the two no longer mesh. The traditional Chinese order came undone, it can be argued, primarily because the Western challenge eroded the traditional value system. The West undermined the value system of the traditional elite. To be sure, the economic system also changed from the 1840s to the 1940s, but to a lesser extent. With some noticeable geographic sectoral exceptions, the basic division of labor in society in 1949 was still similar to that of a century before. The first task of the Chinese Communist Party, achieved by the mid-1950s, was to reintegrate the society by providing an ideology still suited to the low level of economic development, but which effectively responded to the Western challenge. Then it turned its task to transforming the division of labor in society.

The source of America's lack of sychronization is different. Our economic system, technologies, means of production, and resulting division of labor have changed first. The crisis is not due in the first instance to the erosion of values but to the material changes. The search is for values suited to the new material conditions. The Chinese reconstruction of its value system was facilitated by the similarity of its means of production to the means of the traditional era and of other countries. The Chinese could adapt from their past and from abroad. But the American situation appears to be new: it is the first society seeking values commensurate with its increasingly automated productive process.

Finally, American and Chinese societies contrast in their relationship to the rest of the world. As Albert Feuerwerker stresses below, the Chinese Revolution was a response to the Western presence. The goals are national regeneration, termination of perceived humiliations, and a major role in world affairs. The search for dignity is an essential ingredient of almost all Chinese policies, whether domestic or foreign. The desire to preserve independence and national integrity also helps explain many Chinese actions. For example, the Maoist quest is not only intrinsically appealing to Chinese, but it is attractive precisely because it enables them to believe that they have a contribution to make to mankind. Mao's preservation of traditional medicine is an even better example of this spirit.

On the other hand, America's problems partly stem from excessive global power, interests, and involvement. Americans suffer not from feelings of humiliation but from hubris. Chinese policies can aim at strengthening the nation, knowing that the inequitable gap between the rich and poor lands would automatically be reduced. The American task is different, for, alas, there is little coincidence between increasing America's wealth and the just goals of reducing the gap between the rich and poor lands. In sum, efforts at domestic change must take into account America's involvement abroad, which often appears exploitative and frequently impedes domestic change. Moreover, Americans ought to consider whether *all* self-improvements which widen the gap between the United States and poorer lands are desirable. Perhaps the enlightened policy would be to terminate the exploitative involvements abroad, at a cost to Americans, in order to help create a more stable, just world order. Perhaps the American long-run self-interest dictates spending less on ourselves and being willing to pay more to foreign labor. These are obviously complex questions, and the answers are not clear. But the point here is that these considerations do not plague the Chinese.

Conclusion

The Chinese Revolution challenges widely held assumptions about the nature of the state and of society. China's considerable achievements during the past twenty-three years clearly merit close attention. But this does not mean that they offer immediate lessons to our condition. The differences between American and Chinese societies are too great to permit simple cultural transfers.

The advantage of studying the Chinese experience, it seems to me, rests in the contrast. The comparison calls accepted dogma into question and provides new insight into our situation.

Beyond this, the Chinese Revolution is an optimistic statement about the capacity of man to solve his problems. Perhaps, given the mood of pessimism in the United States, the nation needs such inspiration. The Chinese dedication to building a more decent, just society might also spur us. Beyond such broad generalities, the Chinese Revolution stresses that any program of change, to succeed, must grow out of the particular society's traditions and the well-understood needs of the majority of its people. If American intellectuals and students wish to draw a specific lesson from the Chinese experience, therefore, it is this: to be effective agents of change, they must better understand and work with the majority of their countrymen. They certainly cannot afford—as the Chinese Communists never felt they could—the luxury of being aliens in their own society.

China's Developmental Experience, 1949-72

BENJAMIN SCHWARTZ

The notion that the recent history of developing societies should always be analyzed in terms of "growth" or "development" is by now conventional wisdom. In the academic community, there is also the notion that economic development should be discussed by economists, while political scientists should confine their attention to "political development."

I find, however, that while the concept of economic development is relatively tangible and central to an understanding of the recent history of China, the various concepts of "political development" seem to be of limited use in understanding the political history of China since 1949. Does the term "political development" refer to a "rationalization" and bureaucratization of state (and military) structure in the Weberian sense? The state, Party, and army have in fact remained in an unsettled and critical condition for over ten years, and there has even been conscious resistance within China to certain Western definitions of "political growth." Does "political development" refer to the growing stability of political institutions? The cohesion of China over the past fifteen years or so has by no means been due to the established stability of its political institutions. Then does "political development" refer to "mass participation in the political process"? The notion of participation is in itself unclear and the question of whether there is more or less participation in 1972 than in 1962 remains a moot point. Politics in China, as elsewhere, is concerned with a variety of matters which may be unrelated or only tangentially related to development.

On the other hand, economic development has remained a central and sustained concern of the People's Republic—a concern which has certainly played a large role in all the shifting policies and crises of its history. This does not mean that events in China have simply been a function of economic-development strategy or that other considerations have not been as important. Indeed, during the Cultural Revolution other considerations for a time may have pushed the concern with economic development to the sidelines. Questions of economic strategy, even when they have been a central focus of attention, have always been deeply implicated with debate on a wide range of issues of general social policy. The concern with creating a wealthy and powerful China (a concern which inevitably relates to economic development), however, has never been absent even from Chairman Mao's most soaring visions.

In dealing with the general history of the People's Republic since 1949, it is convenient and sensible to emphasize the various periods stressed by the Chinese Communists themselves—the period of recovery, the First Five Year Plan (which might be called the period of maximum Sovietization), the period of the Hundred Flowers, etc. Yet in dealing with the evolution of economic strategy in the narrow sense, one might prefer another scheme of periodization in which the early 1960s mark a decisive turning point.

It has often been pointed out that the years immediately following the assumption of power (1949-53 circa) were years of economic rehabilitation. Yet the relative success of the measures adopted during these years—in the realm of monetary policy, taxation, restoration of communications, and even in the turbulent land-reform campaign—when considered together with the amazingly swift establishment of political control and relative order, may go far toward explaining the sense of legitimacy which the People's Republic has continued to enjoy through all the crises of its later history.

When the attention of the leadership did turn to the tasks of economic development, it soon became obvious that the Stalinist strategy of development would provide the basic model. There were, to be sure, debates about the tempo of implementation of this model, and Li Fu-ch'un's speech of 1953 makes it clear that there were those who opposed total implementation. Yet there is little evidence that any of the leading figures of the Party, such as Mao Tse-tung, Liu Shao-ch'i, Chou En-lai, and Teng Hsiao-p'ing, did not accept as a package the main features of the Soviet design for "building socialism."

The term "building socialism" suggests that one of the main features of what is here called the Stalinist development strategy was the nationalization of the means of production. There can be no doubt that Chairman Mao and other Party leaders were deeply committed to this aspect of the Soviet experience, although some had thought that the "new democracy" might last much longer. There is, of course, no necessary connection between socialization of the means of production and the specifics of the Stalinist economic strategy. The Stalinist model involves not only the collectivization of agriculture, but also the total subordination of the agricultural sector of the economy to the needs of rapid industrial development and the lopsided priority of heavy and capital-goods industry over light industry and consumer-goods industries. It is known from the industrialization debates during the 1920s in the Soviet Union that many Soviet economists had quite different visions of how socialism should be built. Yet there is little evidence that the top leadership of China, including Chairman Mao, was not prepared to accept all the major features of the Stalinist strategy.

Chairman Mao had displayed such a spirit of independence in stressing the peculiarities of the Chinese path of revolution before 1949 that one might ask why he was so receptive to the Soviet path of economic development. Some have suggested that this was the price to be paid for the policy of "leaning to one side" and relying exclusively on Soviet aid. It seems, however, that Mao's ready acceptance of the Soviet design for building socialism was based on a genuine conviction that the Soviet experience did indeed provide the universal model. Mao was, after all, acutely conscious of the difference between the revolutionary strategy required for attaining power and building socialism. Precisely during the Yenan period when he asserted the unique features of the Chinese Communist movement, he also read much Soviet literature on Soviet development. He may have rejected Stalin's authority as a political and military strategist for the Chinese Revolution, yet the rejection went hand in hand with an enormous respect for Stalin as a "builder of socialism." During the early 1950s a campaign was launched to expose all cadres to an intensive study of Stalin's *Short Course* as a kind of catechism of economic development. In the early years of the regime, Mao humbly acknowledged that China had everything to learn in the realm of building socialism from the superior experience of the Soviet Union.

In his *Ideology and Organization in Communist China*, Franz

Schurmann has stressed the degree of tension between the Chinese Communist Yenan "style of work" and the style associated with the Soviet model, particularly in such realms as industrial management.[1] These tensions may have indeed arisen, but they were only to become evident in the course of practice. There is no reason to think that they were anticipated. On the other hand, there were elements of the Maoist Yenan outlook which accorded quite well with the Stalinist strategy. A forced draft industrialization imposed on society by the Party was in keeping with Mao's deep faith in politically induced social change. To the extent that the motive behind the Stalinist model was to achieve quickly the bases of superior military power, this was certainly in keeping with Mao's own nationalist preoccupations. One difference from the Soviet model which is significant is that unlike Stalin, who was prepared to allow agricultural production to stagnate, the Chinese were aware throughout that agricultural production must be increased. In a well-known speech of July 31, 1955, urging the speedup of collectivization, Mao said that precisely because of the particularities of the Chinese Revolution it would be possible to carry out a Stalinist strategy of economic development without the baneful consequences suffered in the Soviet Union.[2] He thought that the Chinese Communist Party had established particularly close relations with the peasants and would be successful in inducing them to accept socialism, particularly since the vast majority of these peasants were poor. Mao was undoubtedly aware that, while collectivization in the Soviet Union had led to firm state control of the channels of grain procurement, it had not led to an increase in production. Yet his own speech expresses an ebullient faith that in China collectivization would lead to a rapid rise in production sufficient to meet not only the subsistence needs of China's vast population but also the demands of the state "which grow year by year." His presuppositions heightened his confidence in China's ability to appropriate the Soviet model.

To be sure, the Chinese economy was by no means completely Sovietized before 1956. Labor-intensive Yenan methods which relied on the mobilization of manpower were still widely applied in many

---

[1] Franz Schurmann, *Ideology and Organization in Communist China*, 2nd ed. (Berkeley: University of California Press, 1969).

[2] Harvard University East Asian Research Center and Harvard University Center for International Affairs, *Communist China 1955-59: Policy Documents with Analysis* (Cambridge: Harvard University Press, 1952), pp. 94-105.

areas. The huge reservoir of handicraft skills continued to be used to fill all sorts of pressing needs. Yet most foreign observers found it reasonable to assume that these phenomena were survivals of the past and that the Soviet model represented the wave of the future. There was nothing in the official Chinese literature of 1953-55 which seemed to run counter to such expectations.

Outside the strictly economic sphere, one finds more evidence of a determination to maintain China's uniqueness. In political control and indoctrination, there was still a heavy reliance on the Maoist techniques of "thought reform," remolding, and the "mass line." Although in muted tones, certain Maoist contributions to Marxist-Leninist ideology were still being stressed, such as the "peaceful transformation of the bourgeoisie" and the notion that Chinese socialism would be achieved by a coalition of classes under the "hegemony of the proletariat." On the other hand, Sovietization was not strictly confined to the area of economic strategy. There was growing imitation of Soviet methods in education, military modernization, literature, and other areas of social and cultural development. Those who argued for an ever-growing approximation to Soviet models felt that the evidence was on their side.

As indicated previously, Franz Schurmann has argued that, in the field of industrial management, tensions between the Chinese and Soviet "working styles" began to appear at a fairly early stage of the effort to approximate Soviet practices. Nevertheless, it can be argued that the first serious questioning of the applicability of Soviet models to Chinese realities began with the Hundred Flowers Campaign in 1956. The death of Stalin, the changes taking place in the Soviet Union, and internal economic difficulties were among the factors behind this departure. While the Hundred Flowers experiment itself did not have any marked immediate effect on economic strategy, it marked the beginning of a new realization that China must find its own way into the future, a realization that was not to be reversed by subsequent changes in policy. Questions were raised not only by those who were later to be attacked as "bourgeois rightists" but also within the Party itself. When Chairman Mao asserted in his "On the Correct Handling of Contradictions" that "full attention must be paid to the development of agriculture and light industry," even while affirming that "heavy industry is the core of China's economic construction," one at first suspected that he was again attempting one of the verbal dialectic balancing acts which are a part of the Communist style. In fact, the speech reflected a vigorous discussion of urgent agrarian needs within the Party. By 1957, it had become apparent that the simple act of collectivization would not solve the problems of Chinese agriculture. The problems of the agrarian economy could not be bracketed as they had been in the case of the Soviet Union. The problem of sheer survival for China's vast rural population pointed to an irreducible difference between the Soviet Union and China.

The recognition of these objective realities did not result in the same response from all elements of the leadership. There were some within the Party who called for a relaxation of collectivization and a lightening of the procurement demands of the state. Yet Mao was not prepared to accept this "rightist" solution. Instead, we have the launching of the Great Leap Forward.

In many ways, the Great Leap Forward marks the triumph of the Maoist approach over Soviet models. The new revelation was that the Yenan maxims which had worked when applied to the tasks of revolution would, in China, also work when applied to the tasks of modernization. Since the details of the Great Leap Forward have been amply described elsewhere, it is necessary here to indicate only that, while it is from many points of view the high point of Maoification, it does not mark a decisive break with one of the main features of the Stalinist model when viewed strictly as economic strategy. There was to be no diversion of investment inputs from the heavy industrial sector. In spite of the enormous concentration of attention in the agricultural sector and on small industries and handicrafts during 1958 and 1959, it was expected that the most spectacular leap forward would take place in the advanced industrial sector and that agriculture would continue to rely on organizing human energy without the diversion of material capital. While "politics in command" and moral incentives were employed in the modern industrial sector, even Chairman Mao did not believe that heavy industry would develop without enormous capital investments. Thus the concentration on agriculture as well as the new theme of developing light industry by "walking on two legs" were still based on the assumption that a Maoist approach was favorable to a Stalinist conception of capital allocation.

It is from this perspective that the decision during the crisis of the early 1960s to take "agriculture as the foundation" must be viewed as the decisive break with the Stalinist economic strategy. It is, of course, extremely risky to speak of irreversible turning points in the history of the People's Republic. Reversals are always possible. In spite of all the upheavals of the Cultural Revolution, however, it appears that the essential features of the policy of "taking agriculture as the foundation" have survived. The policy was restated in the *Peking Review* in August 1972.[3]

Although "agriculture as the foundation" is always accompanied by the phrase "and industry as leading factor," it has been made clear in the course of exposition that to the extent possible this means bending industry itself to the service of agriculture. As early as July 17, 1960, a *People's Daily* editorial stated that "each and every industry, mining and communications enterprise and each and every worker should adopt the idea that agriculture is the foundation of all things. . . . China is a great agricultural nation with more than 80 percent of its population living in rural areas. Without developing agriculture there will be no advance in light industry and it would be difficult to build up a powerful heavy industry. . . . Only a modernized agriculture is able to guarantee that the entire national economy will achieve continued forward leaps in its development."[4] This involved more attention to the production of fertilizer and agricultural tools, the improvement of seed, electrification, etc. It involved, above all, a reconciliation to a slower pace of development in heavy industry. However, this did not imply any decrease in the relative weight of "national-defense" considerations.

How then did this reordering of priorities relate to the vehement controversies which subsequently shattered the unity of the Chinese Communist leadership? The *Peking Review* article of August 1972 mentioned above indicates that the "revisionist" Liu Shao-ch'i had pushed the policy of "developing heavy industry at the expense of agriculture." Others have contended that while Mao Tse-tung was forced to accept the retreat from the Great Leap Forward in the early 1960s, he fundamentally rejected the whole "revisionist" line of the subsequent period, including the new ordering of priorities. A third possibility is that Mao Tse-tung and his opponents accepted this re-

[3] "Relationship between Agriculture, Light Industry and Heavy Industry," *Peking Review*, August 25, 1972.

[4] Economists say that the rate of growth of heavy industry continued to be much higher than the rate of growth of agriculture even after 1960. This by no means detracts, however, from the significance of the policy of "agriculture as foundation."

ordering of priorities in the critical period of the early 1960s, and perhaps even later on. Mao as well as his opponents realized that the needs of agriculture in China required not only the physical and moral energies of the peasant masses but also capital investments and even a slower rate of growth in heavy industry. It is significant that the statements of the tenth plenum of 1962, which presumably enunciated the new Maoist "left" line of class struggle, continued to speak of "taking agriculture as the foundation."

If one can assume a common acceptance of the constraints imposed by Chinese agrarian realities, what were the issues which divided Mao from his opponents? Perhaps Mao's opponents felt that "taking agriculture as the foundation" required not only large investments in agriculture but a relaxation of the "socialist," "collectivist" organization of the countryside. What was required, in their view, was not only investments in agriculture as an economic sector but also more attention to the material incentives of the farmers. Hence the new stress on private plots and free markets. Mao Tse-tung, while accepting the view that agriculture as a sector required large material investments as well as mobilization of moral and physical energies, was adamantly and genuinely opposed to the "spontaneous tendency toward capitalism among some of the small producers" and continued to believe that a more sustained "socialist education" would in the end lead to the type of internalization of the Communist ethic which he had hoped to achieve at one fell swoop during the Great Leap Forward. While he had not given up the faith that a new collectivist ethic would lead to great economic development, his attachment to this collectivist ethic was by no means conditional on its relations to economic results. A dimension was added to these considerations by Mao's reflections on the "bourgeois" course of the Soviet Union. In a sense, at stake was not the relationship of agriculture to industry but the preservation of the Maoist vision of the good ethical order against the inertial pull toward the "restoration of capitalism" as he understood the term. Mao may have continued to believe in his ability to transform the moral nature of man. It is not clear whether he still believed that agricultural production could be raised by a simple reliance on moral force.

With the retreat from the Cultural Revolution, it became increasingly evident that there had been no departure from the policy of "agriculture as the foundation" during the Cultural Revolution.

While the disruption of communications and dislocation of industry undoubtedly affected agriculture, to the extent that industry continued to function, the policy of orienting it to the service of agriculture seems to have continued. Basic decision-making power within the commune appears to have remained on the village level. The extent to which the Cultural Revolutionaries restored private plots and replaced "work points" by "moral incentives" is obscure. Yet it is now clear that those who pressed these policies are being severely attacked as "a priori idealists" who fail to recognize the objective realities of the socialist stage of development.

The policy of "taking agriculture as the foundation" seems to be firmly established. In fact, the maintenance of this policy throughout the Cultural Revolution and into the present may be one of the major reasons for the resiliency with which Chinese society has been able to absorb the turbulence of the Cultural Revolution. Assuming the continuation of this policy, one might briefly ponder its significance and implications.

First, the departure from the Soviet model and the policy of "taking agriculture as the foundation" clearly prove the capacity of the Chinese leadership, in spite of its internal conflicts, to learn the lessons of an unfolding experience. The policy of putting agriculture first involves the recognition of the constraints imposed by Chinese realities. At least in one area of economic strategy, there is a clear recognition of the leadership's limited ability to induce social change by *force majeure*. The implications of this recognition extend beyond the area of the strictly economic. Both the Soviet and Western definitions of "respectable modernity" involve the notion of an overwhelming urbanization of the population and a drastic shrinkage of the rural population. If the Chinese economic strategy is now based on the presumption that the bulk of China's vast population will continue for some time to reside in villages, what are the implications for Chinese modernization?

Many in the West are prepared to see idyllic possibilities in the survival of the Chinese village. They see the opportunity to avoid all sorts of abuses of Western "consumer" society. While China may avoid, by necessity or by choice, some of the unpleasant concomitants of Western consumerism, this still does not eliminate the possibility of all kinds of social, political, and cultural abuse. On the other hand, some will refuse to grant China the coveted attribute of "modernity" so long as much of its population continues to live in comparative rural poverty. This refusal tells us very little, however, about the viability of a society of this type. There is no real reason to choose between the idealization of the village or the megalopolis. The important point is that China will have to find its own way into the future.

The Values of the Chinese Revolution

TANG TSOU

Of all the revolutions in modern times, the Chinese Revolution has proved to be the most protracted, the widest, and the most penetrating, surpassing the Russian Revolution in all of these aspects.[1] It has brought about fundamental changes in social, political, and economic institutions and values. It has attempted to alter the attitudes and thought-patterns of man. In many ways, the Chinese society after the Cultural Revolution stands at the opposite pole to the American society. It rests on a fundamentally different ordering of values and principles. Moreover, China tries consciously and proudly to be different from the West and to be true to itself, thus sharply reversing the attitude of some of its intellectuals and officials who prior to the 1960s endeavored self-consciously, humbly, and awkwardly to imitate first the West and then the Soviet Union.

Of the many contrasts between modern Western and Chinese values and principles, none is more basic and more striking than that between the two notions of the individual and of his relationship to society. Since actual practices seldom conform exactly to ethical and political theories, the contrasts between Chinese and Western practices may not be as sharp as those between their ideologies. They are nonetheless

The author is indebted to Duncan MacRae, Donald Munro, and Mitchell Meisner who read a preliminary draft of this paper and offered many good suggestions.

[1] The Vietnamese Revolution may turn out to be more protracted than the Chinese Revolution, but its impact on the society and the individual may not be as penetrating and wide.

easily observable. In the liberal, democratic tradition and value system of the modern West, the individual is considered an end in himself. Preserving and enhancing the dignity of the individual is believed to be the goal of the society. The individual is served by and placed above the group, and the assent of the individual is the standard of political legitimacy. Private judgment, private willing, and private conscience are considered to be the inviolate basic units from which social and political life is built. But as the sociologists seek to show, the individual is, in practice, enmeshed in a complex network of groups, organizations, institutions, and classes; his interests, duties, and obligations are shaped in a group setting. The freedom and dignity of the individual are ideals which actual practices do not always promote.

In the Maoist social theory, man is given a central place in historical development. As Mao has written, "The people, and the people alone, are the motive force in the making of world history"[2] and "the masses have boundless creative power."[3] In contrast to Western ethical and political philosophy, man is not seen primarily as an individual. As it occurs in Mao's writing, the term *individual* is generally used in a pejorative sense. Man is viewed as a member of collectivities at various levels of comprehensiveness and concreteness, and is always bound by a number of social and political ties. "In class society everyone lives as a member of a particular class," Mao wrote.[4] He becomes a member of the "people" only in his capacity as a member of a definite class, not as an atomistic individual removed from his class moorings. Mao wrote in 1949: "Who are the people? At the present stage in China, they are the working class, the peasantry, the urban petty bourgeoisie and national bourgeoisie."[5] The interests of the people are the interests of these classes, not of individuals in their separate and private existence. Moreover, these classes have different standings in the society and polity, with the working class in the leadership role. Mao also elevated the peasantry above the other two classes (i.e., the urban petty bourgeoisie and national bourgeoisie) when he wrote that "the people's democratic dictatorship is based on the alliance of the working class,

[2] Mao Tse-tung, *Selected Works*, 4 vols. (Peking: Foreign Languages Press, 1961), 3:257.
[3] Mao Tse-tung *Mao Tse-Tung's Quotations: The Red Guards' Handbook* (Nashville: Peabody International Center, 1967), p. 118.
[4] Mao Tse-tung, *Selected Works*, 1:296.
[5] Ibid., 4:417.

the peasantry, and the urban petty bourgeoisie, and *mainly* on the alliance of the workers and the peasants."[6] The individual enters society as a member of the "masses." In 1949, the "masses" were the members of the four classes in their relationship with the leaders in a revolutionary movement and society.[7] Instead of the assent of atomistic individuals in Western political theory, the Communist movement and regime rely on the support of the people and the "masses" as a source of political legitimacy.

Below the level of the classes, the people, and the masses, the individual is viewed primarily as a member of a network of groups, organizations, institutions, and local communities. At the lowest level, he is a member of face-to-face groups. His existence has little meaning outside these subcollectivities. The individual in the liberal, democratic societies in the West also exists in a social network. But theoretically he can always move in and out of subcollectivities on his own initiative, and not infrequently he does. He can make one subcollectivity the primary object of his loyalty, view the common good of the whole society largely in terms of its interests, and push its demands as far as possible. In the search for the common good, attitudes such as interest articulation and aggregation are permitted if not encouraged by Western notions of group process in a pluralistic society.

In contrast, the individual in Chinese society cannot simply move in and out of these subcollectivities on his own initiative without the approval of his peer group and the leading bodies. The interests of society are supposed to override the interests of its subordinate units, and the interests of a given subcollectivity have precedence over those of its component units. In viewing the interests of any subcollectivity, the individual must first consider the larger interests and then determine how the interests of the subcollectivity fit into the interests of society. As Mao has written, "They [the Communists] must grasp the principle of subordinating the needs of the part to the needs of the whole. If a proposal appears feasible for a partial situation but not for the situation as a whole, then the part must give way to the whole. Conversely, if the proposal is not feasible for the part but is feasible in the light of the situation as a whole, again the part must give way

[6] Ibid., p. 421. Italics added. Note the omission of the national bourgeoisie in this statement.
[7] Ibid., p. 415.

to the whole."[8] Although the common good is supposed to prevail over special interests in both China and the West, the intellectual and political process in the search for the common good starts from opposite poles.

In China, emphasis is placed on the individual's duties and responsibilities to society and its subcollectivities. There are, however, no compensating "natural" rights and liberties recognized by society, embodied in legal rights, or liberties protected by a constitution, as in the case of the West. This view of the individual who enters the societies as a member of a class, the people, the masses, and subcollectivities with duties and responsibilities but without social recognition of his "natural" rights and liberties resonates to the traditional stress on the social ties of the individual. Behind this view of the individual lies the collectivistic heritage of the base areas and guerrilla warfare. In the background, there is a country with a huge population and only limited resources readily usable at this stage of its technological development. It has been threatened by repeated crises in its foreign relations, and must compete with industrially and technologically advanced societies.[9] These historical and objective forces combine with the Communist ideology to produce what Benjamin Schwartz calls "the emphasis on the individual's total self-abnegation and total immersion in the collectivities as ultimate goods."[10] The individual is urged to restrain selfishness and to concentrate on the public good. His worth is measured by his service to the people, the masses, and the subcollectivities. If he has achieved a complete identification with the collectivity, he may feel a sense of liberation and find fulfillment not in individual accomplishments but in the promotion of the common good and collective goals. He must transform himself spiritually to live and work in and for a new society. Although the spiritual trans-

[8] Ibid., 2:201. Here Mao was talking primarily about the relationship between the whole Party and its parts, but this notion also governs the way in which the Party must handle the problems of a society under its rule. In a revolutionary situation in which a revolutionary movement challenges the existing social order, the relationship between the whole and the parts is viewed in a fundamentally different way.

[9] Even John Rawls writes: "It is only when social conditions do not allow the effective establishment of these rights, i.e., basic liberties, that one can acknowledge their restriction. The denial of equal liberty can be accepted only if it is necessary to enhance the quality of civilization so that in due course the equal freedoms can be enjoyed by all." John Rawls, *Theory of Justice* (Cambridge: Harvard University Press, 1972), p. 542.

[10] Benjamin Schwartz, "Modernization and the Maoist Vision," *China Quarterly*, no. 21 (January-March 1965), p. 11.

formation of an individual is ultimately a private act, all the individuals in a society cannot be transformed without a collectivist setting which inevitably intrudes on the privacy and mental life of the individuals. This runs counter to the first principle of liberal, democratic society. According to John Rawls's recent formulation, "each person is to have an equal right to the most extensive basic liberty compatible with a similar liberty for others."[11] John Rawls's notion of a lexical order of principles and his ranking of the principle of equal liberty above the regulation of economic and social inequalities constitute one illustration of the contrasts between the Chinese and American value systems and societies, while his second principle is a prescription for a society more equalitarian than the existing American society and corresponds more closely to that underlying the Chinese society.[12]

If in China the individual's duties and responsibilities toward society are not balanced by liberties granted by the society, they are reciprocated by the society's assumption of full responsibility for the individual. If the individual must transform himself spiritually to conform to the needs of the society, the society must also transform itself to make it a worthy object of the individual's loyalty and service. In transforming themselves, the individuals are also helping to transform society. Public virtue and moral men living in a moral society—these are the Chinese aims.

It is in this reciprocal relationship between the society and the individuals viewed collectively that one must find the strength or weakness, the prospects of success or failure, of the Chinese polity. Since Chinese society has, in effect, rejected individual freedom, it relies heavily on this reciprocal relationship as one of the sources of political legitimacy. Thus Mao urges selflessness on the part of the individual, and at the same time enjoins the Party to take care of the interests of the people. He has written: "Every word, every act, and every policy [of the CCP] must conform to the people's interests. . . ."[13] He has also stated: "To link onself with the masses, one must act in accordance with the needs and wishes of the masses."[14] Since the interests of the

[11] Rawls, p. 60. For his fuller statement, see p. 302. This principle has, in Rawls's theory, priority over all other principles.

[12] Ibid., pp. 42-43. His principle of priority means that "liberty can be restricted only for the sake of liberty." See ibid., p. 302. Therefore, liberty cannot be restricted on the ground that such restriction promotes socioeconomic equality or the total welfare of the society—a reasoning which is sometimes invoked to justify the restriction of freedom in China.

[13] Mao Tse-tung, *Selected Works*, 4:16.

[14] Ibid., 3: 236-37.

people and the masses are seen in terms of social classes, some of which are excluded from the category of the "people," and since even within the ranks of the people the various classes occupy different positions, the violent destruction of the landlord class and the compradores and bureaucratic capitalists was considered a measure to promote the interests of the people. So was the "socialist reconstruction of private industries, commerce, and handcraft" which in effect destroyed the economic power of the national bourgeoisie, though it did not eliminate completely its political influence and special economic privileges. Accompanying the change in the class structure, there has also been a process of redistribution of wealth in which the lower classes gained some benefit at the expense of the upper classes.

Mao's definition of the working class as the leading class in China and the peasantry as its principal ally, as well as his sympathies with the poor and middle peasants who furnished the main power for his guerrilla army, in effect means that promotion of the interests of the people signifies primarily assistance to the most deprived groups (or from Mao's view, the most oppressed groups) in Chinese society, which happen also to be the two largest classes in China.[15] Thus, in the reciprocal relationship between the society and the individual, there is a strong drive toward social and economic equality. The political importance attributed to the poor and lower-middle peasants and perhaps even a solicitude for their welfare were the basis of Mao's drive to establish cooperatives in an attempt to prevent further "differentiations of classes in the countryside" and to avoid the danger of the "rupture of the worker-peasant alliance."[16]

But no existing society can eliminate inequalities entirely, certainly not China at its present level of economic development. The Chinese Communists recognized this from the beginning. In the famous Kut'ien resolution of December 1929, which was drafted by Mao, "absolute equalitarianism" and "ultrademocracy" were condemned in no uncertain terms.[17] But two interrelated problems have continued to trouble the Chinese leaders. One is how to justify inequalities. The

[15] Within the working class, the most disadvantaged group is the contract workers. According to the organizer of a nationwide organization of contract workers, there were 10 million contract workers in 1967. See Ko-chih chan-pao, March 1, 1967, p. 2. The theoretical problems raised by the demands and the subsequent suppression of this organization by the regime cannot be discussed here.

[16] For a general discussion of this point in the context of the differences between Liu and Mao, see Tang Tsou, "The Cultural Revolution and the Political System in China," China Quarterly, no. 38 (April-June 1969), pp. 63-91.

[17] Mao Tse-tung, Selected Works, 1:108-111.

other, which is much more important, is to what extent inequalities should be allowed to exist. Besides the obvious Marxist principle of "from each according to his ability, to each according to his work" and the notion of the stages of social development from feudalism to Communism, the Chinese leaders implicitly or explicitly invoked principles familiar to Westerners. In the Kut'ien resolution, Mao justified inequality between officers and soldiers on the basis of the principle of efficiency.[18] He also invoked the notion of maximizing the sum of advantages.[19] In addition to these two ideas, Liu Shao-ch'i employed the principle that social and economic inequalities are to be tolerated if they bring greater benefit to the least advantaged. In his much criticized statement made in 1949 to a group of capitalists, he said: "To exploit more workers is better [than to exploit fewer workers]. Unemployed workers ask for jobs and they want to work in factories run by capitalists. That is to say: 'Please exploit me.' They want you [the capitalists] to exploit them. 'If you can exploit us, we will feel happier. Otherwise we will be miserable.' "[20] Mao's predisposition toward equality may go no further than the basic principle underlying Liu's offhand and impolitic remark.[21] But his identification with and sympathies for the most deprived indicate that this is his minimum position.

From the very beginning of the regime, the use of the welfare and quality of life of the lower classes as the standard for measuring permissible inequalities was combined with the notion of open access to all positions and offices. Equality of opportunity was subject only to the criterion of class origin, even though this criterion was sometimes weakened by circumstances, policies, and practices. This combination made equalitarianism a strong operating principle in the Chinese society. Moreover, the Chinese policies, at least in education, reflect an attempt to redress the inequalities of birth and natural endowment and to compensate for these inequalities by giving more attention to the

[18] Mao cited and condemned the following views as an example of absolute equalitarianism: "When officers rode on horseback, it was not regarded as something necessary for performing their duties but as a sign of inequality." See ibid., p. 110. The term "principle of efficiency" is used here loosely without the precise meaning given to it by John Rawls. See Rawls, pp. 66-70.

[19] Mao reported: "[Absolute equalitarianism] went so far that when there were two wounded men but only one stretcher, neither could be carried away because each refused to yield priority to the other." See Mao Tse-tung, *Selected Works*, 1:111.

[20] *Selections from China Mainland Magazines*, American Consulate General, no. 652 (Hong Kong, April 28, 1969), p. 11.

[21] This basic principle is essentially what John Rawls calls the difference principle.

least advantaged and by imposing restrictions on the most advantaged.

From this perspective, the differences between Mao and Liu in the years prior to the Cultural Revolution can be described in the following terms. From Mao's point of view, the overlapping and interlinked privileged groups at the top had formed a new class and the resulting inequalities could no longer be justified by whatever benefit accrued to the least advantaged under the existing social arrangement. Mao wanted to redress this balance by first maximizing the welfare and the quality of life of the most disadvantaged groups, as indicated in his instruction of June 1, 1965, on public health. He wished to push the principle of redress much further in education than Liu did. Most important, he gave greater weight to equalitarianism than to economic efficiency and technocratic values. He assigned less weight to economic efficiency based on material incentive, specialization, and hierarchical arrangement and more weight to economic efficiency through the use of all available human resources. The Cultural Revolution, which resulted in the repudiation of Liu's views, pushed equalitarianism even further. The period of consolidation may now have put a limit to this trend and pushed it slightly back in order to give more weight to other considerations. But what cannot be denied is that the society has endeavored to use its political power systematically to offset inequalities based on birth and cultural deprivation as well as the tendency of all organizations to create socioeconomic inequalities.[22]

Assuming that the reports of recent visitors reflect the actual situation in China, it is clear that Chinese society has endeavored to provide a floor under the income of the least advantaged and a minimum level of economic security. Even if one is completely skeptical about these reports, one is still justified in considering them as indicative of the value system of the Chinese. If there is greater opportunity for field research, an attempt can be made to ascertain the extent to which this value system is taken seriously and implemented throughout China. Jan Myrdal reports that in Liu Ling (Liu Lin) in northern Shensi, the "five guarantees" of "enough food, enough clothes, enough fuel, an honorable funeral, and a decent education for everyone's children" were put into effect.[23] In providing for these guarantees, eco-

---

[22] See Tang Tsou, "A Talk with the Senior Editors of *Time-Life-Fortune* Magazines," (Talk organized by the University of Chicago, May 1971.) The present paper is an elaboration and revision of this talk.

[23] Jan Myrdal and Gun Kessle, *China: The Revolution Continued* (New York: Pantheon Books, 1970), pp. 50-55.

nomic incentive is not entirely ignored. For example, the basic guarantee for grain was 172 kg. per person or 43 kg. below the average grain consumption of 214 kg. It was regarded as "a citizen's right and did not stand in any relation to how much work he or she does."[24] Obviously an individual must acquire additional income from work. But those who cannot obtain the minimum daily necessity would receive "special help from the collective [i.e., the revolutionary committee of the brigade] under the 'five guarantees.' "[25] The existing wage and salary differentials between the lowest and highest paid workers and employees are probably not as wide as those in economically developed nations or other developing countries. In comparison with countries in the West, the whole system of income distribution looks more equalitarian because the most economically advantaged class in the West is not found in China.[26] The relatively high differentials are explained partly as the legacy of the past and partly as a result of the seniority principle, i.e., reward and recognition for past contributions to the society, partly by the level of skill, and partly by the people's expectation of what is "fair." It is clear that the economic needs and welfare of the least advantaged class are given a very high place in the Chinese value system and constitute a measure of the equity of the social system.

In the realm of politics, the relationship between the individual and society can be discussed in similar terms. Since political power and influence are more elusive than income, however, this relationship is much more difficult to ascertain. If it is true that the Chinese system stresses the reciprocity between the individual and society, one can suggest that the mobilization of individuals by the society to undertake social and political actions is reciprocated by their participation in the political processes granted by the society. Prior to the Cultural Revolution, the Chinese political system was highly centralized and hierarchical, with a clear-cut separation between the elite and the masses and a trend toward increasing bureaucratization in all spheres of social life. The Cultural Revolution brought about several significant changes. First, through the system of triple alliance and the principle of combining the old, the middle-aged, and the young in leader-

[24] Ibid., p. 53.
[25] Ibid.
[26] The author is indebted to Dwight Perkins for this idea which he expressed in a seminar organized by the Adlai Stevenson Institute in autumn 1971, and hopes that the view has not been misrepresented.

ship groups, Mao has attempted to enable selected representatives of the least advantaged groups to participate in governing bodies in all fields of human activity throughout China from the Central Committee downward. In addition to bringing about greater equality in the political sphere, this system brings into governing bodies persons needed by the regime because of their "correct" political standpoint and reliability. It has also institutionalized collective units combining individuals with different skills and intelligence to elevate the status and skill of the least advantaged persons in the hope that the resulting whole is greater than the sum of its parts. Although in practice individuals do not have equal opportunity to occupy positions of authority, these offices are open to all in theory. Even if one assumes that the men and women from the least advantaged groups (i.e., the representatives of the revolutionary mass organizations and the young Party members as distinguished from the veteran and middle-aged members) do not have actual political power, the new system is a reaffirmation of the principle of equality, and their presence may eventually bring important changes in the whole political and social system.

Second, by mobilizing the non-Party students and worker-rebels to destroy the Party apparatus and those outside the establishment to attack the establishment, Mao has made it clear that persons in authority are not immune from attack by their subordinates, however remote the possibility. The process of rebuilding the political system has proved to be slow and difficult with many problems still to be solved, particularly those at the top levels. In the existing political structure and in various organizations and institutions, the governing bodies will probably have less ability to act and may be less efficient than before. But this loss may well be balanced by the officials' newly acquired fear and respect for the masses—attitudes that are not out of place in a system where individual rights and freedoms are not defined and guaranteed by a legal system. This change may well be one of the many factors which account for the more relaxed atmosphere among lower-level workers which many visitors have reported.

Third, the Cultural Revolution brought about a decentralization in the performance of various functions to the provinces and below. The reports that planning and "staff" offices have been developed at the shop levels in some factories suggest that this process of decentralization has reached the lowest level in some organizations.[27] Little is

[27] See Mitch Meisner, "Report from China: The Shenyang Transformer Factory—A Profile," *China Quarterly* (October–December 1972), 717-37.

known about the actual operations of the new system and the consequences of this change, but the hope is that decentralization will bring the decision makers closer to the masses, render them more responsive to social needs, and make them more aware of the local situation.

Fourth, organizational units performing similar or allied functions were in some cases merged into one unit, thus resulting in the reduction of the number of units and personnel under the slogan of "better troops and simpler administration." This change may reduce specialization and it may also eliminate unnecessary duplications. With a smaller number of units in a bureaucratic organization, coordination among them can be achieved even when the levels of hierarchy are reduced. This means that a "flatter" hierarchy will replace a "taller" one. If this development does occur in China, one can test Anthony Downs's hypothesis that "inequalities of power, income, and prestige are greater in tall hierarchies than in flat ones."[28] It will also be interesting to see to what extent the reduction of the level of hierarchies has made it easier for the opinion of the masses to percolate to the highest level of an organization, thus rendering it more likely that high-level officials will have direct contact with the people under their jurisdiction. The combination of this feature with the preceding one may mean that the decision-making units at the lower levels have acquired greater authority and more functions in works dealing directly with the masses.

Fifth, Mao at one point condemned the extensive use of "secretaries" by responsible officials and urged them to handle personally as many of the written documents as possible. This condemnation may have been extended to the use of staff officers generally and may have resulted in the reduction of staff agencies. If it has, this reduction would have weakened the planning and technical function of an organizational unit and the control of the top official over it. But at the same time, it would reinforce the process of decentralization of function and authority to lower levels.

Finally, Mao extended and regularized the participation of officials, cadres, and intellectuals in low-level labor at regular periods of time. The workers' participation in management is reciprocated by managers' participation in productive labor—a principle enshrined in the Anshan Charter. This system of managers' participation in labor may reduce efficiency in the performance of routine work and impose some

[28] Anthony Downs, *Inside Bureaucracy* (Boston: Little, Brown & Co., 1967), p. 265.

hardship on the officials, cadres, and intellectuals, but it may enable them to know through their personal experience the conditions at the lowest level and the feelings and sentiments of the masses. It may lead to the adoption of a new perspective on policy matters and on the exercise of control which considers more fully the expectations of the least advantaged groups in any political or social unit. It may enable them to have an intimate understanding of the problems of production at the lowest level, thus helping them to arrive at a solution and to improve economic efficiency. It forces the officials, cadres, and intellectuals to occupy temporarily but at regular intervals positions at the very bottom of the society. When combined with the attempt to open up top-level offices and positions in every collectivity, group, and organization to the least advantaged, this policy establishes symbolically the principle of opening up all positions, at the top as well as at the bottom, to everyone. It reduces the social and political gaps between leaders and followers, though it does not eliminate them. It represents the analogue in a mobilization system of a democratic, liberal society's principle of fraternity, which represents "a certain equality of social esteem, the absence of manners of deference and servility."[29]

In the liberal, democratic societies of the West, particularly in the postindustrial era, individual creativity is considered both a sign and a cause of social progress. Thus far, the Chinese have shown creativity in the development of a distinct social arrangement to govern a vast population with meager resources in accordance with a social ideal. The immediate goals of this mobilized society are national survival, a proper place in the international community, social equality, and economic development. In endeavoring to achieve these goals, the Chinese have shown a measure of creativity in their collective effort and in the technological spheres. Many art forms of the masses have also been elevated to a new height and popularized for the enjoyment of the masses. But creativity of the individual in the realm of literature, art, and social thought has certainly lagged behind. Critics in the West generally explain this lag in terms of the political and ideological control imposed on the individual.

The notion that literature and art must serve the working class and the peasantry is merely the application to these two spheres of the basic principle of serving the least advantaged groups in the Chinese

[29] Rawls, p. 106.

society. In itself, it need not inhibit creativity.[30] The problem is whether this demand is imposed on the individual or whether the individual voluntarily accepts it as a part of his society's tradition. There is also the question of how to serve these groups—through spontaneity, variety, and originality in the creative efforts of the individual or through conformity, uniformity, and banality.

As the educational level of the masses gradually increases, as their attachment to old cultural ideas is destroyed, and as their political consciousness changes, the literature, art, and social thought which are intended to serve them will have to show a higher level of achievement. As inner-Party conflicts subside, a more relaxed atmosphere may permit a larger measure of spontaneity, variety, and originality. But ultimately, the creativity of the individuals in literature, art, and social thought depends on removing the conscious and unconscious mental inhibitions imposed not only by political control but also by the culture and the subcollectivities. The basic notion that the individual has meaning *only* as a member of a group would seem to have continuing inhibiting effect. This is perhaps a price which must be paid by the present Chinese society. These hasty observations on such a vast subject are merely an indication of an awareness of this problem in any discussion of this relationship between the individual and society.

There is little doubt that since 1949 China has made tremendous progress in economic reconstruction. The contrast between the past and the present is particularly obvious in the countryside. China's economic development is impressive in comparison with other developing nations, especially when one considers the relatively small amount of foreign aid received, the termination of this aid at a critical moment, the expense incurred in fighting the Korean war, and the hostile international environment which has necessitated the diversion of urgently needed resources and scientific manpower into national defense. It is quite clear that this progress has been achieved with tremendous personal hardship and sacrifice. In the process, many mistakes were made. But the hardship and sacrifice have been borne, and the mistakes corrected.

Even more impressive is China's attempt to build a new society in which the principle of socioeconomic equality has probably been

---

[30] Even Aleksandr I. Solzhenitsyn affirms the tradition that "a writer can do much for his people—and must." See "Art—for Man's Sake: II," *New York Times*, October 7, 1972.

pushed further than in any similar society at the same level of economic development; at the same time, the interests and needs of the least advantaged have been used as a guide for socioeconomic policies and institution-building. The Chinese themselves have recognized that the building of an egalitarian society is their greatest achievement. In the past two years, they have been relatively successful in giving visitors a direct experience, personal impression, and "sense perception" of their egalitarian society. There has not been, however, a systematic attempt to communicate to the outside world the rationale, justification, and significance of their social experiment, as well as the problems, weaknesses, and difficulties involved. The situation has not been presented in a way that convinces people with many different political traditions and ideological perspectives of its merits.

Within China, two other problems demand solutions. The first is balancing egalitarianism with economic efficiency and scientific-technological values at different times and in different circumstances. During and immediately after the Cultural Revolution, the Chinese leaders gave priority to socioeconomic equality. But in its peaceful competition with the West and Japan, China must show that a society built upon this priority can also catch up economically. It may be necessary to give greater weight to economic efficiency and the development of science and technology without reversing the priority.

The second problem lies at the heart of the Chinese social system. This crucial problem is raised when attempting to answer two interrelated questions: Who is going to decide what constitute the interests of the working class, the needs of the people, the demands of the masses, and the requirements of the various subcollectivities—in short, who decides what is the public interest? Who is going to decide what reciprocal relationship between the individual and the society is the correct one? The answer is that within the very broad constraints imposed by objective circumstances it is the leadership which is going to turn the "scattered and unsystematic ideas of the masses into concentrated and systematic ideas" and to "synthesize their experience into better, articulated principles and methods."[31] The problem of defining public interest is linked to the ideological view that for every problem there is a single correct solution.

Therefore, everything depends on far-sighted leadership and political unity at the top, although social and international conditions do

[31] Mao Tse-tung, *Selected Works*, 3:119, 158.

have their effects. Without a clear-cut boundary between the individual and the society, their relationship fluctuates in accordance with the policies of the leadership and the unity of conflict at the summit. If a far-sighted leadership continues to exist, political unity can be maintained, if the succession problem can be successfully handled through the development of adequate institutions, and if China can demonstrate that an egalitarian society in a developing peasant society can catch up with the West economically and technologically, then Mao will have made a contribution to social practice as significant as his theory of "peasant and guerilla organization and government."

Relating to the International Community

ALBERT FEUERWERKER

The People's Republic of China (PRC) relates to the international community in myriad ways. Like other states, it participates in international organizations such as the United Nations, conducts formal state-to-state negotiations, maintains and deploys armed forces, engages in trade and foreign assistance, disseminates propaganda, and selectively uses the mechanisms of international law. In addition, the PRC relates to other states through its own nationals who reside abroad, foreign sympathizers and friendship organizations, visiting delegations, and foreigners who reside in China. Chinese attempts to influence other states are not limited to such activities, but also include relations with other Communist Parties and cryptodiplomatic encouragement of revolutionary struggles.

These disparate activities have primarily the same purpose: to enhance the ability of the PRC to influence other states and their peoples with respect to its national interests. However, less universalistic motives also sometimes intrude into the process of policy formation in China as elsewhere: vanity, expediency, the working out of personal and ideological differences among rival domestic leaders, and efforts to reduce domestic disequilibrium by deflecting unrest onto a foreign adversary.

A question frequently arises at this point as to what national interests the PRC sees as salient, and more broadly whether it conceives these ends to be attainable within the present framework of international relations. Is it correct to assume that Peking's participation in a very imperfect "bourgeois" or "revisionist" international system, composed of formally equal and sovereign states of varying real power which interact in changing combinations, is more than a temporary and tactical maneuver? Would the achievement of an identifiable list of specific objectives turn the PRC into a status quo power? Or will China pursue the unlimited objective of overthrowing the present international system and substituting a Maoist, if not traditional Confucian, world order?

One approach to answering these questions is to examine the influence of late-imperial and pre-1949 republican China on the foreign policy of the PRC. Two different views exist. On the one hand, it is argued that something peculiarly Chinese, derived from millenia of a separate and remarkable cultural tradition, motivates the foreign relations of the PRC. This assertion underlies the more extreme doubts about the genuineness with which the PRC, as the inheritor of China's past, accepts the nation-state system, the central organizing concept of the international community. Others argue that the sources and execution of China's foreign policy are only a variant of the common article manufactured by other states.

Even dismissing for a moment the ecumenical vision of utopian Maoism, is not the PRC driven to attempt to reestablish the Sino-centric world order which crumbled in the nineteenth century when China was reduced to a semicolonial status? Is not the tone of superiority—Chinese "arrogance," some say—which is directed not just toward the "imperialist" United States but also toward the "modern revisionist" Soviet Union, directly linked to a traditional assertion of the superiority of the Confucian moral order which identified China as "civilization" and all outside its influence as "barbarism"? The contemporary claim to leadership of the Third World is perhaps a continuation of the ethnocentrism of the past, in which the "Middle Kingdom" by its ruler's "virtue" irresistibly drew the non-Chinese world into a hierarchic system of interstate relations whose center was Peking. And is not the wining and dining of numerous "embassies" to Peking from the small states of the Third World, and of Communist and non-Communist leaders from other states, only the most recent form of the "tribute system" by means of which the imperial dynasties granted trade privileges and political support in return for the kowtow and acknowledgment of Peking's suzerainty? Even if the embassies of Richard Nixon and Tanaka Kakuei to the

People's Republic of China were not sufficient evidence to lay to rest this vision of a People's Middle Kingdom, it would still be highly questionable that these alleged continuities from the imperial past are operative factors in shaping today's foreign policy. Resemblances in style and tone—and probably even in menus and manners—should not be mistaken for unchanged substance.

Confucianism and the Thought of Mao Tse-tung

Let us examine more closely one of the supposedly more important parallels between traditional Chinese international behavior and the modern international behavior of the PRC, namely, that today's or-thodox Marxist-Leninist-Maoist ideology plays a central role in shap-ing policy similar to that performed by the Confucian orthodoxy of the past. Consequently, it is suggested, the PRC strives to achieve broad objectives—such as recreating a Chinese world order based now on the thought of Mao Tse-tung rather than on imperial Confucian-ism—which are inimicable to the present international system.

Before the intrusion of the West, late-imperial China was charac-terized by a remarkable degree of integration. At least among the liter-ate elite there were no dissenters or "Sunday" Confucians. Though the pre-modern Chinese intellectual might sometimes have been hard-pressed to earn his livelihood, he was rarely alienated. The source of this integration was a broad commitment to a single social and political ideology which historians call Confucianism. This ideology played a role in defining the international system in which the Chinese state participated, just as it shaped other aspects of society. Its central premise of the universal kingship of the Son of Heaven, the emperor of China, precluded in theory the acceptance of an equal status for any other political entity with which the Chinese state might have relations. The result was the tribute system, a congeries of institu-tions for the conduct of international relations for which the Chinese had no specific term and which constitute a system only in the eyes of later historians. The tribute system asserted China's cultural supe-riority and its expectation that other states would relate to the Chi-nese emperor only as vassals. It emphasized the sufficiency of the emperor's "virtue" to win the peaceful submission of "men from afar" without the employment of force or threats. The tribute system also gave priority to political over economic relations.

Does not Mao Tse-tung, like the emperors of old, dwell inaccessibly in the Forbidden City in Peking and once again proclaim the true, but now Marxist-Leninist rather than Confucian, "way" to the "barbarians" in the Kremlin and the White House? A striking image which resonates with traditional overtones, but as a historical analogy it is belied by the pragmatic flexibility with which the emperors of old conducted their foreign relations while the dynasty and its social elite still retained an undiminished belief in their values and institutions. This flexibility has also characterized the PRC since its establishment in 1949. The point is not that ideology is unimportant, but that, in contrast to its domestic saliency, it serves as a most unreliable guide for predicting specific international behavior or even for understanding it post facto.

So long as China remained the center of its universe and its ideological assumptions were not directly challenged, there was no need and indeed no possibility of insisting on a full and literal implementation of the tribute system. It may be seriously misleading to treat the impact of the tribute-system ideology of the Chinese empire as radically different from the force of such ideologies as free enterprise in contemporary America or the mass line in the PRC. The important factor in all these cases is that the integrating myths of tribute, free enterprise, and mass line never be contradicted *within* their respective societies, even though the practice of foreign relations or economic enterprise may not conform in all respects and at all times to the ideology in its purest statement. The spatial-ideological imagery of the sinocentric and moralistic tribute system was a critical component of the legitimation of imperial rule in China. Its domestic function of raising the Son of Heaven to a moral height above all other men was as important as its role as a practical medium for China's international relations. The essential thing was that the Chinese documentary record and as far as possible the behavior of foreigners in China did not depart from the ideology. Thus Lord Macartney, although he refused to perform the ceremony, is recorded as having kowtowed—the three kneelings and nine knockings of the head—when received by the emperor. Nor did George III present tributary gifts to the Chia-ch'ing emperor in 1804, though the Chinese documents so assert. Many similar examples could be cited. And lengthy evidence could be offered that, notwithstanding the tributary ideology, the Ch'ing empire used armed force when it appeared necessary, rather than relying on moral virtue alone, in its relations with smaller neighbors in central Asia. At the same time, however, the Chinese empire dealt realistically and on terms of equality with the expanding power of Russia, as indicated by the treaties of Nerchinsk in 1689 and Kyakhta in 1728. Moreover, the tribute embassies from the small maritime states of southeast Asia did no more than opportunistically acknowledge the Chinese definition of the world order in an effort to further their trade with the mainland. If Korea, which sent 664 embassies to China in the period 1637-1874 (an average of almost three a year) was truly under the influence of Chinese culture, the diligent Ryūkyū tributary was in fact under the domination of the *han* of Satsuma in Japan which utilized the Ryūkyū Island kingdom as an entrepôt for an unacknowledged Sino-Japanese trade.

Similarly, the Maoist version of Marxism-Leninism plays only a secondary role in formulating contemporary China's foreign policy. But is not the support of "wars of national liberation" in Asia, Africa, and Latin America a central focus of that foreign policy, and does not this support derive directly from Maoist ideology? Does it not, moreover, signify that the penultimate goal of the People's Republic of China is dominion over a Maoist commonwealth of "have-not" nations, as a step toward the final conquest of all the industrialized world from the Third World "countryside" in the same manner that Mao's peasant armies purportedly came to power in China? The facile response to these questions is that Lin Piao (the author of the famous manifesto of September 1965, "Long Live the Victory of People's War!") disappeared from the Chinese political scene in the summer of 1971 after apparently being purged by Mao Tse-tung and is now reported dead. An equally correct but only somewhat more helpful response would be that Lin Piao's manifesto is "intellectually absurd and politically impractical." There are two additional and possibly more germane observations.

First, support of wars of national liberation by the PRC—in the form of clandestine arms shipments and military training, but more importantly and more commonly by favorable propaganda and political relations with revolutionary organizations—has been more a product of the short-range tactical needs of the Chinese nation-state than of any ultimate Maoist program. Such support has been turned on and off as it suited the policy makers in Peking, without concern for ideological consistency. In 1965, for example, China endorsed 23 out of a possible 120 revolutionary and armed struggles in Asia, Latin America, and Africa. And the pattern of this endorsement, which mostly took the form of propaganda support, indicates that this policy is the tactic of a relatively weak state attempting to keep the United States off balance and to coerce support from other Third World states for a larger and recognized role by China in the international system. From the point of view of the revolutionary movements themselves, China has as often ignored or even betrayed their interests as it has supported them.

As additional evidence of the dominance of political pragmatism rather than millenary ideology, there is China's Security Council veto of the admission of Bangladesh to the United Nations on August 25, 1972. It was China's perception of its immediate national interests against the Soviet Union and India, rather than revolutionary ideology, which led to this support of its most unrevolutionary ally, Pakistan. The familiar phenomenon of other states acting from misperceived national interest may be true of China in this instance. If so, it is only further evidence that one need not take seriously either the claim that its policies are irrevocably based on Marxism-Leninism-Maoism, or the PRC's denial that it is a great power—for example, in the Shanghai joint communiqué of February 27, 1972, which stated, "China will never be a superpower and it opposes hegemony and power politics of any kind."

While the cryptodiplomatic encouragement and support of insurgent movements in the Third World will continue, it will probably become a less important tactic and be increasingly subordinated to more conventional diplomacy as the PRC is fully incorporated into the ongoing system of world politics through participation in the United Nations and normal diplomatic and commercial relations with other states, especially the United States and Japan.

The ideology of a Maoist ecumene is far more important as a determinant of China's domestic politics and of relations with other Communist Parties than as a source of China's foreign policy in general. Its primary role is akin to that of the old Confucian tribute-system ideology, because it serves as a source of legitimacy for the rulers of the PRC *within* the nation and among the Communist nations and Communist Parties of the world. The description of external events for this internal audience in terms which seem to endorse the infallibility of the Maoist leadership helps secure domestic support for a genuinely ideological program of reshaping Chinese society.

Chinese Nationalism

The question is whether anything from the past influences the international behavior of the PRC. In China it would be absurd to expect that there would be no historical residue at work in the present, even after the profound revolutionary changes of the past century. That influence is not to be found, however, in the misleading analogy between imperial Confucian sinocentrism and the ecumenical ideology of Mao Tse-tung.

In broad terms, two reinforcing concepts illuminate the study of international relations. One focuses on a putative international system made up of actors known as nation-states. It attempts to explain the relative and changing power of these components and the ways in which they combine and recombine into competing subsystems. A complementary concern is with the individual states which constitute the system. This approach initially focuses on the sources of foreign policy and its conduct within one or more of these actors. By looking at China's foreign relations from both of these perspectives, the historical factors which influence contemporary policy may be illuminated.

Prior to the major intrusion of the West in the first part of the nineteenth century, imperial China was not part of the same international system which the European states had developed in the post-medieval period. Intermittent trading and missionary contacts in the seventeenth and eighteenth centuries had little impact on China's image of itself as the center of the universe or on its genuine self-confidence in the superiority of its civilization—attitudes expressed in the tributary system. As the discrepancy between China's assumed superiority and its actual weakness grew in the early nineteenth century, romantic traditionalism was substituted for genuine belief, and an irrational insistence upon the letter of the tribute system replaced a previous flexibility in its application.

At that time, Europe was pursuing the combination of "civilizing mission" and squalid greed which led to temporary domination of the world. The confrontation between arteriosclerotic late-imperial China and nineteenth-century Europe dissolved the traditional Chinese world order as a political ideology and as an actuality. The intrusion of European, American, and Japanese power into the Middle Kingdom, the Opium Wars with the resulting unequal treaties, the loss of imperial China's nominal dependencies to the imperialist powers, large war indemnities to the foreigners, and a scramble for economic concessions all helped shatter the old self-image of China's cultural superiority and political centrality and resulted in the incorporation of China into the European-dominated international system as a second-class participant. During the period of the unequal treaties, from 1842 to 1949, a politically shattered and economically weak China was more frequently a passive subject than an independent actor in its relations with other states.

By the end of the Ch'ing dynasty in 1911, the foreigners in China had by force acquired extraterritorial rights, i.e., immunity from Chinese legal jurisdiction, had established foreign-governed enclaves in the treaty ports, had deprived China of tariff autonomy, and freely navigated China's inland waters not only with their merchant vessels but also with their gunboats. The foreigners were competing among themselves for railroad and mining concessions and to place loans with the Chinese government which would enhance their influence over its decisions; they had penetrated into the interior of the country with their missionaries who challenged the dominance of the rural social elite; and they had begun to nibble at the territory of the Chinese empire in Manchuria, Shantung Province, and elsewhere. Nevertheless, before 1911, the imperialist bark was more ferocious than its bite. Foreign political influence in late-imperial China was less than the powers thought it was or hoped it would be. While the foreign role in the very small modern sector of the economy was a significant one, the great bulk of the Chinese economy was not dependent upon an export market for primary agricultural or mineral products, as in parts of Southeast Asia and Latin America. Contrary to the common view, the foreign merchant in late-Ch'ing China increasingly served rather than controlled the traditional Chinese commercial system.[1]

If the direct effect of imperialism on China in the nineteenth century was a limited one, the Chinese elite magnified its consequences out of proportion to the actual derogations of China's sovereignty by the imperialist powers. Here can be seen a source of the particular power of Chinese nationalism, and here also—if anywhere—traditional forces helped shape modern actions. For the modern nationalist (anti-imperialist) sentiment which began to appear at the end of the

[1] See Albert Feuerwerker, The Chinese Economy, ca. 1870-1911, Michigan Papers in Chinese Studies No. 5 (Ann Arbor: Center for Chinese Studies, 1969); Chi-ming Hou, Foreign Investment and Economic Development in China, 1840-1937 (Cambridge: Harvard University Press, 1965).

century, especially after the shocking defeat that Japan inflicted on China in the war of 1894-95, gained intensity by incorporating the culturalist xenophobia of Confucian tradition. Most of China's first nationalists were men of elite background socialized in the traditional society. If they now focused their efforts on the survival of the Chinese nation (*kuo-chia*) rather than on the Confucian cultural ecumene (*t'ien-hsia*), the pain of losing the latter was still a great one and added a fervid emotionalism to the expression of nationalist sentiment.

The first Chinese reactions to the incursions of postindustrial-revolution Europe in the 1840s and 1850s were a combination of blind antiforeignism and futile attempts to play off one "barbarian" against another. This was a variation on the old cultural theme that had worked when the dynasty was domestically secure, self-confident, and isolated from any really powerful external challenge. In the decades between 1860 and the Sino-Japanese War, these reactions gave way to a more pragmatic effort to prevent further foreign demands by honoring the treaty privileges which they had exacted while attempting a modest military and economic self-strengthening which was immediately directed to the repression of internal dissension but might ultimately deter the foreign powers from enlarging their foothold. The Boxer uprising of 1900 was a brief and partial reversion to the xenophobic response of the midcentury. Thereafter, the field was held by modern Chinese nationalism. From the end of the nineteenth century until 1949, nationalist strivings to combine domestic reform (primarily to achieve the political and material basis for ending foreign special privileges) with an attack on the imperialist prerogatives themselves have constituted the main content of China's history. Each of the successive centralizing efforts of this half-century—the late-Ch'ing reform program, the brief rule of Yuan Shih-k'ai in the first years after the republican revolution of 1911, the nationalist revolution of the 1920s from which the Kuomintang emerged victorious and established its government at Nanking, and the rise to power of the Chinese Communist Party—has in its own manner been a response to this two-pronged nationalist program of domestic reform and anti-imperialism. When, after the brief or conditional successes but ultimate failure of their predecessors, the Chinese Communists came to rule China, they did so as the legitimate and authoritative inheritors of the leadership of this nationalist revolution.

But in the fifty-year transition of leadership from the late-Ch'ing statesmen to Mao Tse-tung, two critical developments increased the intensity and saliency of Chinese nationalism over the already high levels of the first decades of the twentieth century. Before World War I the imperialist powers had collectively nibbled at the margins of China's sovereignty and territorial integrity; but after 1915, Japan undertook its all-out political and military effort to turn China into its exclusive dependency, an attempt which culminated in the war of 1937-45. The memory of Japanese imperialism in China remains deeply etched in the minds of the present leaders of the PRC. These men, now in their sixties and seventies (Mao Tse-tung is seventy-nine, Chou En-lai is seventy-five), devoted their prime years to fighting it. Not surprisingly, they continue to challenge vigorously any distribution of international power which might lead eventually to a repetition of that struggle and to a possible derailment of the domestic goals of development and social revolution.

The second related development applies to the people of China rather than to their leaders. One major consequence of the fifty-year nationalist revolution was the mobilization or politicalization of ever-broader sectors of the population. While this process primarily affects domestic affairs, it has some bearing on foreign relations. Chinese nationalism in the late nineteenth century was confined to members of the elite. The motivation for at least some of them was the protection of their traditional political and economic privileges against foreign competition. Those who were not members of the traditional social elite, including merchants, Western-type professionals, the new intelligentsia, and even some workers and peasants, began to participate in the nationalist movement during the 1920s. The movement, however, was still largely an urban phenomenon removed from most of the people and only ambiguously related to the goal of domestic social change. During the war with Japan from 1937 to 1945, largely through the efforts of the Chinese Communist Party, a significant part of north China's rural population was mobilized under the banner of nationalism and for a concomitant program of social change (though not yet in support of the ultimate collectivist program of the CCP). Thus, China's modern history produced not only nationalism, but modern mass nationalism.

During the first phase of its modern contact with the West, China was located at the center of a distinct and autonomous international system of its own construction. During the second phase it was a victim in an international system dominated by Europe, America, and Japan. In the most recent phase, the People's Republic of China has progressively assumed the role of an autonomous actor in the post-World War II international system. This transformation took more than two decades, largely because of American obstruction. Its realization is marked by the PRC's entry into the United Nations in October 1971 and by the establishment of formal diplomatic relations with eighty-six states. During the century of the second phase, China's one area of successful adaptation to alien patterns of international relations was in the matter of style and protocol. Paraphernalia of the European international system such as a foreign ministry, ambassadors, second secretaries, and international law were sometimes utilized with skill, but to little avail in changing China's inferior status. With the reestablishment of a strong and unified polity after 1949, which eliminated the special privileges of foreign interests, style was joined with substance, and China began to acquire an international status commensurate with its size, population, and resources.

To summarize, imperialist incursions in the nineteenth and twentieth centuries have been of central importance in determining current Chinese attitudes and policies. The mental residue of that experience, for example, continues more than anything else to prevent normal relations between the PRC and the United States. The way the Chinese view their recent past and the fervid nationalism which arose gradually in response to the cataclysmic impact of imperialism on traditional China, not any Maoist version of sinocentrism, constitute the primary historical force which influences the foreign policy of the People's Republic of China.

If the content of modern Chinese nationalist demands is familiar to any student of recent world history—sovereignty, territorial integrity, equality with other nations, security, autonomy in determining its path to the future—there is an unusual intensity, almost vehemence, in their expression. It is as if the "classical" contours of nineteenth-century nationalism had been replicated in exaggerated form. The sometimes violent, even outrageous, rhetoric of Chinese foreign policy at times seems like a plea that its past oppressors acknowledge the immorality and long-run ineffectiveness of their deeds, and thereby clear the air for realistic negotiation in terms of present national interests. Chinese demands on the Soviet Union for the return of territories incorporated into czarist Russia in the nineteenth century may not be mere verbal ploys in a political battle.

The leadership of the Chinese Communist Party is legitimized by more than its perhaps dubious Marxist-Leninist credentials, and in this sense its ideological basis is not fully analogous to the role of Confucianism in imperial China. The claim to universal kingship was a central pillar of the traditional Chinese political system; when it was rejected, the whole edifice began to crumble. In contemporary China, even when Marxist-Leninist orthodoxy is compromised, the CCP can still legitimize its rule by falling back on its expulsion of imperialists from China. In this light the recovery of Taiwan, the one significant tear in the nationalist integument, is a more important force in Chinese international policy than the achievement of a worldwide Maoist utopia.

While nationalism as a commitment to the protection of the integrity and security of the Chinese state is a major factor in the formation of foreign policy, it is not the only determinant. Since 1949 several shifts and unanticipated changes in both foreign and domestic matters indicate that immediate national interest has been modified or distorted by ideological and policy clashes at home and that there have been problems of definition arising from the misperception of other nations' actions. The "leaning to one side" alliance with the Soviet Union of the early 1950s contrasts sharply with the armed clashes on the Ussuri River and in Sinkiang in 1969, the "spirit of Bandung" of the mid-1950s with the anti-imperialist offensive in the Third World from 1958 to 1965, and the xenophobia and isolation of the Cultural Revolution with the entertainment of Richard M. Nixon in February 1972.

Since 1949, China's foreign policy has generally been characterized by relatively cautious actions, however harsh the anti-imperialist and antirevisionist rhetoric which has accompanied them. While the ideological goal of overthrowing the bourgeois, modern-revisionist international system has been of some importance in China's domestic politics, the actual basis of the PRC's relations to the international community has become increasingly indistinguishable from that of other great powers. Although China may appear to be modest about accepting the designation, let there be no mistake: China is a great power. This suggests that the PRC's manner of relating to the international community is neither particularly benign (in accordance with its own self-image) nor malevolent (in the view of its rivals or adversaries).

China's national interests are not likely always to correspond to the perceived interests of the other powers. There will inevitably be misunderstandings, disputes, threats, and counterthreats as well as hard bargaining and subtle negotiations in which victories and defeats will be shared by all parties. These confrontations will most likely take place within the present international system which, with all its shortcomings, permits no claim to universal hegemony except the rhetorical.

There appear to be few lessons that the rest of the world can learn from China's conduct of foreign relations, either in the late-imperial period or in the twentieth century. This unremarkable conclusion has one exception: the usefulness of being aware of the historical reasons for the particular sensitivity with which China approaches all its external relations. The memory of the century of imperialist intrusions which ended in 1949 remains quite potent. Recognition of its continued influence may increase the possibility that the optimistic view expressed here will indeed turn out to be an accurate assessment.

Development of Agriculture

DWIGHT H. PERKINS

China's agricultural development over the past two decades has been unique in several important ways but similar to that of a number of developing economies in others. The similarities are obvious. China feeds nearly a quarter of the world's population on 7 percent of the globe's cultivated land. Like India, Korea, and several other less developed nations that are short of good land, China is over-supplied with labor. Unlike most other countries just beginning their modern economic growth, however, China has had to rely almost exclusively on its own resources. The large grain surpluses of the American midwestern plains, supplied virtually free to many nations suffering from harvest failure, have not been available to China. Thus circumstances have forced China to find its own solutions to its difficulties.

This article describes the Chinese experience in agricultural development and assesses its relevance for other countries in similar circumstances. The first part of the analysis will deal with Chinese efforts to raise farm output through improvements in technology and accelerated investment. The latter part will be concerned with China's attempts to reduce the wide disparities in income among farmers and between urban and rural workers, without harming agricultural productivity.

China must raise its farm output to keep up with its rapidly growing population and to allow for increases in per-capita food consumption. Birth-control efforts may eventually reduce some of the pressure to increase production, but such efforts by their nature take effect only slowly under the best of circumstances. Thus for the immediate future China will have to achieve an annual growth rate in agricultural output of over 2 percent simply to stand still. To improve living conditions, the rate will have to reach 3 percent or more.

During the past two decades, Chinese efforts to achieve a level of growth of this magnitude have gone through several major transformations. In the 1950s, output increases were attained by the massive application of essentially traditional techniques such as the pooling of land, the extension of double cropping, and the mobilization of labor for water-control construction activities. But these techniques had been used for a thousand years or more, during which time Chinese land productivity had risen well above that of most of China's neighbors (e.g., India and southeast Asia). By the late 1950s the potential for further advances by these methods had been largely exhausted. Beginning in the 1960s, therefore, a search began for new methods that would make it possible to break through the spreading stagnation of the late 1950s. These new methods relied more heavily on modern science and technology and included increasingly heavy application of chemical fertilizers, mechanization of key functions, and the like. These efforts will be described in some detail below.

A few indicators of the results of the past two decades of effort are presented in table 1. From these figures it is apparent that, in spite of massive efforts, Chinese agricultural production has managed to keep only slightly ahead of the increase in the number to be fed. This over-

TABLE 1

Indicators of Agricultural Performance in China

	1952	1957	1970	Annual percent of increase	
				1952–57	1957–70
Gross value of farm output (in billions of yuan)					
1952 prices	48.4	60.4	—	4.4	—
1957 prices	—	53.7*	72.0*	—	2.3*
Grain output (in millions of metric tons)	154.4	185.0	240.0	3.7	2.0
Population (in millions)	575	647	800+	2.4	—

Source: Official Chinese statistics except for the 1970 figure for population.
*The 1957 and 1970 gross-value figures may not be precisely comparable and hence there may be some error in the 1957–70 gross-value growth rate.

view, however, obscures the fact that during two periods (the early 1950s and from 1963 to the present) farm output kept well ahead of population growth. From 1963 to 1972, for example, grain output increased at an average annual rate of 3.1 percent. Between 1956 and 1963, in contrast, there was no increase in grain output at all (and a substantial per-capita decline).

In the discussion that follows, an attempt is made to explain the causes of these periods of growth and stagnation. An effort is also made to speculate about the future.

To begin with, there has been little scope for the extension of China's cultivated acreage at a reasonable cost. In fact, owing to the development of cities, factories, and water-control facilities between 1957 and 1958, the cultivated acreage actually fell from 112 million hectares in 1957 to 108 million in 1958 and to 102 million in 1965. Edgar Snow refers to an addition to the cultivated acreage of some 12 million hectares of marginal land from 1960 to 1970. But it is not clear whether this increase raised the total cultivated acreage or offset the effects of land used for other purposes. In either case, China's agricultural problems will probably not be solved by such efforts. And any extensions that do occur will depend heavily on complementary investments to provide an adequate water supply.

The key to China's future success in this area is therefore increased yields, just as increased yields account for most of the rise in output over the past decade. Efforts to raise yields have been concentrated on improving seeds, applying more and more fertilizer, constructing irrigation and drainage facilities, and, to some extent, mechanization.

Better Seeds and More Fertilizer

Enormous publicity has been given during the past several years to the impact that improved seeds have had on grain output in Asia and elsewhere. The new varieties developed by scientists at the Rockefeller-financed institutes in Mexico and the Philippines have been given credit for bringing about a "green revolution." Economists have even begun to worry about a second generation of problems caused by this revolution, problems of storage, of income distribution, and of marketing.

Unfortunately, available evidence does not allow one to assess precisely the spread of improved seed and chemical fertilizer in China. Such efforts have been made, of course. The problem lies in appraising the degree of their success. The Chinese claim, for example, that the grain-crop area sown with improved seeds rose from 4.7 percent in 1952 to 55.2 in 1957 and 77.5 in 1958. But given the near stagnation in grain production between 1956 when the output was 182 million tons and 1963 when it was 183 million tons, one can reasonably conclude that the new seeds were probably only a marginal improvement over their predecessors. Similarly, the use of improved seeds for edible oil crops had no apparent effect on output whatsoever.

Cotton is the one crop upon which improved seeds do appear to have had a substantial effect in the 1950s. The best available evidence suggests that the area devoted to cotton did not change much between the 1930s and 1957. Output, however, appears to have risen 74 percent, from 940,000 tons to 1,640,000 tons. The introduction of improved American varieties of cotton had begun in the late nineteenth century and had made some progress against the older varieties in the 1920s and 1930s. In 1952, when government extension efforts were just getting underway, roughly half of the cotton acreage was already in improved varieties, and that figure rose to 94 percent in 1957. Yields rose commensurately from roughly 23 catties per mou in the 1930s to 31 catties in 1952 and 38 catties in 1957. Better seeds did not account for all of the increase, but it is likely that they did account for much of it.

Data available for the 1960s on this subject are considerably skimpier than even that for the 1950s. For example, in the late 1960s the Chinese introduced a new strain of rice with a small stalk, few leaves, and higher yields, which rarely collapsed prematurely—a description that sounds much like the strains developed by the International Rice Research Institute (IRRI) in the Philippines. Some evidence suggests that the Chinese may have experimented with some varieties developed by the IRRI, but it is not clear that the IRRI varieties, which were developed for tropical climes, will be suitable farther north. Similarly, Mexican wheat, for the most part, is grown in the spring while most Chinese varieties are grown in the winter, except in the northwest section of the country. Thus, research to improve Chinese seeds must be essentially an indigenous effort.

Improved seeds are commonly effective in raising yields only when combined with large amounts of fertilizer. In fact, one of the principal purposes of new seeds is to make possible the application of chemical fertilizers. Whether or not because of the introduction of new varieties, China's use of chemical fertilizers in the 1960s increased dramatically. The expansion in the domestic production and import of this class of commodities is the clearest single indication of the shift in Chinese investment priorities after the rural crisis of 1959-61 from machinery and steel to greater emphasis on agricultural support industries.

In the 1950s chemical-fertilizer production remained at a very low level. After collectivization, a great effort was made to ensure that peasants continued to make effective use of organic fertilizers. Hogs were valued as much for the fertilizer they produced as for the supply of pork. But, obviously, one could not increase the number of hogs and draft animals unless one could feed them, and that in turn required more grain.

Figures for the production and import of chemical fertilizer are presented in table 2. This table clearly indicates that both domestic production and imports have increased rapidly throughout the 1960s. Although many problems are involved in estimating the effect of this fertilizer on crop yields, its use undoubtedly accounts for most of the rise in grain output between 1957 and 1970. It is likely that chemical fertilizer accounted for about 80 percent of the 55-million-ton increase in grain output in this period.

The Japanese currently apply slightly over 300 kilograms of fertilizer to a cultivated hectare, or over 60 kilograms of nutrient equivalent, while the Chinese apply approximately 10 to 14 kilograms of nutrient equivalent per hectare. A simple projection of these figures would imply that China could raise its fertilizer application roughly four to five times, but such a projection would be highly misleading. The use of large amounts of fertilizer is generally possible only where there is an accompanying supply of water for irrigation. Most Japanese farmland is planted in rice and is irrigated. Such is not the case in

TABLE 2

Chemical Fertilizer Production and Imports

	Production	Imports	Total
		(in thousands of tons gross weight)	
1952	188	137	325
1957	871	1,313	2,184
1960	1,930	1,134	3,064
1965	7,300	2,500	9,800
1970	14,000	6,000+	20,000+

Source: Production data have been reconstructed from official Chinese sources, and import data from reports of China's trading partners.

China where only 20 percent of the cultivated acreage was in rice (in 1957) and only one-third was irrigated (in 1963).

Indeed, the application of fertilizer to irrigated land in China may already be approaching Japanese levels. If all available fertilizer in 1970, for example, were applied only to this irrigated land, the amount per cultivated hectare would be about 80 kilograms (in terms of nutrient), which would be above the Japanese rate of application. In actual practice, fertilizer is not distributed in this manner, but irrigated land in China today may be receiving 40 kilograms a hectare or more. Chou En-lai may have recognized that China was nearing an upper limit on how much fertilizer it could use effectively, given the existing technology. He spoke to Edgar Snow in 1971 of a target of from 30 to 35 million tons to be achieved in 1975, and said, "Thirty million tons of chemical fertilizer may be more or less sufficient but we need more because not only grain crops but cash crops need fertilizer."

If 30 to 35 million tons is China's upper limit, what will come after that? Even under favorable circumstances, the additional 10 to 15 million tons will allow grain output to rise only another 30 to 45 million tons, or enough to feed an additional population of 150 million in seven to ten years at existing levels of consumption. China will remain on a vicious treadmill with one key difference from the 1960s. One major way of staying even or pushing ahead—raising yields through the application of more fertilizer—will be closed.

One solution to this approaching challenge would be to develop new and better seeds that would respond to increased fertilizer applications with even higher yields. As indicated above, it is not known how much progress China is making in this area. It is clear, however, that such progress is essential to China's economic future.

If China does succeed in developing new and better seeds, this achievement could provide both technology and hope for other developing economies. That is, the new seeds might be of some use in other countries in spite of differences in climate and soil. Hope would come from knowing that current maximum yields in places such as Japan do not constitute an upper biological limit. In fact, if there is such a limit, the planet will soon be unable to support continued massive increases in the population. Because China's yields started in the 1950s from a level much higher than those of most other developing economies, it will either reach or break through this assumed barrier ahead of the others.

It is possible to look on this coming challenge to Chinese ingenuity pessimistically, but pessimism is probably not warranted. Chinese science and technology have proved themselves in a variety of complex areas ranging from nuclear weapons to computers. There is no reason to think they will fail in the task of growing plants that yield more food content per acre. Furthermore, once the new technology is available, it is likely to spread rapidly across the countryside. The rise in rural educational levels, the small-scale industry movement, and the transfer of many technicians to the countryside ensure that the new techniques will find a ready market.

Irrigated Land and Underemployed Labor

New seeds and more fertilizer are not the only ways of raising farm output. During the 1950s China concentrated on expanding its water-control facilities. The most interesting feature of this program was the method of implementation.

Economists and others have long hoped that somehow the great masses of labor power in rural areas of developing nations could be mobilized. Under existing conditions, it has been commonly believed, these farm workers are underemployed or, at best, occupied in low-productivity activities. Other countries have only talked about making use of this resource or have instituted very modest programs, but China has mobilized rural labor on a large scale.

Underemployed labor has been used in China for a variety of purposes, including reforestation, road building, and terracing of land. Most of all, however, it has been used in the construction of water-control facilities such as irrigation and drainage. In judging the effectiveness of this source of increased productivity, therefore, it is necessary to consider whether the use of underemployed labor leads to a substantial extension of China's irrigated acreage and related improvements. With this background, one can begin to appraise the significance of the Chinese experience for other developing countries.

The record through 1957 is reasonably clear. By the end of the First Five Year Plan, China had succeeded in raising its irrigated acreage from about 21 million to nearly 35 million hectares. Thus the prewar levels of 26 or 27 million hectares were recovered and expanded. There were also many improvements to existing facilities.

In 1958, however, labor-intensive methods were applied on a much grander scale so that virtually all of China's acreage could be irrigated in a brief period. It was reported that the total irrigated acreage increased from 35 million to 67 million hectares between 1957 and 1958. Most of the increase was in central and north China, where the percentage of land irrigated in such provinces as Shantung and Shansi rose from 23 to 70 percent and 19 to 54 percent respectively. Even allowing for considerable exaggeration as a result of the dismantling of the statistical reporting service, there is little doubt that there was an enormous outpouring of effort.

But most of that effort went for naught. Beginning in 1959, China suffered through three poor harvests. The North was hit particularly hard. By the time recovery had been achieved in 1962 no one heard claims of vast new increases in irrigated acreage. Although the reports are somewhat vague, it appears that the total amount of irrigated land is not much higher than it was in 1957. What went wrong?

The answer appears to be that labor-intensive methods by themselves could not bring about the kinds of water-control construction required. Rivers in north China flood frequently, carrying with them great quantities of silt. This sediment clogs irrigation facilities almost as soon as they are completed and renders them useless. Irrigation is also made difficult by the fact that land in the North becomes water-logged easily.

The ultimate solution to this problem is to bring the great rivers of central and north China (the Yellow, Hwai, and Hai) under control, eliminating floods and removing most of the sediment which they carry. But this will involve the construction of large, modern dams at a great number of locations on the upper reaches of these rivers. Labor corvées can undoubtedly play some role in this process, but only a modest one when compared to the building of local facilities in the South where workers lived at home, only rudimentary machinery was required, and few if any modern materials were used.

Control of the northern rivers, therefore, is likely to prove expensive. One estimate puts the total cost of controlling just the Hwai and Hai rivers at 12.6 billion yuan (in United States currency, $5.3 billion), and control of the Yellow River would presumably be even more costly. Such sums, however, are not beyond the realm of the possible. The Chinese GNP today is probably over 200 billion yuan (in United States currency, $100 billion), and this investment could be extended over a decade or more if it begins soon. Some parts of a program to control the northern rivers have, of course, been underway or completed for some time. In any case, if extension of the irrigated acreage proves to be the principal or only means for making possible the greater use of chemical fertilizers and hence of raising yields, the Chinese government will have little choice but to push ahead with a scheme to control the Yellow River at almost any cost.

What, then, are the lessons of this experience for other developing economies? Even if one puts aside all the problems involved in mobilizing rural labor power, the initial inclination is to look on China's experience in this area as a negative example for others. Mobilization of this labor has led to only marginal gains in construction at the cost of considerable disruption in other more fundamental activities such as the raising of crops. But such a conclusion would be misleading. China's inability to achieve large gains from these efforts is in part a result of the fact that such activities have been used there for over a thousand years. So there was not much left to be done by the middle of the twentieth century. Other countries, including India and many in southeast Asia, have accomplished much less and might well benefit from labor mobilization like that practiced in China.

Whether these other countries could avoid the costs of such great mobilization efforts, which disrupt other activities, is problematic even if their governments possessed the necessary political power to initiate them. Much would depend on whether these governments could avoid the campaign atmosphere that has surrounded so many Chinese activities of this type. In the midst of a campaign, work is often done shoddily and on the basis of hurriedly drawn-up plans, with unpredictable results. But if one does not use the campaign technique, how does one arouse the enthusiasm of millions of peasants for the task at hand? It is a dilemma with no easy solution.

Mechanization

In recent years, visitors to China have increasingly mentioned the spread of mechanization in the countryside. To some this may seem surprising, given China's great quantities of "surplus" labor, but there are uses for machinery even under the conditions that prevail in rural China. First, many kinds of farm machinery do not in any way involve a reduction in the demand for labor. Better plows and improved hoes, for example, raise the quality of cultivation, but still have to be wielded by men.

Second, certain mechanizable tasks must be carried out during periods of peak labor demand. A considerable body of evidence indicates

that during such peak periods a shortage of manpower—not a surplus
—exists in rural China. In areas where double cropping is possible,
for example, farmers must harvest the first crop, reflood the fields, and
transplant the second crop in a short period. Several kinds of labor-
saving machines are clearly helpful under these circumstances, if ob-
tainable at a reasonable price. Power threshers allow the harvest to be
moved from the fields more quickly, power pumps move great quantities of water to the fields more quickly and efficiently than a man or
ox turning a waterwheel, improved transport devices move the grain
to storage bins and markets more swiftly and with less loss, and mechanized transplanters reduce the amount of labor required for that arduous task.

Of these three types of machinery, only power pumps appear to be
extensively used in China, although there has been some increase in
threshers. There has also been talk of the use of mechanized transplanters, but if Japanese experience is any guide, these machines tend
to be quite expensive and have yet to find much acceptance from farmers even in Japan where there is a labor shortage. The predominance of
power pumps on China's mechanized farms can be seen from 1964
figures, which indicate that of the total of 7 million horsepower
for all machinery employed in agriculture, pumping equipment accounted for 4 million, or over half.

Most of the increased use of power equipment, like that of chemical
fertilizer, occurred after the 1959-61 difficulties and was also part of
an apparent recognition that labor-intensive methods of raising yields
alone were not enough. By 1963 rural consumption of electricity had
risen 1,600 percent above the miniscule level of 1957. In the same
year the total horsepower of farm machinery had risen from 0.56
million in 1957 to 5.20 million and rose further to 7.00 million, as
already mentioned, in 1964.

Tractors have been introduced on a modest scale. Their main use has
been on the sparsely populated farms of the Northeast and Northwest,
although a few are found elsewhere.

The lessons of this experience for other countries with limited mechanization are rather prosaic. The Japanese were the first to develop a
wide range of mechanical implements suitable for the labor-intensive
farming that prevails in most of Asia. China is demonstrating that
such equipment can be beneficial even when rural wages and productivity are much lower than those that prevailed in Japan when the
mechanical devices were first introduced.

Communes and Income Distribution

The most important lessons of the Chinese agricultural experience lie outside the realm of technology. Although many nations have begun to raise agricultural productivity, few have made any attempt to come to grips with the great inequalities that exist in the distribution of rural income, inequalities that are sometimes exacerbated in the early stages of development. China is one of a small number of exceptions to the pattern in that it has experimented widely with policies that would reduce income disparities without harming productivity. Both its successes and failures are instructive.

In many poor countries today a small percentage of the rural population owns half or more of the land, while many millions of others have no land at all. Frequently those at the bottom of the income scale do not even have enough to stave off malnutrition. Furthermore, only those with enough money to save and who have some education and knowledge of the outside world are in a position to take advantage of various technical innovations. Thus a favored minority tends to develop faster than its neighbors.

The Chinese solution to this problem was first to confiscate the land of all who did not farm it themselves, generally well-to-do absentee landlords. Thus they swiftly eliminated the largest single source of income disparities, but large differentials in land ownership between rich and poor peasants remained. These latter differences were eliminated in the winter of 1955-56 with the formation of high-level agricultural producers' cooperatives in which income was earned solely on the basis of work done, except in a limited number of welfare cases. No special credit was given to those who had previously owned more land.

Although these measures did reduce disparities between the rich and poor in rural areas to a substantial degree, they did not eliminate them. Differences continued as a result of the fact that some cooperatives had good land while others' was of low quality. Also, some families had several skilled, hard-working members while others had only one or none. The families of good workers in the best co-ops probably had incomes per capita that were many times those of the least fortunate.

A further source of differences in income among families has been the existence of the private plot. Certain activities of farmers, most notably the raising of vegetables and hogs, have not lent themselves to collective management. When private plots were abolished in 1958 and 1959, for example, shortages of vegetables and pork appeared almost immediately. As a result, private plots (representing roughly 5 percent of the cultivated acreage) were quickly restored and have not been abolished since.

The problem that these plots create for collective activities is that individual farmers are constantly tempted to divert resources from collective to private use. Those who are successful can often increase their income to a considerable degree, particularly if they can produce items in heavy demand in a nearby city.

The Chinese leadership has never been happy about these continuing differences in income. In 1958 with the formation of the rural people's communes, in addition to abolishing private plots, it attempted to take another giant step toward egalitarianism. The amount of pay one received on the basis of need as contrasted to skill and effort was increased sharply, and the size of the basic collective unit was increased from about 200 families to 4,000 to 5,000 families. Before, in effect, the income of 200 families had been pooled and divided on the basis of work accomplished, but in 1958 the pool consisted of twenty to twenty-five times that number. This step thus eliminated differences in income that had been the result of differing qualities of land within the area covered by a single commune, although it did not eliminate disparities among the communes.

The rural commune, of course, was never designed for the sole purpose of redistributing income. One of its prime objectives was to create a vehicle for the mass mobilization of labor for water-control construction. Productivity was not ignored; it was at the heart of rural reorganization efforts.

But, as indicated earlier, productivity in the 1959-61 period did not rise. It fell precipitously. There were many reasons for the farm crisis of 1959-61, including bad weather, but two other important factors were the managerial and incentive problems connected with farm units of such great size. A few cadres simply could not manage thousands of workers producing hundreds of different products on many kinds of land and doing so with techniques that had more in common with gardening than with the kind of extensive farming practiced in, say, Nebraska. Nor could individuals see much connection between effort expended and what they received as income. In particular, any extra effort that was not explicitly rewarded with "work points" would only lead to an increase in farm output that would then be divided equally among 4,000 families.

The only solutions to the latter problem were to educate people to work for the good of society, not material reward, or to reduce the size of the farm unit so that people could see clearly the connection between extra effort and more income. The "socialist education campaign" initiated in the early 1960s and reinforced by the Cultural Revolution in 1966 was designed to accomplish the first goal. But human values are not changed overnight and many may not be subject to change by these kinds of campaigns at all. What was needed were changes that would make possible immediate rises in agricultural productivity.

The solution found in the early 1960s and continued to this day was to reduce the size of the basic unit which controlled the management of crops and upon whose income individual wages were based. This was done by dividing large communes and all their subunits of production brigades and teams into smaller communes and teams and then transferring most authority over crop management and the calculation of individual incomes to the smallest unit of all, the production team. The end result of this process was that the basic collective unit for most agricultural production had less than fifty families throughout the 1960s, including the period of the Cultural Revolution.

Thus China has found a compromise between the demands of productivity and the goal of a more equal distribution of income. It has avoided the depression of many decades that followed collectivization in the Soviet Union, and it has eliminated at least the worst forms of rural poverty that seem to be characteristic of private landownership in rural societies with surplus labor, such as India or Bangladesh. If the Chinese have failed to reach fast and easy solutions to the worldwide problem of rural poverty, they have at least found a path that over the long run promises to eliminate it in nearly a quarter of the world's population. Other nations will have to find solutions compatible with their own resources and values, but the Chinese experience appears to hold lessons for them.

Rural Economic Planning

JON SIGURDSON

This paper describes economic development in rural areas of China, relating it to methods of national coordination and planning. More precisely, it considers these questions: What type of investment policy do most rural counties follow? Who makes the decisions? And why? The discussion is based mainly on information from the Chinese press during the past few years and on a visit to two rural counties in China in December 1971. The analysis must remain tentative and impressionistic, however, because of the absence of firm data and because time has not yet put events in perspective. The scarcity of industrial and economic statistics since 1960, when the Chinese authorities stopped publishing aggregate figures, makes it virtually impossible to describe and analyze the development precisely. Further, the consequences of China's economic priorities and its methods of industrialization are not yet clear because the policies have been fully implemented for only a short time.

Since 1957, economic planning has stressed the importance of local initiative, local industries, and the systematic use of small and medium enterprises to achieve rapid industrialization. The rationale for these economic policies originated in the Party discussions of 1957 or earlier. Mao Tse-tung's comments on industrialization in his 1957 essay, "On the Correct Handling of Contradictions Among the People," is often quoted when Chinese planners discuss industrial or agricultural policies officially:

Heavy industry is the core of Chinese economic construction. This must be affirmed. But at the same time, full attention must be paid to the development of agriculture and light industry. . . . With the development of agriculture and light industry, heavy industry will be assured of its market and its funds, and thus grow faster. Hence what may seem to be a slower pace of industrialization is actually not so, indeed the tempo may even be speeded up. . . . What we must do now is to cut the time to gain experience in economic construction to less than it took us to get experience in revolutionary work and not pay such a high price for it. We'll have to pay some sort of price, but we hope that it will not be as high as that paid during the revolutionary period.

In sum, since 1957 the leaders of China have recognized the crucial importance of developing agriculture and rural industry. Only these sectors of the economy can provide adequate employment for the nation's increasing manpower. Even the most rapid expansion possible of the urban industrial sector could not absorb the annual increase of the labor pool. Only development of agriculture and light rural industry can meet the basic demands of the increasing population for food and shelter. Moreover, these sectors can generate much of the funds necessary for further growth. The leadership also stresses rapid development of heavy industry. It is committed to minimizing differences between urban workers and peasants.

The political and economic program for pursuing these goals is stated in a series of principles known as "walking on two legs," attributed to Mao. There are five principles: develop industry and agriculture simultaneously; develop heavy industry and light industry, but give priority to heavy industry; develop national and local industries; develop enterprises of all sizes; and use modern and indigenous methods of production. The successful implementation of these policies requires considerable decentralization; but planning, "proper" division of labor, and coordination under centralized leadership have always been considered necessary.

Because of decentralization, the number of central ministries and agencies in China today is less than half of the number before the Cultural Revolution. The number of people engaged in the central administration may have been reduced even more drastically. At the same time, local governments, particularly those at the regional and county level, have been expanded to cope with transferred responsibilities for industrial development, education and culture, and public health. Functions and powers have thus been dispersed from the central authority to local governing bodies. Industry and certain categories of the population have at the same time been redistributed away from the urban centers. These changes indicate some decentralization, but it is not true that central authority has been substantially reduced. Authority and power are likely to be shared among more people than previously, but the changes in the central organization seem to be mainly a question of delegating less urgent matters to local governments while concentrating on those which are essential for promoting overall economic development and rapid industrialization.

Local industry includes a wide range of undertakings. One form of local industrial expansion, where resources permit, is the development of small metallurgical plants and of small coal, iron, and other mines. Another important field of local industry is the making of farm machinery, fertilizer, insecticides, and other products for agriculture. Textile mills, sugar refineries, and food-processing and other consumer-goods factories are also being established.

Local industries now operate at all levels—in the 29 provinces, nearly 200 regions, about 2,000 counties, about 75,000 communes, and roughly 750,000 brigades. The counties in the populated areas in China cover and area of about 2,000 square kilometers and each has about 300,000 residents. The average population of a commune is almost 10,000 but varies considerably from one area to another. County factories concentrate on building hard-core industries to manufacture the means of production necessary to equip commune and brigade factories and also supply agricultural inputs. Commune factories make agricultural implements, process foodstuffs, and provide raw materials to county factories. Brigade factories assemble and repair agricultural implements, mill flour, and mine ores for the county factories.

According to Chinese industrial policy, all levels should engage in industrial production, and the size and sophistication of the enterprises should increase from the brigade upward. Many products are manufactured at several levels. Nitrogen chemical fertilizer, for example, is produced in large national or provincial plants, in medium-size regional plants, and in small plants run by the counties. The lower cost of transportation to and from local plants probably offsets part of the diseconomy of scale which results from small-plant production.

Ball bearings are also produced by large national enterprises, by medium-size plants run by the provinces or large municipalities, and by small enterprises run by counties or communes. In this case, the small enterprises have a very limited range of size and quality. Available information indicates that it is practical to substitute labor for capital expenditures at the local level. Part of the explanation, however, seems to be the considerable wage differential between the large national enterprises and the small county and commune enterprises.

Industrial coordination occurs at all administrative levels. The interaction of agriculture and industry can be best understood in the context of a county industrial system. Figure 1 shows the kind of eco-

FIGURE 1

Rural Industrial System

Commodity Flow

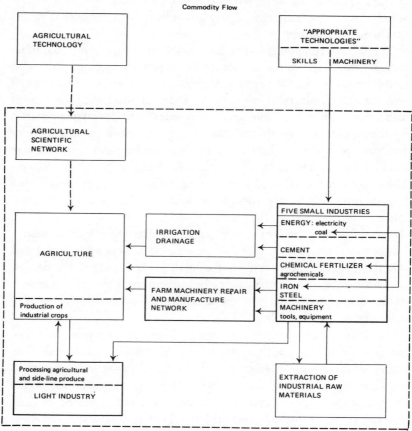

nomic and industrial system which is evident today in many counties.

The commodity flow in the figure indicates that the county industrial system primarily serves agriculture. The agricultural sector is provided with agricultural technology (including high-yielding seed strains), improved irrigation and drainage facilities, chemical fertilizer, and farm machinery. This creates the basis for increased agricultural productivity, which, when a certain level is reached, means that production of industrial crops can be expanded. Industry can then be supplied with more raw materials, and more light industrial products can be manufactured for local consumption. With increasing mechanization, more manpower can be released for industrial employment.

The industrial activities of a county are usually made up of four components. The first is the "five small industries." These produce energy, cement, chemical fertilizer, iron and steel, and machinery, which directly or indirectly supply agriculture with the inputs necessary to raise productivity.

The second component—the farm machinery repair and manufacture network—produces simple farm implements, tools, and also heavier equipment. Of primary importance is the repair and maintenance of agricultural implements in order to sustain a high rate of utilization. While the "five small industries" are operated primarily by the county, the repair and manufacture network has a three-tier structure with the smallest units run by the brigades, medium-size ones by the communes, and the relatively large units by the county. There is a clear division of labor among units on different levels; the brigade units are mainly engaged in simple repairs and manufacturing.

The third component of county industrial activity is light industry. The primary responsibility of this sector is to process agricultural and side-line produce and to provide the locality with many of the needed consumer goods. The expansion of light industry is closely dependent on increased productivity in the agricultural sector, which provides much of the raw materials.

The fourth component, the extractive industries, provides raw materials such as coal and iron ore to the "five small industries." The mining of minerals is often carried out by the brigades and communes.

The manpower for all the industrial activities comes almost exclusively from agriculture. Certain activities are greatly affected by considerable seasonal fluctuations in the supply of agricultural manpower. This is the case particularly in the construction of drainage and irrigation facilities and in mining and some light industrial activities. These activities are particularly labor-intensive. The farm-machinery repair and manufacturing network is less seriously affected by changes in the supply of manpower since it is less labor-intensive. The seasonal changes in demand, however, require great flexibility. The "five small industries" are, as far as the process industries are concerned, capital-intensive and thus not greatly affected by manpower fluctuations.

Industrial expansion is financed primarily by capital accumulated within the county. Initially, the agricultural sector expanded through low-cost, labor-intensive investment projects, such as the construction of irrigation and drainage facilities. The focus has shifted to the expansion of light industry where the expansion is coupled with generation of profits which then can be used for financing the expansion of the other industrial components. Seventy percent of light industry's raw materials come from agriculture, and their cost, compared to the price charged for the finished product, results in considerable capital accumulation.

Although the county industrial system is basically self-sufficient, larger units provide the county system with two important inputs. First, technology is fed into the agricultural scientific network, a multi-tiered (county, commune, brigade, and team) mass organization, in order to obtain rapid increased yields and productivity. Second, appropriate technologies and certain critical equipment are fed into the industrial structures, mainly the "five small industries" but also into light industry, mining, and the manufacture of farm machinery.

The important aspect of this local industrial system is its primary emphasis on providing agriculture with the necessary inputs for ultimate, full mechanization. This is to be achieved with local raw materials, local manpower, and local capital accumulation.

Obviously not all of China's counties have the resources to create a complete industrial system of this kind. The size and the diversity of a county industrial system depend on the natural resource base and the level of economic development. Some counties are well advanced, with the value of their total industrial production exceeding that of agriculture, but most are likely to be still in the initial stages of developing their industrial systems.

A similar analysis of a region's economic and industrial system would reveal the same interaction between industry and agriculture. But even though the regions run their own enterprises, they are primarily concerned with promoting the development of the counties within their region.

The management—not related to the daily routine—of most enterprises is handled by local (province, region, and county) authorities. They are responsible for stimulating the enterprises to achieve their potential production. Hence, the relationship between local political figures and enterprise managers is close and direct. Since the income of local governments is directly affected by the profits or losses of the enterprises, which in turn have a bearing on local economic development, the local governmental authorities will be more concerned with the production and construction of the enterprises and will make every attempt to increase production.

Local industrial and agricultural development depends upon the use of small-scale technologies, sometimes called "appropriate technologies," which are usually less efficient than those used in modern large-scale enterprises. The primary justification for this is that a large number of localities can set up medium and small enterprises which, compared with large plants, can still produce at reasonable costs.

Another reason for the use of appropriate technologies is China's growing manpower and the increased employment provided by these technologies. A February 1958 article in the *People's Daily* discussed ways to solve the country's population problem. It pointed out that medium and small enterprises could provide additional employment even though these local industries had shortcomings such as higher production costs. The article noted:

> Socialism has no preference for medium and small enterprises alone to the exclusion of large modern enterprises, but under certain conditions the policy of a combination of large, medium and small enterprises will help overcome the difficulties and accelerate industrialization. . . . The exclusive pursuit of large enterprises employing advanced techniques will result in the engagement of a part of the labour force in actual production which requires the allocation of a large part of the available means of production. As a consequence, another part of the labour force will not be engaged in actual production through lack of sufficient means of production. The result is that that part of the labour force engaged in actual production has to support the other part which is temporarily not engaged in actual production, thus wasting much available labour power. Furthermore, so far as the acceleration of the rate of accumulation of capital is concerned, the exclusive pursuit of large enterprises employing advanced techniques is not wholly reasonable under certain conditions.

The same article also argued that in order to attain full employment, wage scales should be reformed to minimize the differences in living standards between workers and peasants. This would prevent urban migration and the expansion of urban unemployment.

Some of the appropriate technologies, particularly in small process plants which produce items such as iron and steel or chemical fertilizer, are as capital-intensive as those used in large plants. This is because of the need to maintain quality standards and to make use of the economies of scale. For other types of production which are not faced with these constraints, the appropriate technologies are very labor-intensive. In enterprises which are subject to great seasonal shifts in the available manpower, labor-intensive technologies are often used. The application of capital-intensive technology in such cases would raise capital costs because the plant would be underutilized. This problem is especially acute in local industries such as sugar refining and oil pressing, which process raw materials available only for a limited period each year.

The development of local industry and agriculture is accompanied by considerable expansion in communications, trade, culture, education, and public health facilities. Increased manpower must be channeled into these areas.

However, labor-intensive technologies and local industries cannot solve the employment problem alone. Indeed, statements by Chinese planners indicate that agriculture will probably absorb most of the increase in manpower in the foreseeable future. Thus, the appropriate technologies are developed and used to expand local industry, which in turn enables an increasingly diversified, productive agriculture to absorb more manpower.

There is another important aspect, closely related to resource mobilization. In many places, local industries based on appropriate technologies expand simultaneously with the introduction of improved seeds, irrigation, and more chemical fertilizer. The consequent increase in agricultural output—the Chinese equivalent of the "green revolution"—creates potential savings. The local industries facilitate the tapping of these potential savings, for the peasants have the incentive to invest their surplus in order to get industrial goods for themselves as well as further inputs for their agriculture. In sum, local enterprises induce investments; therefore, the level of private consumption rises more slowly than would otherwise be the case.

The importance of local initiative is clearly stressed in economic planning in China today. This policy would seem to favor development of already well-developed areas of the country and may therefore increase regional inequalities. This may be partially correct in the initial stages of local development, but the higher authorities (region, province, and nation) have several ways to control the distribution of industrial activity and thus the income distribution among localities.

Control of investment funds is an important means of guiding the geographical distribution of industrial activities. Construction or expansion of some new local industries, such as iron and steel mills or chemical-fertilizer plants, usually cannot be undertaken by the locality itself. The distribution of electrical generating plants and the drawing of feeder lines from the main electrical networks is another way of forcing coordination between local and central planning. Still another measure has been devised which affects the income distribution within a county. Peasants who are temporarily working in industry are paid only about half of their wages, and the remainder is returned to their original brigade. This cash flow to the brigade then benefits all brigade members and is usually used to purchase new equipment. Peasant labor, then, is drafted according to which brigades need extra money to buy more farm machinery.

The distribution of critical skills and equipment may be a more important means for the center to coordinate central and local planning. A county industrial system will never manufacture special alloy steels or specialized ball bearings. Such products will be needed in the future but are likely to be manufactured only by some of the national enterprises at the top of the industrial hierarchy. As the demand for specialized equipment increases and as local industry expands and becomes more sophisticated, the localities will become more dependent on the center for certain critical equipment.

The higher levels will continue to control admission to the advanced educational institutions and probably will direct the allocation of highly skilled manpower. As more and more sophisticated skills are needed for further industrialization in the localities, these levels (region, province, and nation) will be able, within certain limits, to use the admission of students from the localities and the allocation of skilled personnel as a means to control or direct local economic development.

There appear to be short-term contradictions in the simultaneous development of rural and urban industries. The urban-based, predominantly large and modern enterprises are affected in two important ways by the rapid development of local industry. First, as local enterprises in rural areas begin to manufacture producer and consumer goods, the urban-based industries which previously supplied such goods lose part of their markets. Since local industry is expanding all over the country, large industrial producers are probably increasingly affected. This necessitates changes in the urban-based production profile. It also requires a decision on the division of labor between urban and rural industries. Many of the large industries are increasingly specializing in larger and more complicated products. Future industrial development in the large industrial cities will certainly emphasize products of high quality and complicated manufacture.

As the rural local industries become more numerous, more sophisticated, and larger in scale, this shift in direction for the large industrial cities is likely to continue for some time. One effect will be to hasten the obsolescence of urban machinery. However, since rural industries badly need such equipment, it may be transferred to rural areas and adapted to the different economic conditions and their smaller scale of production.

The growth of rural industry has affected industry in the cities in a second major way. Rural industries are critically short of industrial technology. Part of this need is fulfilled through mutual study and exchange among local industries in rural areas. However, a large number of problems cannot be solved locally and must be resolved with the assistance of engineering and technical personnel from the urban-based enterprises. A considerable amount of the training necessary for personnel in rural industries is also carried out in the large enterprises.

These two problems—the gradual shift of industrial production from urban to rural areas and the lack of personnel for problem-solving and technical training—require a system of planning that reduces the independence of the individual enterprises. If the urban enterprises were allowed to maximize profits, they would certainly have little interest in providing industrial training and problem-solving know-how to rural industries. In addition, few urban enterprises would be willing to give up their markets. As a result, much of the responsibility for individual enterprises must rest with local-government planning agencies.

What, then, is the role of the central ministries? They operate enterprises of an experimental nature and a small number of special enterprises, many of them producing for the defense sector. The central-government departments seem to concentrate on overall planning, nationwide coordination, and problems of balance. They also organize research for the adaptation of new techniques and provide technical guidance. There is no doubt that these tasks are far more complicated than concrete management.

China appears to be making considerable progress in solving the employment and regional problems which are becoming serious in a large number of developing nations. A well-organized Party, increasingly competent administration at all levels, and collectively owned enterprises have contributed to the results. The necessary interaction and close cooperation among the small local industries and between rural industries and urban industries would probably not have been possible if the enterprises were privately owned. However, the issue of ownership in China raises problems for the future.

The many local industries which mobilize resources in order to speed up economic and social development have been made economically feasible by a number of factors. The use of appropriate technologies is part of the explanation. Moreover, the wage differential (and sometimes a quality differential) between small and large enterprises is a crucial explanation for the feasibility of the small enterprises. Chinese planners apparently have created a temporary dual economy, where the rural industries with lower wages and lower productivity are producing goods which are mainly used within the agricultural sector, while the urban-based industries with higher wages and higher productivity continue to support the building of a modern industrial base. These differences must not continue to exist except in the transitional stage.

Socialist development requires an increase in ownership by all the people while ownership by small collectives decreases. The secular economic trend facilitates this social change: the value of industrial output increases more rapidly than that of agriculture. Since industry is run by larger collectives than agriculture, it appears that the trend is toward socialist transformation in rural areas. Many small industries, however, are collectively owned by brigades or communes, or jointly by the collectives and the state, while the big enterprises are owned entirely by the state. Since the small local enterprises are responsible for an increasing share of total industrial production, this may mean that fairly small collectives will have a considerable influence in the disposal of industrial profits and investments. This may result in certain contradictions in long-term planning even if the higher levels (region, province, and nation) utilize the previously mentioned instruments to control local development.

Resource mobilization in rural areas, which was initially important, will eventually become less important. As transportation networks are developed and the level of industrial technology raised, many of the small enterprises may become obsolete. They must then be closed down, expanded, or transformed to other relevant production. These problems will require constant attention and foresight by the planning agencies at different levels to make the partially decentralized economy work.

Science and Technology Policies*

C. H. G. OLDHAM

Almost twenty-five years have passed since Mao Tse-tung proclaimed the founding of the People's Republic of China and committed that country along a path toward his concept of a Communist utopia. Throughout these years the cornerstone of China's science policy has been that science must serve the people. Most of the Chinese investments in science and technology have been governed by this dictum, and hence an assessment of the current status of science and technology in China must be measured against Mao's objectives.

Twenty years ago, this would have been a more difficult assessment to make. At that time, a nation's scientific prestige was measured almost entirely by its ability to produce new knowledge and, to a lesser extent, to use knowledge in producing sophisticated weapons and generating wealth. In the 1970s, policy makers in most countries are more concerned with the utilization of science and technology to achieve a gamut of objectives which are frequently summed up by the phrase "improvement in the quality of life." That science should serve the people has now become the cornerstone of policy in the United States, Europe, and indeed in most countries.

Although a utilitarian viewpoint has dominated Chinese thinking about science, the precise ways in which science should serve the people have been the subject of heated debate. Specific policies have

* Adapted from the 1973 *Britannica Yearbook of Science and the Future*, copyright 1972 by Encyclopaedia Britannica, Inc., Chicago, Illinois.

changed frequently and sometimes dramatically over the past twenty-five years. Indeed, the changes and the novel approaches of the Chinese make a study of their science and technology interesting—and tantalizing. It is interesting because of the inherent interest of China's social experiment and because of the possible relevance of the Chinese experience to other developing countries. It is tantalizing because, although one can form a rather good idea of Chinese policies from their press, it is difficult to judge their success in achieving the desired goals.

This paper attempts to summarize the changing Chinese policies on science and technology and, in the conclusion, speculates on the reasons behind Mao's strategy. Throughout, it refers to the major issues currently discussed by those concerned with the use of science and technology as tools to aid development.

To start with, China exists in a world where 98 percent of expenditures for research and development take place in the industrialized countries. This maldistribution of world research has profound implications for developing countries. Not only is much of the world's research irrelevant to the needs of poor countries in the tropics, but some of it, such as research on the development of synthetics, is harmful to their trading prospects in materials. It is against this background that the Chinese priorities and experience must be viewed.

Although China's commitment to modern science is relatively new, the country has a long history of scientific discovery and technological invention. As Dr. Joseph Needham of Cambridge University has well documented in *Science and Civilization in China*, China can lay claim to more technological firsts than almost any other civilization.[1] The Chinese first invented the seismoscope, in the first century A. D. The magnetic compass, gunpowder, and the printing press with movable type are further examples of technologies first developed in China and many years later developed independently in the West.

However, for some unknown reason, the scientific revolution took place in Western Europe rather than in China. The Industrial Revolution and the growth in material wealth of Europe and the United States followed the scientific revolution. China and the rest of the developing world changed slowly.

[1] Joseph Needham, *Science and Civilization in China*, 4 vols. (Cambridge: At the University Press, 1954-71).

Apart from a few early contacts with missionaries such as Matteo Ricci, until its defeat by the British during the Opium Wars in 1842, China remained isolated from the changes which were sweeping through Europe. From that point the slow, painful process of modernization took on a new dimension as some Chinese reformers urged that China begin to adopt what they thought of as Western science and technology. Their voices had little effect, and it was not until after the Manchu dynasty was overthrown in 1911 that the efforts to transplant modern science onto Chinese soil began to have much effect.

Even then it was not until the 1920s that the major intellectual break with Confucianism was made and politicians were committed to build a new China based on modern science and technology. By the mid-1930s, the Nationalists had begun to organize scientific endeavors and had established several research institutes and universities. Although this scientific effort was severely disrupted during the late 1930s and throughout the 1940s because of the state of war which existed in China, a nucleus of competent scientists and engineers still existed in 1949 and a start had been made to build an indigenous scientific system.

The Organization of Science

The nucleus of scientists and an organizational framework, which Mao inherited, though in a fragmented form, proved valuable. For many years, experts on development have put a low priority on the need for developing countries to have an indigenous scientific capability. They argued that the industrialized countries were a veritable supermarket of technologies and all the developing countries had to do was to shop around for what they wanted. Mao has always rejected this argument. Most other developing countries are following his line.

To begin with, most industrial technologies developed in the advanced countries cater to conditions of large-scale production; capital is relatively abundant and labor scarce. This situation is hardly found in China or other developing countries. Most of the agricultural and medical research done in the developed countries is even more inappropriate for developing countries. But probably the most important reason why China and other developing countries want their own scientific establishment is that without one they are dependent on foreigners to make the important technological decisions affecting them. They find this dependence economically unpalatable and politically unacceptable.

The network of research institutions and facilities for training scientists and engineers developed in China in the 1950s was based largely on the Russian system. The Academies of Science, Agricultural Science, and Medical Science operated their own research institutes and carried out most of the advanced research in the country. Overall strategy was set by the state Scientific and Technological Commission. Applied research was sponsored and carried out by the relevant ministry. Few universities carried on advanced research, and most new research workers received their training on the job at the various institutes of the academies.

Since an initial period in the early 1950s when the academies determined their own research priorities, the work of the various institutes has been subject to the overview of a planning authority. In 1956 a twelve-year plan for science was drawn up with a great deal of Russian help. China planned to catch up with the advanced world in ten priority areas by the end of the twelve-year period. However, during the Great Leap Forward (1958-60), a mammoth campaign which mobilized China's masses, the earlier concept of central planning of research priorities seemingly was abandoned in favor of encouraging all innovations which originated with peasants and workers in whatever field they occurred.

During the 1960s there was little reference to the state Scientific and Technological Commission in the Chinese press, although it continued to be the main policy-making body for science and technology. It either operates quietly or it is largely ineffective.

The Great Leap Forward also coincided with another event which had a major impact on Chinese science, as well as on foreign policy: the withdrawal of all Soviet aid. Between 1958 and 1961 all the Russians were called home and the massive technical-assistance program came to a halt. The Russians even took the blueprints of unfinished plants home with them. This event still deeply disturbs the Chinese. Even in 1972, visitors to China were still being told with evident bitterness about the fickle Russians. There can be little doubt that the Chinese attitude toward the Soviet Union is heavily influenced by this event.

The effect on Chinese science policy was immediate and long-lasting. It made the Chinese distrustful of foreign aid, and "self-reliance" became the key slogan of the early 1960s. More and more resources were injected into the Chinese science system, and by 1965 it seemed that the Chinese plan to catch up with the advanced world in certain priority areas was on the way to fulfillment. In 1964 and 1965 contacts with Western scientists were considerable, and formal scientific exchanges were arranged with many Western European countries. Reports of the foreign scientists who visited the country indicated that China was creating a solid foundation in most scientific disciplines. Chinese scientists were apparently well informed of work in their disciplines in other parts of the world and in a few areas were already making important new contributions themselves. But by and large there were few surprises. The adjective most commonly used by the foreign visitors was "sensible." By the mid-1960s, judged by Western scientific standards, the Chinese science system appeared vigorous and was producing good work. But apparently Mao felt otherwise.

When the Cultural Revolution began in 1966, scientists were specifically excluded, but not for long. By early 1967 the activities of scientists came under close scrutiny. For several months the Chinese press was full of accounts of upheavals within the institutes of the Academy of Sciences. The criterion was whether the institutes had served the people. Many scientists were accused of being too greatly influenced by the foreign scientific literature and too little influenced by Chinese problems; they were too eager for scientific awards and titles, and they were more interested in personal fame than relatively unglamorous work. In short, scientific research was not sufficiently integrated with the needs of society.

In the early 1970s, similar charges were directed against the scientific community in most of the world's developing countries and increasingly in the more industrialized countries. The initial Chinese solution was to put the research institutes under the control of the revolutionary committees made up of representatives of the People's Liberation Army, the political cadres, and "revolutionary" workers. China has also experimented with different ways of integrating research with education and production, but too little is known about the details of these experiments to judge their success.

Contacts with foreign scientists were broken off during the Cultural Revolution. Since the publication of Chinese scientific journals also stopped, it became difficult to assess the impact of the Cultural Revolution on Chinese scientific research. In the early 1970s, however, China made a dramatic reentry into international affairs, and Western scientists were once again able to visit the research institutes of the Academy of Sciences. They found that the institutes were working on more applied problems than had been the case in the mid-1960s and that despite the criticism of scientists in the Cultural Revolution and the time many had spent working in communes, most were again doing research. They also found less familiarity with the latest research in the rest of the world than there had been before the Cultural Revolution, especially among younger research workers, even though they were receiving foreign scientific journals. In 1972 delegations of Chinese scientists began visiting Western countries again, and scientific exchange agreements were negotiated with several foreign academies of science.

Although the long-term effects of China's isolation from the mainstream of world scientific research remain unknown, in some areas of research Chinese scientists have probably pioneered novel approaches. But the rate of growth of scientific knowledge in the world is such that by cutting itself off from much of this knowledge, China must delay reaching its stated goal of catching up with the advanced countries of the world.

Scientific and Technical Education

Although the Communist government inherited a nucleus of scientific institutions when it came to power in 1949, not many fully qualified scientists and engineers were available. A major effort was launched to increase the number of technical personnel, and certainly the number with some technical training has increased dramatically. It is difficult, however, to make comparisons either with other countries or between different periods in China. This is because there seem to be no definitions of "manpower" which are generally adhered to. The best manpower estimates, based on conflicting Chinese evidence, indicate that the number of scientists and engineers rose from 600,000 in 1955 to 2.4 million in 1967. Approximately 670,000 of the 2.4 million had been trained in full-time institutes of higher education in China since 1949. The rest were either promoted to the rank of scientist or engineer without receiving full-time training or were already trained in 1949.[2]

It has been estimated that the number of college-trained scientists and engineers had reached 1.3 million when the Cultural Revolution began and all the schools and universities were closed. The universities remained closed for four years and only began teaching scientific subjects again in 1971. This closure represents a major loss of technical manpower. But even though schools and colleges were closed, the research institutes of the Academy of Sciences remained open, and many of them tripled their staff during the Cultural Revolution. Most of the new recruits were secondary-school graduates, and the Academy of Sciences must therefore have played an important role in continuing to provide a scientific education, at least to some.

When reopened in 1971, the colleges and universities had implemented many reforms. The new entrants were drawn mainly from families of working-class origin. The children of the former bourgeois classes found it more difficult than before to gain admittance. The length of instruction was cut from four and five years to two or three years, and higher education was linked more closely with production, both through changes in the curricula and through students' working part-time in factories or communes. The latter practice existed before the Cultural Revolution, but was now integrated into the students' schedule more systematically. These new policies mean that the new scientists and engineers will enter the work force as scientific and technical generalists rather than as specialists.

As important as the education of highly trained members of the society may be, perhaps equally important in a developing country is the scientific education given to the population as a whole. The Chinese have given this aspect a high priority. Full-time secondary schools stress scientific and technical subjects, and a wide variety of part-time education is available, especially to workers in factories. In fact, one of the most important educational accomplishments has been the training of paratechnical personnel. This has been particularly successful in the medical sphere where large numbers of so-called barefoot doctors have brought rudimentary health care to millions of peasants. Great emphasis has also been put on providing an elementary scientific education to all members of society. The leadership considers this particularly important since they expect the work-

---

[2] Yuan-li Wu and Robert B. Sheeks, *The Organization and Support of Scientific Research and Development in Mainland China* (New York: Praeger, 1970).

ers to provide many of the technical innovations adopted by industry. They claim that workers' innovations are more relevant to production than those generated by the experts. This is a controversial issue in China, but certainly during the Cultural Revolution greatest publicity was given to the workers' innovations.

Industry

So far this article has focused attention on the ways in which China has built up its indigenous science system. However, research carried out in a country's laboratories is only one way in which its production sectors can acquire new technologies. The other way is by importing the technology from abroad. One of the most important science and technology decisions for any country is to decide how much and what to import and how much and what to generate indigenously.

Most developing countries have relied heavily on the importation of technology, but it is now recognized that this can lead to economic and political dependence on the foreign countries, and many developing countries are trying to find ways to diversify their sources of technology.

China has made a big issue of "self-reliance." Just how self-reliant has China been and to what extent has it, too, depended on foreign technology? In the choice of techniques, to what extent have Chinese policy makers been concerned with goals other than economic growth? These questions need to be considered as they apply to different sectors of the economy.

The industrial sector affords the clearest view of the policy conflicts over choice of techniques and issues of importing foreign technology. But here, as in almost all phases of Chinese development strategy, no single approach has dominated Chinese thinking throughout the period of Communist rule. Rather, the evolution of policy can be divided into several periods.

In the first period immediately after 1949, Chinese industrial policy was clearly aimed at copying the Soviet model. Emphasis was placed on heavy industry, and the technologies used in this sector were mostly imported from the Soviet Union and were capital-intensive. Rapid economic growth was China's principal goal.

This period lasted until 1958 when the whole Chinese approach to development dramatically changed. A period of mass involvement and mobilization, called the Great Leap Forward, was launched. Many foreign observers tend to write this experiment off as an economic failure. Certainly the high pitch of total involvement was only continued for about three or four years, and some of the experiments initiated at the time, such as the backyard blast furnaces, were later abandoned. But the emphasis which was given to local initiatives and the development of rural, small-scale industries has continued to the present day. Indeed, it was during this period that the much-quoted slogan of "walking on two legs" was promulgated. Not only was China to achieve its national developmental goals by stimulating the growth of a modern state-operated industrial sector, it was also to develop its second leg by promoting local commune- and district-run industries using more labor-intensive technologies. The Great Leap Forward, however, can be identified as a time when relatively greater emphasis was given to the second leg and the importance of the technical expert declined.

The next period began in 1961 and lasted until the Cultural Revolution in 1966. It began with the severing of Soviet aid, the withdrawal of Soviet technicians, and the cancellation of Chinese orders for new Soviet plants. The enormous flow of Soviet technology into China, which had characterized the 1950s, became only a trickle. Self-reliance was the order of the day. The call for self-reliance led to a boost in indigenous research and revived the prestige of the research worker and the expert, but it did not mean that China became autarkic. Although cut off from Soviet technology, China began to import modern technology from Japan and Western Europe. Orders were placed not only for equipment and machinery, but also for entire plants.

The Cultural Revolution once again led to new policies. Egalitarianism became the principal goal. Scientists and engineers were accused of becoming a new elite and of being the forerunners of a return to capitalism; the earlier policies ascribed to the president of the People's Republic, Liu Shao-ch'i, were criticized. Once again emphasis was given to innovations which originated with the workers, and the importation of foreign technology declined from its previous levels, but, despite the emphasis given to self-reliance, never stopped.

Finally, in 1971, the policy began to change. The importation of sophisticated technologies increased in volume, and the policy of "walking on two legs" with roughly equal emphasis on modern large-scale industrialization and local small-scale industries appeared once again to be the main guideline.

Other developing countries might learn some relevant lessons from the changing Chinese policies on technology and industrialization. Undue reliance on one source of foreign technology can have disastrous short-term economic effects, since the source could suddenly dry up. The short-term economic disruption caused by the loss of a single source of foreign technology may have beneficial effects in the long run because it encourages both self-reliance and a process of shopping for alternative foreign technologies more appropriate to local conditions. In China, great self-reliance and inventiveness were needed to cope with a situation in which plants were left unfinished, blue prints were taken away, and an embargo was placed on the importation of spare parts. (Cuba was in a similar situation vis-à-vis the United States when the latter placed an embargo on goods exported to Cuba in 1961. Some Cubans argue that the "technical learning effect" which this generated among Cuban engineers will in the long run be more beneficial for Cuban development than the short-run economic losses which the embargo caused.)

The goals of creating employment opportunities and egalitarianism will likely require technologies different from those which maximize short-term economic growth. The Chinese approach has been to utilize both kinds of technologies, but the coexistence may be possible only in planned and command economies. It is doubtful whether China's relatively inefficient, labor-intensive technologies could compete with more efficient, growth-oriented technologies in a market economy. Thus, although many developing countries have great interest in technologies to create employment, the Chinese experience may not be particularly relevant if the country is also committed to maintaining a market economy.

Finally, the Chinese experience indicates the considerable economic and social advantages which can accrue by encouraging innovation among workers. On the other hand, the vacillating policy toward experts indicates that China appears to have as much trouble as most countries in getting scientists and engineers to work on relevant problems, and the Chinese solution—reform of political thought—seems no more successful than less dramatic solutions elsewhere.

Agriculture

In the early years of Communist rule, little attention was given to developing new agricultural technologies. But when the decision was made in the late 1950s to give agriculture first priority, two technical issues predominated. The first was how to increase yields; the second was the more ideological issue of agricultural mechanization.

Technology plays an important part in increasing production by contributing to the development of irrigation, fertilizers, pesticides, and new seeds. During the period of the Great Leap Forward (1958-60) when the communes were introduced, the greatest emphasis was placed on improving irrigation. Labor was mobilized on a massive scale to dig ditches and build dams. During the 1960s much greater emphasis was placed on improving production by producing and applying more chemical fertilizer. The need for fertilizer led to the invention of new techniques which enabled small-scale plants to produce ammonia and urea efficiently. By the end of 1971 nearly half of all chemical fertilizer was produced by local industry. It has been estimated that most of the increased grain output in the 1960s was due to the application of chemical fertilizer.

There is no evidence that Chinese scientists have been able to breed new strains of rice and wheat with yields as high as those produced by the International Rice Research Institute in the Philippines or the Wheat Research Institute in Mexico. The new grains that have contributed much to the "green revolution" in a large part of Asia are not particularly appropriate to Chinese conditions. But one can assume that the Chinese will put high priority on research to develop new varieties with high yields.

Ideological considerations complicate the mechanization issue. Mao has advocated that in the long run China should aim for the maximum agricultural mechanization possible. The tactics to achieve this long-term objective were debated during the Cultural Revolution. The supporters of Liu Shao-ch'i argued for a concentration of the agricultural machinery to be allocated by the state to those areas most suitable for machine operations, i.e., large areas of arable land where draught animals are scarce. They also favored a concentration of research resources into a few centralized research institutes. Mao's supporters, on the other hand, were in favor of decentralization or of giving the initiative to the communes. If a particular commune wanted to mechanize and acquire its own tractors, they believed it should be encouraged to do so. Mao's supporters also favored decentralization of research. Instead of one or two large research stations, Mao favored the establishment of dozens of semimechanized stations so a peasant with a worthwhile innovation could try it out locally. In this way, it was hoped, there would be a flow of new innovations, and all peasants would have a sense of involvement in the development of their country. Mao argued that, although some resources should be allocated to advanced research, most should go to semimechanized institutes. This issue became controversial during the mid-1960s, and the extent of the debate was revealed in the Chinese press during the Cultural Revolution. As in almost all debates, the press assured its readers that Mao's ideas were "correct" and were being implemented.

This approach suggests obvious lessons for other developing countries. Mao's policy is not only more appropriate for generating labor-intensive technologies, but also has the other social benefit of providing more opportunities for individual peasants to be personally involved with development.

Medicine

Probably the Chinese experience in the field of public health and medicine has the greatest relevance for other countries. A few notable aspects of the Chinese approach will be mentioned here. First, the Chinese have put more stress on preventive than on curative medicine, although even with the latter they have in some branches surpassed the level of success achieved in the more industrially advanced nations. They have been notably successful in rejoining severed limbs and in treating burns. Second, they have given a high priority to training paramedical personnel, especially peasants, for service in rural areas. Third, they have been remarkably successful in combining traditional and modern medicine. Herbal drugs have had widespread therapeutic value, and acupuncture has received worldwide attention.

But most significant and important have been the concentration on preventive medicine and the introduction of a curative service in rural areas. How this has been done is graphically described by Dr. Joshua Horn, who has returned to England after working as a doctor for fifteen years in China. His book *Away with All Pests* described what happened in his hospital in Peking after the start of the Cultural Revolution.[3] When the decision had been made to speed up the rate at which rural areas were to receive health care in 1967, all hospitals

[3] Joshua Horn, *Away with All Pests: An English Surgeon in People's China* (New York: Monthly Review Press, 1971).

in urban centers were ordered to send one-third of their staff to rural medical centers in Hopeh for a year at a time. At the end of the first year some chose to stay permanently in the country, while the rest returned to Peking to be replaced by another third of the hospital staff.

Dr. Horn describes in some detail the work of the hospital staff in the countryside. First, rural teams stressed preventive medicine by focusing on public-health measures and sanitation. They helped organize campaigns to eradicate pests such as flies and mosquitoes. The teams also organized the training courses for the barefoot doctors. During the first winter, new recruits from the communes received five months of medical training. Thereafter, they could give inoculations and first aid, and they knew when to call the hospital doctors. They returned for a second five months of training the next year, and were scheduled to receive three such sessions. Afterwards, they returned to the communes that had sent them and provided grass-roots medical service, instruction in family planning, and assistance to local medical units in both traditional and modern medicine.

The widespread move to bring health services to rural areas must be reckoned among the most outstanding of all China's accomplishments. Nowhere else has the movement of doctors from poorer to richer areas and from poorer to richer countries been reversed.

Defense

Although the application of science and technology to the fields of economics and health has the greatest relevance to other developing countries, Chinese achievements in developing military technologies have also caught world attention. The timing of these achievements is well known, although the technical details are still obscure. China's first hydrogen bomb was successfully exploded only eight years after the inauguration of its first research reactor, and less than three years after its first atomic explosion. China has also demonstrated its capability in rocket technology by launching a guided missile and putting a space satellite into orbit.

The scientific and technical work behind these successes was led by two Chinese scientists who had worked in the United States but who returned to China in the mid-1950s. Their work has obviously had massive research and engineering support, and although defense science and technology did not entirely escape political criticism during the Cultural Revolution, it did not suffer from the same sort of disruption that civilian science experienced. The existence of a high-technology enclave in China has important ramifications far beyond its military value. Especially important are the demands on Chinese industry for high-quality, technically sophisticated products. It would be interesting to know the extent to which the Chinese experience in linking industrial production to research and to defense requirements has been transferred to the civilian sector.

Conclusion

Sufficient examples of Chinese science and technology policies have been given here to permit a brief synthesis. What appear to be contradictory and even at times irrational policies make sense if Mao's long-term objective is kept in mind. That is to set China firmly on the road to a truly utopian Communist society in which there is no exploitation, no dichotomy between manual and mental labor or between urban and rural areas, and where everyone is both ideologically committed and technically competent.

As early as 1964-65 it was clear that Mao was disappointed with the progress toward this goal. He apparently decided that a major midcourse correction was needed, and in 1966 he launched the Cultural Revolution.

In the years preceding the Cultural Revolution, Mao had taken the experts, many of whom had been trained abroad, and tried to make them Communists with only partial success. As China developed economically, an elitist technocracy that was pragmatic rather than idealistic began to emerge. Mao believed that the pragmatists would lead China back into the capitalist camp. Clearly, from Mao's point of view, drastic action was needed if the younger generation was not to be misled permanently. If he could not make Communists out of the experts, then he must try to make a new kind of expert out of the Communists. This was to be accompanied by an even greater effort to reeducate the scientists and other intellectuals in what seems to be an almost desperate attempt to attune them mentally to Mao's utopia.

The growing dichotomy between manual and mental labor seems to have been one of the key reasons for starting the Cultural Revolution, and explains much of what has happened in the research institutes and universities. Once the revolution got underway, the dichotomy between city and village became increasingly important. Mao's efforts to decentralize education and health services and to encourage small-scale industries and intermediate technologies are consistent with his aim to narrow the development gaps between different parts of China.

The Cultural Revolution undoubtedly caused a major interruption in education and scientific research, but apparently for only a relatively brief period. There appears to have been less interruption in industrial and agricultural production, and in some sectors with military significance there have been major technological feats such as the satellite launching. There have also been major gains in public health. The objective of self-reliance means that Mao's determination to use science and technology to build a modern China has not faltered, but whether a truly modern country can be built without creating a technocratic elite remains to be seen.

Ecology and Environmental Control

J. B. R. WHITNEY

For many centuries China has provided a model for advocates of political, social, economic, and educational reforms in the West.[1] Distance and differences in culture made China an eminently suitable choice, since general ignorance of the country permitted the reformers to clothe it with all the ideals they wished to introduce into their own societies; no one was in a position to challenge them. Recently, and perhaps for the same reasons as in earlier periods, China has been held up as a model of the way in which a country should conduct relations with its environment.[2]

Although the present leaders of China have espoused many causes, apparently they have not considered themselves in the vanguard of the worldwide ecological crusade that some of their admirers in the West feel they should lead. Indeed, as is seen from their statements at the United Nations Stockholm Conference on the Human Environment, the Chinese make only a modest assessment of their ecological achievements.[3] They do, however, see themselves as spokesmen for Third World countries that oppose imperialism and international capitalism and the various kinds of moral and social pollution that, they believe, are engendered by them. An increasing number of statements in the Chinese press and radio, moreover, indicate a growing concern

[1] See, e.g., Harold R. Isaacs, *Scratches on Our Minds* (New York: John Day Co., 1958).
[2] *Globe and Mail* (Toronto), June 6, 1972.
[3] Tang Ke, "China's Stand on the Question of the Human Environment," *Peking Review*, June 16, 1972, pp. 5-8.

to reinterpret policies and programs in terms of ecological considerations even though they were originally undertaken for other reasons. One may therefore speculate that within the next few years the rest of the world will study Chinese ecotactics as assiduously as it now studies Chinese revolutionary tactics.

Ecology and Environmental Management in Traditional China

In traditional China, apart from a few large environmental engineering schemes (such as flood-control projects on the Yellow River) that were under the control of the central or the provincial government, the greater part of man's impact on the environment and on ecosystems took place at the local level as a result of decisions made by millions of peasants and a few thousand gentry families. (In this paper the term *environment* refers to the basic inputs of air, solar energy, water, and minerals and gases that control ecosystems. *Ecosystems* refers to the network of biological processes and forms through which elements from the environment flow.) For the most part, these decisions took place in the organizational framework of the *hsien* (county) and, at a still lower level, within the some 70,000 market areas that formed one of the basic social and economic units in China.[4] Each of these small units was largely self-sufficient and was linked rather weakly by trading networks to its neighbors and to higher-order economic regions.

Figure 1 depicts, in a highly simplified form, the flows of plant minerals and nutrients in one of these local cells.[5] For the most part, farm animals were used for agricultural purposes, and the modest flows of plant nutrients which they utilized (E in figure 1) were obtained from those portions of the crop that man had not used as food.

High productivity per unit of land was obtained by utilizing human and animal energy to accelerate the flow of energy and nutrients through local farming ecosystems in partial imitation of natural ecological processes. Labor-intensive mulching techniques sped up the process of bacterial decomposition and returned minerals more rapidly to the soil for further plant growth (F and G), and, in many parts of

[4] The economic and social aspects of these units are fully described in G. William Skinner, "Marketing and Social Structure in Rural China," *Journal of Asian Studies* 24 (November 1964), 3-43.
[5] One of the best accounts of the traditional Chinese farming system is Franklin H. King, *Farmers of Forty Centuries* (London: Johnathan Cape, 1949).

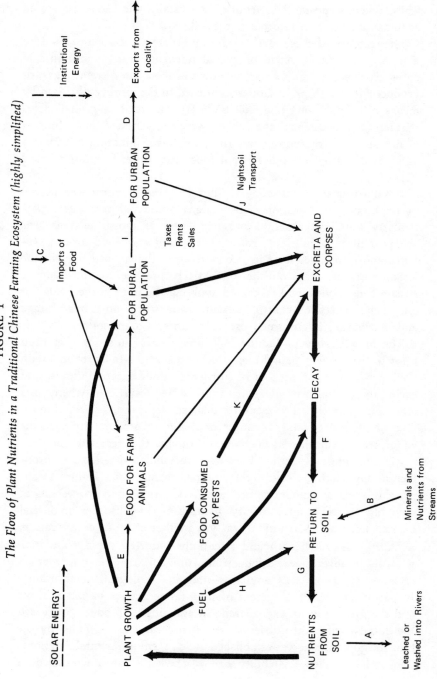

FIGURE 1

The Flow of Plant Nutrients in a Traditional Chinese Farming Ecosystem (highly simplified)

China where a substantial part of a crop's stalks and leaves were used as fuel, the ashes were returned to the soil (H).

The stability of these local farming ecosystems was maintained by a highly organized system of spatial nutrient cycling. Nutrients in crops exported to the local market town in the form of rent, taxes, or produce for sale (I) were, in part, returned to the locality of origin by means of a flourishing nightsoil trade (J). The relatively small flows that left the ecosystem altogether (D) were compensated for by inflows of nutrients in irrigation waters from streams originating outside the area (B) and from the purchase of food from other farming districts (C).

A vital role in maintaining productivity and stability was played by the human modification of certain environmental parameters, particularly the flow, storage, and regulation of moisture. This was achieved through hillside terracing, irrigation and flood-control systems, and techniques used in rice cultivation that helped prevent the leaching of nutrients from the soil (A). The practice, too, of dredging stream beds, ponds, and lakes and applying the mud to the fields not only benefitted flood-control measures and irrigation-water storage and distribution, but returned lost plant nutrients to the soil.

The long history of famine in China clearly indicates that even prior to the modern period many local ecosystems failed to maintain their productivity. Outflows of nutrients might exceed inflows, and declining fertility would result. There were years, too, when pests took more than their usual one-third share of the crop (K in figure 1). One of the most common causes of declining productivity was the widespread occurrence of floods and droughts that resulted when climatic fluctuations exceeded the safety thresholds that local environmental engineering works were designed to maintain. Failure to apply the levels of human energy necessary to maintain ecosystems at their high levels of productivity, because of civil disorder or official incompetence and corruption, was yet another cause of deterioration.

During the nineteenth and twentieth centuries, rapid population growth, urbanization, and industrialization appear to have further accelerated the process of environmental and ecological deterioration. In particular, the development of long-range transportation systems and the growth of an export trade in agricultural products increased the outflows of plant nutrients from many rural areas. Thus, by the time the government was established in 1949, environmental deterioration and ecosystem instability had reached a crisis unparalleled in Chinese history.

The Basis of Communist Environmental Policies

Chinese ecological and environmental-management policies since 1949 must be viewed in the light of the following demographic and economic constraints: a population of nearly 600 million, growing at the rate of 12 to 15 million a year; a relatively small amount of agricultural land (10 percent of the total area) compared with other major countries and few virgin areas that could be opened up without the expenditure of vast amounts of capital; nearly half of the existing cultivated land subject to a high recurrence of floods and droughts, thus making stable agricultural production impossible to achieve; already high crop yields per unit area of land with each acre supporting twenty times as many people as an acre in North America; and a shortage of capital for industrial development.

The leaders also have strong ideological commitments. They have been determined to generate most of the capital required from internal sources rather than relying on foreign aid. This means that agriculture has had to bear most of the burden, and hence additional stresses have been placed on the productivity of the land. In addition, they desire rapid economic development without, at the same time, subverting the revolutionary principles on which the revolution was founded. These goals of economic and socialist development were to be achieved by a combination of technological innovation, on the one hand, and a condition of permanent revolution on, the other, that involves the total physical, intellectual, and spiritual mobilization of all people throughout the country.[6]

Despite the vital role that environmental and ecological quality has in the great task of national development, the Chinese leaders have seldom singled them out as special problems per se. Rather, they have seen contradictions that arise between man and his environment as part of the wider problem of disharmony among men brought about by exploitative political and economic systems, and hence their belief that there cannot be a transformation of nature without a transformation of man.[7]

Environment and Economic Development

In order to increase agricultural productivity, the Chinese leaders have

[6] For an excellent discussion of conflicts between ideology and economic development, see Franz Schurmann, *Ideology and Organization in Communist China* (Berkeley: University of California Press, 1966).

[7] Rhoads Murphey, "Man and Nature in China," *Modern Asian Studies* 1 (October 1967), 313-33.

insisted that nature must be transformed. This does not mean, as some Western observers have interpreted it, that she should be plundered and raped of her riches, but rather that those manifestations of nature which reduce the productivity of man-made ecosystems should be removed.

Some of the most spectacular transformations of the landscape have involved attempts to eliminate the impact of climatic fluctuations on agricultural production. In the mid-1950s large capital-intensive water-conservancy projects were undertaken on many of China's major river basins, but since then, the major emphasis has been placed on the construction of small-scale, labor-intensive projects that supplement the protection afforded by the larger schemes and also spread the benefits of water control more widely and inexpensively than the larger capital-intensive projects. The result of all these efforts appears to be encouraging. The projects on the Yellow River, for example, are claimed to have increased protection to the lower valley against floods to an average frequency of one occurrence per thousand years, whereas previously the lands were likely to be inundated once every decade. Between 1952 and 1967, irrigation schemes with drought-protection facilities lasting from thirty to seventy days have been extended from 51 million acres to 97 million acres and are expected to increase at the rate of 3 million acres a year over the next decade.[8]

Closely related to the problem of moderating the impact of environmental fluctuations is the need to improve the environment in rural areas. The call by Mao in 1956 to "turn the country green" through afforestation is one of the major attempts in this direction. Prior to 1949, China had one of the lowest proportions of forest lands of any country in the world—10 percent, compared with some 30 percent in both the USSR and the United States. Afforestation improves general environmental quality by stabilizing hill slopes and preventing excessive runoff and soil erosion. In the more arid parts of the country, shelterbelts have been planted for thousands of miles in an attempt to prevent blowing sand and to reduce evaporative losses. The fact that many forests are now owned by communes, in contrast to the situation prior to 1949 when they were under no one's special control, means that they can now be protected from unregulated cutting and managed on a sustained-yield basis.

[8] An account of some of these water-management schemes can be found in Owen L. Dawson, *Communist China's Agriculture: Its Development and Future Potential* (New York: Praeger, 1970).

Another policy designed to raise productivity that is having a major, and probably beneficial, impact on environmental quality, is the exhortation of Chairman Mao in 1964: "In agriculture learn from Tachai." The Tachai model now being emulated in numerous communes is based on the achievements of a small, impoverished brigade in north China that was able to transform eroded and barren hillsides into fertile farmlands. Terraces were constructed to create more flat land and to reduce runoff. Small rock dams were built in gullies to check the flow of accumulated silt. New fields then formed behind the dams. Fertile soil was then carried up from the lowlands and spread on these new areas, and water was led from distant mountain streams along the contours of the hills to irrigate the newly developed farmlands.[9]

A less beneficial attempt to increase farming productivity has been the mass campaigns to eliminate crop pests. In many cases these have been undertaken without adequate knowledge of the complex food chains of which the pests formed an important link. Thus, the great campaigns to eliminate sparrows in the late 1950s resulted in an even greater invasion of insect pests that decimated the crops.[10]

Behind all discussions of the Chinese man-environment problem, particularly in the eyes of Western observers, has loomed the spectre of a vast and rapidly growing population that, year by year, presses harder and harder on the supporting capacity of the environment. The Chinese leaders, on the other hand, have been more optimistic and more pragmatic in their view of the situation. In the first place, even had ideological considerations permitted it, there was little point in bemoaning China's population size and growth, since neither could be reduced for at least several decades. Secondly, as noted earlier, the output levels of the traditional Chinese farming ecosystem depend on the levels at which human energy is applied. Thus, the Chinese leaders believed that the growing population, if properly mobilized, could provide its own food through some of the labor-intensive programs discussed earlier. At the same time, they knew that a population growing too rapidly would make increases in the material and nonmaterial living standards difficult to achieve even if food could be supplied at the subsistence level. Thus, apart from areas of China inhabited by

[9] See Hua-wen Hsin et al., *Tachai—Standard Bearer in China's Agriculture* (Peking: Foreign Languages Press, 1972).

[10] Georg Borgstrom, *Too Many: An Ecological Overview of Earth's Limitations* (New York: Collier Books, 1971), p. 110.

minority peoples who might have religious objections, birth control has been popularized in all densely populated areas, and family planning has been advocated so that "the family can avoid being over-burdened and a better education can be given to the children and full chance of employment provided."[11] As Paul Ehrlich has stated, and as many recent visitors to China have confirmed, China's population-limitation program is probably unmatched by any other nation's in the world.[12] That this should be so is not surprising, for, as Engels noted over a century ago, "if at some stage communist society finds itself obliged to regulate the production of human beings, just as it has already come to regulate the production of things, it will be precisely this society alone, which can carry this out without difficulty."[13]

The Maoist Developmental Model

Environmental and ecological management is not only being affected by some of the direct measures discussed above, but by many of the principles and policies that are part of the general Maoist development strategy. Of preeminence in this strategy is the concept that politics is in command. In economic life, this is interpreted as meaning that the whole economy, rather than a part of it, is to be taken into account when decisions are made. Thus, the benefits and costs of an enterprise cannot be calculated in isolation from the total impact, both social and spatial, that the enterprise will have on society and the environment as a whole.[14] This principle was neglected, for example, when numerous small-scale water conservancy projects were undertaken in the late 1950s by the cooperatives and communes, each designed to benefit a particular locality without regard to the downstream users of water and to regional water balances.

Liu Shao-ch'i, Mao's chief adversary, is frequently accused of causing waste and pollution because of the emphasis that he is alleged to have put on profitability as the sole criterion for judging the success

[11] Second National People's Congress of the People's Republic of China, *National Programme for Agricultural Development, 1956-1967* (Peking: Foreign Language Press, 1960).

[12] Paul Ehrlich and John P. Holdren, "Neither Marx nor Malthus," *Saturday Review*, November 6, 1971, pp. 88-91.

[13] Frederich Engels, letter to Karl Kautsky, February 1, 1881, cited by Ronald Meeks, ed., *Marx and Engels on Malthus* (New York: International Books, 1954), p. 109.

[14] Chi Wei, "Turning the Harmful into the Beneficial," *Peking Review*, January 28, 1972, pp. 5-7.

of an enterprise. With politics in command, however, the valuable resources contained in waste materials must be recovered, not only because the country is poor and cannot afford to lose them, but also because of the harm they do to people and to the environment.

The lack of such a comprehensive view of planning and the failure to take into account the external impacts of enterprises have been two of the major causes of environmental deterioration in both overdeveloped and developing countries, and while many may hesitate to use the same ideological rhetoric as the Chinese, few could find fault with the intent of their efforts in this direction. Nevertheless, in this respect, the Chinese may also be accused of taking a view that is too limited. The overemphasis on man and his relationship to society, which is implied by the slogan "politics in command," may blind people to those still more subtle and elusive ties that bind men to their environment. Thus, even from the purely anthropocentric view of the importance of human survival, it is "ecology" rather than "politics" that must ultimately be placed in command.

"Redness" Versus Expertise

Arising from the concept that politics is in command is the view that expertise should be subordinated to "redness." Technical expertise should, of course, be encouraged, but the ability to see all problems in their total ideological, political, and economic context should be prized above all, since it is only with such vision that the full implications of expertise can be assessed. Thus, the press frequently credits ideologically purified peasants and workers with innovations in environmental management which the restricted vision of experts cannot supply.

If the Chinese do effectively encourage public participation in the planning process, as much evidence suggests they do, their valuable experience offers a great deal to other parts of the world, where the pronouncements of experts are still listened to with religious awe. Indeed, the solutions of experts have had disastrous results upon the environment precisely because they have not heeded the advice of local inhabitants concerning the nature of local ecosystems.

"Everything Divides into Two"

One of China's most widely quoted aphorisms in relation to environmental problems—as in many other situations—is the somewhat esoteric statement that "everything divides into two." According to this dialectical view, environmental problems which initially appear to be harmful can be transformed into something beneficial. In Maoist analytical terms, the creation of waste products is a nonantagonistic contradiction which, if not resolved, could lead to serious consequences, i.e., shortages of raw materials on the one hand and pollution on the other. Thus, the Chinese emphasize that waste and declining environmental quality are part of the same problem, in contrast to the West, which stresses the deteriorating quality rather than the waste. Hence, the Chinese believe that the problem of pollution will be solved only when all wastes are productively utilized.

Numerous articles indicate how multiple-purpose use transforms the "three evils" (waste gas, liquids, and solids) into the "three advantages." Thus, waste heat from a rolling mill can be used in a brewery; sewage and industrial effluents that killed fish in the Nunchiang River in northeast China are now being treated and led into the countryside, thereby reducing the need for chemical fertilizers.[15] Factories reportedly are being linked together by the wastes they produce. Plants that can utilize the wastes of a large enterprise are constructed nearby and thus economize on their own purchases of raw materials.[16]

Failure to analyze the dual nature of pollution is clearly at the root of the failure of most of the industrial world to deal with environmental quality problems effectively. Thus, because it is not profitable for individual enterprises to utilize their wastes, these are either dumped into the air and water, or they are removed by expensive treatment processes. The waste is then burnt or buried, thereby contributing to other kinds of pollution.

Rural-Urban Symbiosis

Mao indicates that, in the process of economic development, new contradictions constantly arise. All these initially are nonantagonistic in nature, but if not satisfactorily resolved they may eventually subvert the revolution itself. Some of the most dangerous of these contradictions are the social, economic, and ecological tensions that exist be-

[15] Chiang-wen Lung, "Tsitsihar Saves its Fish," *China Reconstructs* 21 (June 1972), 8-10.

[16] Ch'ing-yuan Hua, "In Multiple Purpose Use of Materials, It Is Necessary to Prevent What Is Harmful and Promote What Is Beneficial," *Hung Ch'i*, September 1, 1971, trans. in *Survey of China Mainland Magazines* (October 1971), pp. 66-72.

tween rural and urban areas. The Chinese have instituted a number of innovations that have important direct and indirect environmental and ecological implications. The *hsia-fang* movement, which involves the transfer of large numbers of urban dwellers from all walks of life to work in the countryside, increases the chances that the country's elite may have a rather extensive knowledge and experience of rural conditions and will presumably be aware of the importance of rural ecosystems upon which the prosperity of the country depends. This policy is in strong contrast to the policy followed in most other parts of the Third World where the countryside is the last place where urban elites would go.

The contradiction between countryside and town as source and sink for plant nutrients is resolved more concretely by the role that the city plays in transferring the nutrients that it has used in food and industry back to the rural areas again. As already indicated, many rural areas are being irrigated with treated sewage from urban centers in the vicinity. Where no such facilities have yet been built there are other ways to achieve the same result. A recent report, for example, describes how half a million citizens of the northeastern city of Shenyang were mobilized to carry nightsoil that had accumulated during the winter and to spread it over the fields before the spring plowing.[17]

The Chinese leaders have expressed their desire to minimize urban-rural disparities by planning towns so that their inhabitants can participate in both agricultural and industrial work. There are "urban villages" or "rural cities" growing up in the Taching oilfield, consisting of a central town providing conventional urban services and four or five satellite communities within a mile radius whose inhabitants engage in both industrial and agricultural occupations.

Walking on Two Legs

Another basic tenet of the Maoist developmental strategy, one that has significant environmental implications, is the utilization of both traditional and modern forms of technology and expertise—the "walking on two legs" policy. Mao supports a native technology and expertise that utilize the available human and resource materials rather than importing them from other sectors of the economy or regions of the country. This strategy incidentally reduces the possibility of eco-

[17] Shen Wen, "How Shenyang Became Self-Sufficient in Grain and Vegetables," *Peking Review*, March 5, 1971, pp. 8-10.

logical disruption. For example, indigenous bacterial fertilizers and microbe insecticides, which are processed locally, are used widely in the fight against agricultural insect pests and in the promotion of animal husbandry. In south China, farmers have put their knowledge of local ecology to practical use by breeding a certain kind of bee that preys on the larva of the riceborer. Large reductions in crop damage are reported. In short, the general encouragement of these "native" practices is likely to be less environmentally harmful than the promotion of widespread modern agricultural technology and land management.[18]

Local Self-Sufficiency

Local and regional self-sufficiency is another principle of the Maoist developmental strategy that embraces elements of all the others discussed so far. This emphasis on decentralization and self-sufficiency originally had nothing to do with concern for the environment, but was based primarily on ideological reasons and the poor transportation system that made regional specialization unfeasible. Strategic purposes also played a part, since a decentralized economy is less susceptible to paralysis in the event of an attack than a centralized one. The reemphasis on the traditional cellular structure of the economy, however, does have at least two important environmental benefits that have not yet received any attention.

In the first place, the partially closed, essentially autarkic local systems provide a more rapid feedback effect when malpractices in one part of the system give rise to environmental deterioration in another, when compared to systems where there is a greater spatial separation between the locations of decision and impact point. Even in the case where large urban areas are physically distant from their rural support base, as shown earlier, the *hsia-fang* system ensures, in theory at least, rapid feedback between the two sectors.

Secondly, although dispersion of industry and population is not the ultimate solution to problems of environmental pollution, the attempt since the First Five Year Plan to prevent the growth of large urban and industrial centers does mean that many local environments do not have to cope with increasingly concentrated loads of waste. This kind of dispersal, in addition to the policy of recycling and multipurpose

[18] The use of natural methods for disease and pest control is discussed in *Man in the Living Environment*, ed. Linda Weimer (Madison: University of Wisconsin Press, 1971), pp. 98-168.

use of wastes, suggests the possibility that local environments will be able to assimilate with minimal detrimental effects whatever effluents may be loaded upon them.

Conclusions

Apart, then, from the policies directed explicitly toward the environment, it would appear that many of the principles and strategies for attaining the goals of economic and socialist development are perhaps indirectly and inadvertently contributing to China's environmental and ecological integrity. Until recently the Chinese have not linked the Maoist model to the solution of environmental problems. Judging from articles that appeared in the Chinese press during the last two years, however, the leadership seems to be reinterpreting policies and programs undertaken for other purposes in terms of their environmental consequences. For example, the Chinese have attributed the crisis of capitalism in the West not to the class struggle and the imminent proletarian revolution but to the environmental degradation accompanying the uncontrolled search for profits by private enterprise.[19] This is contrasted with China's socialist system where the people's happiness and prosperity, rather than profits, are the ultimate goal. Indeed, in view of the failure of a proletarian revolution to materialize in advanced capitalist countries, perhaps a new interpretation of Marx might evolve in which the collapse of capitalism might be attributed not to contradictions between the classes brought about by technological change, but in terms of contradictions between the capitalist system and its environment brought about by the application of technology to the unrestricted search for profit.

Fundamental questions remain, however. Can China achieve rapid economic development and still maintain the environmental integrity which many of its present policies promote? Has China already a foot in the twenty-first century in its attitude toward environmental questions? Or, is China temporarily trying to make the best of traditional man-environment relations, a policy to be discarded as soon as a higher level of technology permits? Judging from statements at the Stockholm Conference on the Human Environment, China is optimistic about its ability to achieve simultaneously both economic development and environmental integrity through the strategies discussed above.

[19] Chi Wei.

One conclusion is that China's experience in ecological and environmental management is no more distinctive or innovative than that of many other countries. Everywhere peasants have attempted to control floods and droughts, have opened up hillsides, planted trees, and used a combination of traditional and modern techniques for dealing with local ecological problems. In the more industrialized countries, too, there are examples of the waste products of one enterprise used by others, and in the sphere of urban planning there have been notable attempts to bring rural qualities to urban life.

The distinctive element of the Chinese experience has been the leaders' attempt to promote these methods and principles as integral parts of the national developmental consensus. Elsewhere, the efforts have been sporadic, uncontrolled, and uncoordinated or dependent on the whims of enlightened planners or industrialists. But in China the latest birth-control device, the multiple-purpose use of wastes, traditional ecological techniques to control pests, the applicability of the Tachai model, and the ways in which town and countryside can cooperate—all these are the subject of serious, if not always well-informed, discussions in the millions of work groups throughout the nation. The value of the Chinese experience, then, lies more in the realm of the techniques that are used to transform the outlook of men than in the specific techniques that are used to deal with a particular environmental problem.

The Chinese experience challenges all countries to look afresh at many of their national developmental goals and the methods used to achieve them, for environmental problems are deeply embedded in culture and ideology and cannot be solved in isolation from them. Apart from special techniques such as the Chinese practice of nutrient cycling and the building of their industrial economy around the multiple utilization of wastes—in both of which they excel—China's experience challenges other countries to make changes in their own procedures of national development.

First, the calculations of the profitability of enterprises, whether urban or rural, industrial or agricultural, must be broadened to consider their impact on ecological and environmental systems. Second, the environmentally disastrous concept that the only road to modernization is through urban and industrial concentration must be reviewed in the light of the Chinese experience. Third, lessons can be learned from the Chinese methods of utilizing public participation in the planning and execution of local environmental engineering projects to lessen the chances of unforeseen or inadvertent ecological deterioration taking place. Fourth, the concept that only advanced technology and its products are suitable for dealing with ecological and environmental problems must be reevaluated in the light of the Chinese experience of "walking on two legs." Finally, the Chinese methods of building a national consensus on issues such as the need to utilize rather than dispose of wastes, family limitation, and other matters of environmental concern must be studied and adapted, if possible, for use by nonsocialist and more pluralistic countries.

Many environmental groups in the West, of course, have also faced such issues. For example, a number of leading British scientists recently endorsed the interesting *Blueprint for Survival*.[20] Although this publication did not mention the Chinese experience, it urges courses of action similar to Chinese policies. Thus, the *Blueprint* advocates the utilization of sewage on the land, the decentralization of urbanization and industrialization, and increased emphasis on mid-level, labor-intensive technology; the establishment of a network of self-sufficient semiautonomous communities, the assessment of real rather than economic costs when any new development is planned, and, of course, a national policy of population limitation—all these courses of action are espoused by the Chinese.

The Chinese, for their part, should be challenged to reexamine their overly anthropocentric view that, with politics in command, all problems, including environmental ones, can be solved. While the application of this principle may remove many of the causes of environmental deterioration, it cannot adequately represent the needs of those all too fragile parts of the earth's life-support system of which mankind is just one part.[21]

[20] The Editorial Staff, "A Blueprint for Survival," *The Ecologist* 2 (January 1972), pp. 1-43.

[21] Barbara Ward and René Dubos, *Only One Earth: The Care and Maintenance of a Small Planet* (New York: W. W. Norton & Co., 1972).

Medicine and Public Health

VICTOR W. SIDEL

In China before the Liberation, medical and public health services, as well as other human services, faced overwhelming problems with totally inadequate manpower and resources. Health statistics for this period are unreliable, but many of the problems are well known. Diseases resulting from malnutrition such as pellagra, scurvy, osteomalacia, beriberi, and nutritional edema were widespread. "Social" illnesses such as venereal disease, opium addiction, and tuberculosis were rampant. There were endemic or epidemic infectious diseases like cholera, smallpox, typhoid fever, typhus, meningitis, encephalitis, plague, and leprosy. Infestations of schistosomiasis, hookworm, malaria, and other parasitic diseases were found in many areas.

To cope with this flood of human disease and misery, China had in 1949 no more than 40,000 doctors trained in Western-type medicine and no more than 90,000 beds in Western-type hospitals. Although comparisons of medical resources in societies with vastly different medical problems and different patterns of medical care are often misleading, China in 1949 would have required more than 600,000 doctors and more than 5 million hospital beds in order to have the same doctor-patient and hospital-patient ratio as the United States in that year. The

This paper is based largely on the observations of the author during two month-long trips to the People's Republic of China in 1971 and 1972 as a guest of the Chinese Medical Association. It also draws on the published experiences of other recent English-speaking medical visitors to China in addition to translations and analyses in English of materials that came out of China over the past three decades.

discrepancy between the number needed by Western standards and the actual number is staggering.

There were attempts to help from outside China. Missionary hospitals and medical schools staffed with doctors were established by several Western countries. The Peking Union Medical College (PUMC), sponsored by the Rockefeller Foundation, was one of the best known efforts from the United States. These efforts were failures, not only because their limited budgets paled in comparison to the wealth which the imperialist powers withdrew from China, but also because they were based on models ill-suited to bring about any basic change in the disease and misery of China's people. The PUMC, for example, with a few exceptions such as the work of John Grant, was based on the academic model of medical schools in highly developed Western countries. This model led to graduates who, through well-trained in Western medical techniques, were too few in number and poorly trained for coping with China's massive health-care problems.

Other efforts from outside China were similar in some ways to the service model pursued in Africa by Albert Schweitzer. Such efforts might have helped the few people who were provided with direct medical services or, in a few cases, a somewhat greater number through the training of relevant local health workers. However, little effort was made to encourage change in the social and economic causes of China's malaise. Quite the contrary, while most of those who participated directly in missionary activities had the highest altruistic motives, many who supported those activities may have done so in the cynical hope that by ameliorating a fraction of the misery they might delay the upheaval which would permit the Chinese people to control their own destinies.

Internally, China was plagued by the corruption and inefficiency of Chiang Kai-shek's Kuomintang government, a problem which was compounded by the disruption and waste of resources resulting from two decades of civil war and Japanese invasion. The limited medical resources were concentrated in the cities on China's east coast. Fee-for-service medical care was the dominant pattern. Preventive medicine was totally inadequate. In the parts of China controlled by the Chinese Communist Party, the People's Liberation Army and its cadres placed great emphasis on medical care and preventive medicine. There was, however, little that could be done effectively in the absence of governmental power and social stability.

From Liberation to Cultural Revolution

When the People's Republic of China was established in 1949, the task of building medical and public-health services to meet China's needs was given high priority. In August 1950, a National Health Congress meeting in Peking adopted four basic principles which guided much of China's health care over the next fifteen years: (1) health services should serve the workers, peasants, and soldiers; (2) preventive medicine should be stressed; (3) the work of doctors trained in traditional Chinese medicine should be merged with the work of doctors trained in modern Western medicine; and (4) health work should be conducted wherever possible with the full participation of the people.

(1) Health services should serve the workers, peasants, and soldiers

Under the leadership of the Ministry of Health, new forms of training for health workers and health-service organizations were developed. These new forms often followed the models provided by Soviet advisers, which were not necessarily the most appropriate ones to meet China's problems. "Middle" or "secondary" medical schools were set up to train "assistant doctors," comparable in many ways to the Soviet feldshers, and to train nurses, technicians, and dispensers. Students entered these schools after junior middle school and studied about three years. "Higher" medical colleges were expanded and some were shifted from east coast cities, such as Shanghai, to the interior. New medical colleges were also founded. Medical education was usually based on the Soviet model of separate faculties for, and early student specialization in, adult medicine, pediatrics, public health, and stomatology (diseases of the mouth, including dentistry). Students entered the higher medical colleges after senior middle school and usually studied five or six years. The China Medical College, which used the facilities of the old PUMC, had an eight-year curriculum designed to train teachers and researchers.

As a result of these efforts the number of Western-type health workers increased rapidly. Leo Orleans has estimated that by 1965 there were 150,000 doctors and 170,000 assistant doctors. Primary-care physicians were increasingly organized into groups bearing a resemblance to the Soviet polyclinics, although in the absence of universal health insurance most of the groups accepted fee-for-service payments. Specialized physicians were largely hospital-based and were salaried. Many of the new medical graduates were assigned to the countryside.

It is reported that the entire graduating class in 1963 was assigned to rural areas.

The number of hospital beds was also vastly expanded, particularly in rural China. Between 1949 and 1957, 860 new hospitals with an average of 350 beds each were built. By 1965, the Ministry of Health was able to make the astounding statement that every county in China had at least one hospital.

Health services in factories were intensively developed, again following Soviet models. Workers receive not only occupational health services but also personal medical services at their place of work. The People's Liberation Army has also developed its own medical colleges and specialized hospitals; an example of the latter, which the author visited in Shihchiachuang in 1972, appeared to be fully comparable in quality to the teaching hospitals of Peking and Shanghai.

Despite these advances in service for workers and soldiers, and despite the training of assistant doctors, the building of rural hospitals, and the assignment of many graduating doctors to the countryside, the peasants who constitute 80 percent of the population still did not appear to be receiving their proportionate share of medical resources.

(2) Preventive medicine should be stressed

Scarce resources were used for preventive medicine rather than medical care. Vast immunization, pest-eradication, and sanitation campaigns were initiated. The institutes for producing vaccines, as well as the neighborhood organizations for administering them and making certain that everyone received them, were among the best organized aspects of Chinese life. Special efforts were devoted to protecting workers in hazardous occupations, to providing maternal and child-care services, and to the prevention of diseases like tuberculosis and schistosomiasis. In every province, city, and district, prevention stations were developed, following the Soviet model.

As a result of these efforts, cholera, smallpox, and plague were quickly eliminated. Nutritional diseases, except for the occasional appearance of rickets in northeast China, have largely vanished. The incidence of tuberculosis and schistosomiasis has fallen sharply. Even more startling, opium addiction and venereal disease have been essentially eradicated at a time when they are apparently spreading in both socialist and capitalist countries.

Despite these efforts, much preventable illness such as trachoma and

pinworm and hookworm infestation remained. Perhaps more important in light of the Cultural Revolution, those working in therapeutic
medicine, especially in its more specialized aspects, apparently com-
manded greater prestige and larger salaries than those working in preventive medicine.

*(3) The work of traditional Chinese and Western doctors should be
merged*

One difficult problem of the People's Republic was dealing with the
hundreds of thousands of practitioners of traditional Chinese medicine, who in 1949 were providing most of the medical care, particularly
in the countryside. These practitioners ranged from highly skilled and
experienced doctors, who understood well the nature of health and disease and knew when referral for Western methods might be helpful,
to poorly trained bonesetters and herbalists.

If traditional Chinese medicine had simply been a collection of empirical remedies such as acupuncture and herbs, the merging of traditional and Western methods might have posed few problems. However, a large body of traditional theory, based on concepts such as
the balance of *yin* and *yang* and the life force *ch'i*, complicated the
relationships between traditional and Western doctors. For example, a
fundamental, traditional diagnostic method was the prolonged and detailed palpation of the pulse, a technique which has far less relevance
in Western medicine.

Since one objective of the People's Republic was an advance from
the "superstitions" of feudalism to the "scientific methods" of socialism, the continuation of traditional medicine, particularly its "theoretical basis," was difficult to justify. Nevertheless, traditional doctors
provided indispensable services for the treatment of most illnesses in
China and were trusted by their patients, most of whom had known
no other system of medical care. There was no attempt to resolve the
issue by eliminating traditional doctors; instead, Mao called for the
study and adoption of whatever was useful from the "treasurehouse
of Chinese medicine" and for traditional and Western doctors to work
together and learn from each other.

Some traditional techniques, such as acupuncture, herb medicine,
massage, and flexible splinting for fractures, were rapidly integrated
into the Western medicine practiced in China. But it was several years
before traditional doctors were even admitted into the prestigious Chinese Medical Association—not to speak of full integration—and many

Western doctors continued to treat the traditional practitioners with condescension.

(4) The people should participate fully in health work

The effort to combine health work with the mass movement is probably the most important of the four principles adopted by the National Health Congress in 1950. It reflects the efforts of the entire society. The concept of a mass movement means that people must fully understand the problem to be faced, and must themselves be involved in solving the problem. In order to involve the masses in health care, neighborhoods are intensively organized for all human services. Various organizations devote much time to sanitation, immunization, health education, the "great patriotic health movements," and other issues related to health. The idea is to involve people as much as possible in the care and prevention of disease.

Opium addiction was eliminated by convincing the addicts, on a neighborhood basis, that use of drugs was contrary to the goals of the society and would not be tolerated. Neighborhoods helped addicts face the problems of withdrawal and cooperated in the effort to make certain that no drugs were available. Those who pushed drugs were dealt with harshly, and the supply was cut off by incorruptible policing and the full cooperation of the people in the communities.

The elimination of venereal disease is another example. The slogan "We don't want to take syphilis into Communism" emphasized the new effort. Checklists of symptoms were posted in every store and community center throughout the country, and those with symptoms were urged to get a blood test and treatment. Again, neighborhood pressure influenced those who might have ignored symptoms to seek treatment. Where the concentration of the disease was great, door-to-door campaigns of examination and blood tests were organized. Prostitutes were identified, and after suitable alternative jobs were created —if necessary, by moving machinery into the brothels and turning them into factories—prostitution was eliminated. Neighborhood committees have the organization and the will to ensure that prostitution and promiscuity are prohibited.

Less dramatic, but perhaps even more important, are the drives to eliminate flies and mosquitos, conducted at the neighborhood level. Immunization is also a neighborhood affair. And when one already has an illness his neighbors encourage him to "struggle against it."

Although the involvement of people in their own care worked well to a great extent, a technological elite nonetheless developed, divorced in its work from the masses. The use of auxiliary personnel such as the "barefoot doctor" was said to have been discouraged by those like Liu Shao-ch'i who were concerned more with issues of "quality" than mass participation and rapid correction of the maldistribution of resources. These issues were basic to the Cultural Revolution.

The Great Proletarian Cultural Revolution

On June 26, 1965, Chairman Mao issued a statement severely criticizing the Ministry of Health. The major point of this criticism was the continuing uneven distribution of medical resources between city and countryside. His watchword, which became known as the "June 26 Directive," widely quoted in China over the past seven years, was: "In medical and health work, put the stress on the rural areas."

During the Cultural Revolution, the Ministry of Health and health services at every level underwent the major disruptions which characterized all aspects of Chinese society. Former leaders were sent to the countryside for "reeducation" by the peasants. Prolonged periods of criticism and self-criticism were conducted in all health-care institutions. At all levels except the most local, statistical reporting was interrupted, although most of the work apparently continued. Medical schools completed at an accelerated rate the training of students already enrolled, but admitted no new classes.

As the Cultural Revolution progressed, all urban health workers, including educators and researchers, were rotated to the countryside for service on mobile medical teams or in production-brigade medical services. In some instances health workers provided services in factories rather than in communes. Their work included direct service, consultation, training, and their own "reeducation."

New types of health workers were also developed and their number rapidly expanded. At the production-brigade and production-team level, over a million "barefoot doctors" provide preventive and treatment services while continuing their agricultural work. Following three to six months of training in the commune or county hospitals, these health workers receive on-the-job supervision by doctors and additional training. Their counterparts in the factories are called worker doctors. Housewives have been trained to become Red Medical Workers. In all these cases, the emphasis is on prevention, health education, and the treatment of common and minor illnesses.

A major task for these health workers since the mid-1960s has been the promotion of family planning. In the city neighborhoods Red Medical Workers go from door to door and talk with married women of childbearing age. The workers stress the importance of population limitation in relation to China's development and offer contraceptives or access to sterilization free of charge. Among the unmarried men and women the importance of late marriage is stressed, and the typical marriage age for men in urban China is now said to be twenty-six to twenty-nine and for women twenty-four to twenty-six. Abortions are free and readily available in both the cities and countryside. Red Medical Workers often set an example by having tubal ligations after their second or third child.

This campaign has been triumphantly successful in the cities. In Shanghai, the reported crude birthrate of six births per thousand a year is not only among the lowest birthrates in the world but is also close to the city's crude death rate. The birthrates for other cities are said to be higher but still quite low in comparison with those in other countries. In rural areas the rates are still higher than in the cities, but appear to be falling at a fairly rapid rate. In the sparsely populated, outlying autonomous areas where "national minorities" live, higher birthrates are encouraged.

Medical education resumed with the admission of classes for experimental curricula of three years—and in some instances even less time —in 1971 and 1972. Most students were selected from among those who had been either barefoot doctors and other part-time health workers, usually after completion of only junior middle school. An important part of the selection process is recommendation by the applicant's fellow workers. In medical schools the practical is emphasized over the theoretical, and considerable time is spent studying in the countryside with one's teachers.

The campaign to integrate traditional and Western medicine has been intensified. Students of Western medicine now receive considerable training in traditional techniques, and the reverse is true for students of traditional medicine. The development of acupuncture anesthesia has been one of the most dramatic aspects, but integration has also proceeded in many other areas.

The financing of health care is a good example of decentralization. Care is free for factory workers, and their families are reimbursed for half the cost of their treatment. Payment for peasant health care varies with the particular commune. In some, care is still provided on a fee-for-service basis. In many, however, there are experiments in "cooperative medical care." Each commune member pays a premium of about 1 yuan (40 cents) a year. The fund is supplemented by allocations from the welfare funds of the commune. This fund covers almost all—in some communes all—medical expenses.

Probably the most important medical developments of the Cultural Revolution involved the relationships of people to one another and to their institutions. By 1972, many institutions had settled into functioning patterns, statistics were being collected, and work was proceeding. But it was no longer "business as usual." The leadership had been "reeducated" or had been drawn from among those previously working at lower levels, and these leaders were apparently much more sensitive to the need to avoid elitism, to involve the masses, and to serve the people.

It remains to be seen whether these principles and goals can be maintained as medical care becomes increasingly technological and as the emphasis of treatment must shift from infectious to degenerative diseases, such as cancer and stroke. There have been recent discussions about the competence of the barefoot doctors and the three-year doctors, and further changes in the role and training of health workers seem likely. Nevertheless, as a result of the Cultural Revolution, health workers appear to have become even more deeply involved with the principles and goals which have been a driving force in Chinese medicine and public health since the Liberation.

The Transferability of the Experience

China has not solved all its health problems. Infectious and parasitic diseases are still more common than in the more economically developed countries. Highly trained medical manpower and more sophisticated medical equipment are needed. Preventive medicine and medical care in the cities are still much better than in the countryside. And the patterns of care, education, and research are still undergoing experiment and change.

Nevertheless, the Chinese people have accomplished medical miracles with limited resources. There is visible evidence of excellent sanitation and of healthy, well-developed children, and no evidence of the alcoholism, drug addiction, and hopelessness once widespread in China and still widespread in other countries. Statistically, data for the first three months of 1972 for Shanghai indicated an infant mortality rate of 13 per 1,000 live births, among the lowest in the world; a life expectancy of over 70 years, among the highest in the world; and a shift in the leading causes of death from diseases of malnutrition and infection to those of older age such as cancer and cerebrovascular disease.

The data are still fragmentary and Shanghai is certainly not representative of all of China. But the accomplishments of the "sick man of Asia" in the face of severely limited resources and overwhelming problems are, after twenty-three years, unmatched in the history of the world. The accomplishments are evidence of what can be done when a goal is set and the population mobilized to do it.

There are several areas in which the application of China's experience in medicine and public health might be beneficial to the United States—techniques of treatment, selection and training of health workers, and organization of public health and medical care. Treatment techniques include acupuncture, both as an anesthetic and for the treatment of specific medical problems; other methods of traditional Chinese medicine, particularly medicinal herbs; exercises and massage; and innovative treatments for severed limbs and widespread body burns. Changes in the training of health workers might include the selection of medical students from relatively untapped strata of society; promotion of lower-level health workers to more important medical occupations; emphasizing practical rather than theoretical training, thereby reducing the length of the initial training period; and widespread on-the-job training and continuing-education programs. A variety of Chinese policies might be applicable to the United States in the organization of public health and medical care, including emphasis on preventive medicine, particularly for "social" illnesses such as venereal diseases and drug addiction and for degenerative diseases such as lung cancer; decentralization of services, with more accessible treatment for common and minor illnesses; standardized referral patterns for specialized care to optimize the use of expensive and scarce resources; and, finally, involvement of the people in the provision of their own health services through community education and community organization.

The transfer of Chinese methods of treatment would be relatively easy. There would be some opposition from physicians who view any change with alarm, cultists who abuse the techniques and give them an unsavory reputation, and problems in transferring techniques such as acupuncture to a different cultural and theoretical context. But these problems can probably be surmounted.

The transfer of Chinese practices in the other two areas would be much more difficult because the educational and job structure of health workers and the organization of health care are closely intertwined with current patterns of education, attitudes toward human services, and the economic and cultural basis of American society. It may be possible to initiate isolated experiments within medicine, but the general applicability of Chinese techniques of education and organization in medicine will depend more on urgently needed changes in the macrocosm of society than on changes in the microcosom of medicine and public health.

Nonetheless, one lesson we may draw from China's developmental experience is that there may yet be hope for the United States to solve problems such as drug addiction, venereal disease, poverty, and the lack of a sense of purpose. Our future may indeed depend on whether we in the United States can grasp the meaning of the Chinese experience, translate it into our frame of reference, and act on it.

Man, State, and School

DONALD J. MUNRO

Conceptions of human nature and political doctrines are intimately related to the functions of education. American and Chinese beliefs about the character and function of government rest on anti-thetical assumptions about man. These assumptions were first articulated in religious and philosophical classics in the two countries, and subsequently entered the mainstream of popular belief. Scientists in both countries know more about human behavior than is reflected in either tradition's politically important beliefs about man. But the dominant traditional and current conceptions do not necessarily contain the most accurate available knowledge.

The essence of the American belief is that all individuals are self-regarding, motivated primarily by self-interest. Among the Puritans, this was a sign of human degradation. Roger Williams maintained that "in the best natural Soul in the World, there is nothing but a Kennil, an Hogstie, a den of Atheisme, Murther, Theft, Fornication, Adultry, and all kinde of Wickedness."[1] The philosophers who influenced the authors of the *Federalist* papers, the Constitution, and the Bill of Rights accepted the egoistic portrait, but most played down the idea that there was anything degrading about it. The American statesmen were far more concerned with the implications of this fact about human nature for the kind of government to be established.

The fact, as they saw it, was that rulers lust for power and wealth. The desire to protect the people against their rulers determined the character of the government. Both the representative form and the

---

[1] Cecilia M. Kenyon, *Conceptions of Human Nature in American Political Thought* (Ph.D. diss., Radcliffe, 1949), p. 40.

separation of powers reflect this concern with protection. James Madison reasoned: "But the great security against a gradual concentration of the several powers in the same department, consists in giving to those who administer each department the necessary constitutional means and personal motives to resist the encroachments of others. . . . Ambition must be made to counteract ambition. The interest of the man must be connected with the constitutional rights of the place. It may be a reflection on human nature, that such devices should be necessary to control the abuses of government. But what is government itself, but the greatest of all reflections on human nature?"[2]

The other dimension to the American conception of man is the belief in an endowment of rights. It, too, helped generate the belief that the function of government should be protection. The belief in rights emerged in a European historical situation that had no parallel in China's past. It arose as the demand for the protection of an "innate" right of freedom of belief or conscience among religious minorities such as Socinians, Baptists, and Anabaptists in countries where they had no possibility of attaining any political dominance. They invented the doctrine of "consent of the governed" to explain why they should obey the state. Eventually, the list of rights was extended by philosophers beyond liberty of conscience to include life, happiness, and property. The existence of rights determined the primary purpose of government as understood by the English philosophers and the Americans who absorbed their wisdom. Government exists to protect the rights of the people against their rulers, and its ideal democratic form is best suited to protect various groups by somehow balancing their interests.

Another principle, which combined elements of the first two, became increasingly popular in the nineteenth century. According to this principle, everyone has a natural right to happiness; happiness is achieved when everyone is able to satisfy his personal interests, except when doing so denies that right to others; and the individual, who is the best judge of what will satisfy his interests, should be protected against interference by others in making those judgments.

If the American legacy is the idea that government is essentially protective, the Chinese legacy is a belief that the function of government is fosterage, i.e., providing the economic and educational condi-

[2] James Madison, Alexander Hamilton, and John Jay, *The Federalist* Modern Library (New York, 1937), p. 321.

tions whereby the social capacities of individuals can be developed in specified directions. Today the term *yang-ch'eng* (to nurture) is often used to describe the act of fostering such development. The idea is conveyed in a Confucian classic:

> In good years the children of the people are most of them good, while in bad years most of them abandon themselves to evil. It is not owing to any difference in their natural powers conferred by Heaven that they are thus different. . . . There is now barley. Let it be sown and covered up; the ground being the same, and the time of sowing likewise the same, it grows rapidly up, and, when the full time is come, it is all found to be ripe. Although there may be inequalities of produce, that is owing to the difference of the soil, as rich or poor, to the unequal nourishment afforded by the rains and dews, and to the different ways in which man has performed his business in reference to it. Thus all things which are the same in kind are like to one another; why should we doubt in regard to man, as if he were a solitary exception to this? the sage and we are the same in kind.[3]

One senses the relevance of the fact that China is an agricultural country in the common analogies between governing and farming, and between human development and plant development. Men are born without innate defects and with the potential to become good citizens.

The function of government and education in traditional China followed from this portrait of human nature. It was to provide the "rains and dews" and thereby foster the growth of social conduct consistent with antecedent views about what kind of conduct is "natural." The question of the individual's protection against his rulers rarely arose. When it did, the preferred solution was the Censorate, a bureaucratic inspection system. One group of rulers checked up on others.

The dominant conception of man in Chinese Marxism perpetuates part of the most influential traditional one: man lacks any dangerous innate qualities, and negative early-childhood attributes need not persist in later life. Hence, Chinese Marxism does not talk of innate aggressive impulses, unchangeable intelligence differences, enduring selfish motivations, or the Oedipus complex. Rather, man is pictured as clay, subject at any age to molding in nearly any form. One can legitimately claim that such a portrait is, relatively speaking, more inaccurate than the American version discussed above. However, potentially it has a positive dimension lacking in the latter; it can act

[3] *Mencius*, 6A.7.

as a self-fulfilling prophecy. The belief that man is malleable can serve as an incentive to create conditions which may in fact make some change possible. The change can be desirable or undesirable. But the creation of those conditions is not so closely linked with the American position. In China, the accuracy of a conception of human nature has rarely been an important consideration in an educated person's acceptance of it. Truth and falsity are Western concerns. More important to the Chinese is the behavioral implications of a particular belief or position, the effect adherence to it will have on people, and the implications for social action that can be drawn from it.

Contemporary Chinese emphasize far more than their ancestors the changeability of man's social nature, which is defined as mental phenomena. One consequence is that the Chinese are more prone than orthodox European Marxists to appreciate the differences between individuals within a given social class, a function of the obviously wide range of influences to which they are subject. As Mao Tse-tung said: "The concept of man lacks content; it lacks the specificity of male and female, adult and child, Chinese and foreign, revolutionary and counterrevolutionary. The only thing left is the vague features differentiating man from beast. Who has ever seen such a man? All we ever see is Chang the Third or Li the Fourth. No one has ever seen the concept of house in general either. They have only seen concrete houses such as a Western style building in Tientsin and a house surrounded by a square courtyard in Peking."[4]

Once again, convictions about the nature of government are associated with this conception of man. The main purpose of government is fosterage, only more forcefully so than in the past. The human clay is malleable, and the state's role is to lessen haphazard influences as it systematically does the molding. If the American government exists primarily to protect the life, liberty, and property of its citizens, the Chinese government exists to nourish the development of the social nature of its people through economic and educational practices. The techniques developed to perform this function concurrently serve to strengthen the control exerted by the central government over the people. Actually, one has a choice as to vocabulary: *fosterage* if one takes the Chinese view, *control* if one is unsympathetic. But only a combination of the two conveys the idea accurately.

[4] *Tsu-kuo* (China Monthly), September 1, 1969, pp. 41-46.

Education and the Nature of Nurturance

Man's essence, his social nature, is ideas. This sets the focus for the government's task. The term *education*, which defines that task, has been broadly conceived in past and present China to include officially sponsored teaching in and out of the school house. Because the teaching activities are aimed at cultivating man's social nature, there has been little appreciation of knowledge for knowledge's sake. The ideas of education and moral education converge. The differences between fact and value or technology and morality are blurred. Specifically, a social-utility criterion determines what materials are included in texts, how they are presented, and how they are taught. In Confucian China, love and nature poetry could be legitimized as part of the Confucian curriculum only when commentaries purporting to explain them as allegories with some social message were appended to them. Today, students are conditioned to think of even mathematical and scientific material in terms of its social functions. One example will illustrate the point: a comparison of the same section (on hygiene) as it appears respectfully in a sixth-grade, natural-science text used in the Communist- and Japanese-occupied areas during the 1940s. The Communist text, which is still regarded as a model, explains worms as they relate to parasitical diseases found in that part of the country, their source, symptoms of the ailment, and prevention suggestions. The homework, called "investigate and do," requires students to instruct neighbors and family members in what has been learned about causes and prevention of parasitical diseases. In the Peking texts used in the Japanese-occupied areas, which were based on Anglo-American models, students study in detail the process whereby germs and parasites affect the body; they survey worldwide epidemics caused by germs, and parasites found all over the world. The homework is to study the morphology of different types of worms.

Three additional factors affect the state's preoccupation with mind-cultivation. One is a traditional sensitivity to the close link between attitude and behavior. In Confucianism it was called the "unity of knowledge and action," and today a dramatic application is in the insistence on attitudinal transformation in convicts prior to release. The second is the belief that innate factors play far less of a role in an individual's ability to acquire a technical skill than do the existence of correct attitudes. "To learn flying well one must first be adept in the control of one's feelings, and struggle against certain incorrect ideological trends. . . . The various psychological dispositions which are closely related to aviation are rapid and correct sensual judgment, flexibility of reaction, etc. . . . These qualities are not pre-natal, and much less are they immutable."[5] The third is the need to achieve some value consensus in China as a necessary condition of political unity.

Other principles underlying mind-moulding and -control practices are consistent with those operative in traditional China. An example is model-emulation theory, which consists of three basic assumptions. First, people learn through the emulation of models. Second, the best way to introduce any mental transformation or inculcate any behavior is to present a model for the people to imitate. These models can be either living or dead, local or national. Normally the models are exemplars of both a significant virtue and a special skill. Individuals are expected to imitate the attitude of the model toward a given subject matter as well as the content of the subject. The emphasis is on mental transformation. The use of models is regarded as a device both for the cultivation of the people and for ensuring an orderly society. In connection with the latter, it has been argued for 2,500 years that when people learn what is correct through model emulation, they develop a permanent, positive attitude. This kind of learning is more stable than that induced through fear of punishment for transgressing some law. Having a permanent attitude, the individual will comply with what is expected of him even when no policeman or supervisor is present. Coercive methods certainly exist, but they tend to be played down and regarded as second best. The third assumption is that group respect, which comes from being imitated as a model, is the legitimate and most desirable form of reward. This is paired with a two-pronged attack on the legitimacy and desirability of material incentives as reward. Such incentives, it is maintained, condition the individual to think of self-interest without relating it to group interest. When the most successful individuals are perceived as pursuing their own interest, others will imitate them. This leads to the loss of social cohesion and the appearance of chaos. Thus group respect, rather than material advantage, is preferred as an incentive to correct behavior.

The functions of models in China are extremely diverse. In addition to the general end of cultivation of the citizens' minds, they serve to

---

[5] Lin Chung-hsien, "Psychological Disposition Necessary for the Study of Flying," *Hang-k'ung chih-shih* (Aviation Knowledge), March 8, 1960, pp. 24-25, translated in *Joint Publications Research Service*, no. 2973 (Washington, D.C., July 6, 1960), pp. 9-10.

ensure political unity by creating value consensus. National models are effective in this connection. They help spread information about new government policies and to disseminate new technical information. They also travel widely, to present themselves for imitation, thereby weakening regional and organizational barriers. The motivational efficacy of group respect is used to increase industrial and agricultural productivity.

Although Stakhanovite emulation campaigns were copied to varying degrees during the 1950s, Chinese model theory and practice are essentially indigenous and differ qualitatively and quantitatively from the Soviet phenomenon. The decentralized nature of the actual selection in which local officials play a significant role, the educational cultivation of a potential model, and the deemphasis on material rewards for the individuals finally selected distinguish the Chinese and Soviet experiences. The quantity selected throughout China is far greater than in any other country, and the belief in their efficacy is taken far more seriously.

Although the use of models achieves many of the goals indicated above, it has an inherent limitation. There has been much talk since 1949 about the need to cultivate independent judgment or problem-solving ability, which is essential in modernizing the economy. Yet the use of models has perpetuated authoritarian tendencies. Traditionally, people have been conditioned to think of a model instead of working out a solution for themselves. This reflexive, over-the-shoulder response is associated with excessive book-worship, because in the past the ways of deceased models were presented in books to be memorized.

The quest for independent judgment is an attempt to minimize rote learning. One solution to the problem is to insist that all models concurrently be examples of excellence in independent judgment. Theoretically, one can learn the proper steps in independent inquiry from a model. But in practice, the negative legacy of the past remains. In the old days, it would have been an unpardonable arrogance to attempt to surpass a model; hence the customary appending of original thoughts as "mere commentaries" to the works of classical figures. Although the present regime wants people to surpass the models in creative judgment, the psychological effects of the reflexive reliance on a model's approach to a problem endure as an obstacle to independent problem solving. The other solution is an obsession with individuals' involving themselves in "concrete situations" in order to learn specific conditions of place and time, thereby avoiding the application of cookbook recipes. If a significant insight of traditional Chinese political theorists concerned the influence of attitudes on behavior, the contemporary and complementary discovery is the fact that action radically alters attitudes and beliefs. Many of the major policy shifts in China recently have represented attempts to gear programs to local needs. Chinese ways are preferable to Soviet ways, as are rural ways in the countryside to what a city dweller considers right for the farmer.

All officials in contemporary and traditional China are expected to serve as models. Mao has said, "Members of the Communist Party cannot but consciously undertake the great responsibility of consolidating the whole nation and getting rid of backwardness. At this point, the function of members of the Communist Party as heralds and models is extremely important."[6] Thus the behavior of cadres and the people's imitative relation to them should be understood in accordance with the principles outlined above. Furthermore, because the gap between ethics and politics is minimized, those individuals who are properly nurtured and become virtuous models in their own work organizations frequently achieve political status as well. They are made members of the Chinese Communist Party (CCP) or delegates to county, provincial, or national people's congresses, all of which strengthens their ability to aid the state in its continuing program of fosterage of others. Mao told labor models in 1945: "You are the bridge between the leader and the masses. The opinions of the masses go through you to the top, and the opinions of the top go through you to the masses."[7]

Language as Evidence of Nurturance

In China, the choice of language is among the most important kinds of evidence that a person's mind has been properly nurtured. Along with other actions reflecting a person's thoughts, his language is called a "manifestation" (of ideas). In addition to merely describing events, an individual's words are believed to perform two tasks, conveying value judgments and influencing other people's attitudes. This may be

[6] Mao Tse-tung, *Selected Writings* (Harbin: Tung-pei Book Co., 1948), p. 915.

[7] Mao Tse-tung, *Mao Tse-tung Hsüan-chi* (Selected Works) (Shanghai: Jen-min ch'u-pan she, 1966), pp. 1013-1019.

purposive or unconscious.[8] Both are accomplished in the specific kinds of words selected by the person to refer to a situation. These are universal functions of language, but the Chinese have long been more sensitive to them than others and normally consider them the primary functions of language. As a result, they pay close attention to a person's choice of words, and consider them clues to his value orientation.

The Chinese regard all nontrivial statements and acts as clues to something unstated, in much the same way as a psychiatrist weighs the discourse of his patient. However, the search is not for the cause of a neurosis but for the person's so-called standpoint. The assumption is that everyone has a set of value priorities that determines how he is willing to regard a situation, and that set of priorities is his standpoint. The Chinese is conditioned to search for a standpoint for two reasons. One is his tendency to perceive phenomena in wholes rather than atomistically. Everything is interrelated. Thus no individual remark or act stands by itself, but is immediately perceived in terms of the links it has to associated phenomena. The other, linked to the philosophical principles discussed above, is the fact that the Chinese child grows up in an environment in which education and moral education have merged. The zones of fact and value converge, and he is accustomed to relating any statement that pertains to the former to the latter.

In addition to concern with these two functions of language, the Chinese also have some distinctive beliefs about language when it is used to describe. In the past, some Confucian scholar-officials had an almost pathological concern to limit the meanings of words so that the link between a word and an actual situation would never become cloudy. Social chaos was the expected penalty when the proper relation of words and things was disturbed. These opinions reflect practices popular to this day in which there is an obsession with choosing, or requiring others to choose, the correct word to describe a situation. This is matched, where feasible, with an equal interest in ensuring that the actuality conforms or appears to conform with the words selected. At times, this need for the two to match passed into the realm of the irrational with an expectation that selection of proper words can really cause the actuality to occur.

For the Chinese a struggle with an opponent can be verbal, with

[8] For a discussion of this topic in classical Chinese thought, see Chad D. Hansen, *Philosophy of Language and Logic in Ancient Chinese Thought* (Ph.D. diss., University of Michigan, 1972).

words performing the two functions of making moral judgments and moulding attitudes. This does not mean that horrors or glories outlined in floods of words will take place, because in actuality praising or blaming someone and attempts to change his thought may be occurring. The dispute may very well be resolved when the opponent accepts the "wording" of the other party, a sign to the Chinese that his "thought" has been changed. For example, a foreign diplomat in Shanghai struggled unsuccessfully to visit a fellow countryman jailed on a rape charge without signing a statement that he had come to visit "Criminal X." When he at last signed that statement, he rapidly gained access to the gentleman. The latter was subsequently found not guilty and permitted to leave China. The foreigner should distinguish this kind of verbal interaction from that of a more formal nature, as used in making agreements or contracts. In this connection, the additional dimension of Chinese language theory associated with the descriptive function comes into play: the Chinese belief that the relationship between words and realities must be tight, at the pain of social chaos and personal loss of face. Great and lengthy deliberation may occur as to the correctness of the wording of even the most simple statement.

Especially in view of beliefs about the power of words to change people's attitudes, the Chinese regard it as legitimate for the government to control their use. This is one factor that accounts for close official attention to the language used in the writing and recent rewriting of textbooks.

The Aims of Cultivation

To what end is fosterage carried out in China? Some of the answers are obvious: the cultivation of a citizenry with cohesive inclinations, which places large-group interest ahead of small-group interest and thus helps ensure national unity; the cultivation of sufficiently positive attitudes toward productive labor to help China move toward great power status and economic modernization. Two other vitally important aims are less obvious. They represent significant breaks both with the past and with the Chinese perception of Soviet practices. They are also distinctive in being treated as intrinsically desirable and at the same time valuable means of fostering other attributes.

One aim is to foster in all officials a sense of obligation to associate periodically with people under their jurisdiction in order to discover their interests, their reaction to government policies, and their suggestions for more effective implementation of them. This is known as "applying the mass line," and it is the closest that the Chinese have come to popular representation in liberal democratic theory. It has never existed in the Soviet Union, except in the urban factory soviets for a few months at the end of 1917. Lenin was at first optimistic about the possibility of dispensing with a bureaucracy aloof from the people. He planned to simplify official tasks so that any workman could perform them and at workman's wages, with every cook having a voice in decisions. The Chinese have never coupled their ideas about mass participation with romantic notions about the elimination of bureaucracy. Two differences between the conditions of revolution in China and the USSR have helped to make the idea of mass participation a possibility in China, although it has not been successfully achieved. One is that the Soviet Party after 1900 was forced to act in an aloof, secretive manner because of the dangers of the Czarist police. The habits of exclusiveness in leadership were retained after the victory. In China, after the debacle in the cities between 1928 and 1934 in which much of the urban Party was destroyed, the CCP operated openly in certain geographical regions and was not regularly forced to act in such furtive ways. The other difference in conditions of revolution is that the Soviet intelligentsia constituting the Bolshevik leadership had little organized support among the Russian masses prior to 1917. In 1917, they gained the support of city factory workers who understood little about their ideology but liked their promises. The Chinese Communists, in contrast, came to power with mass support. Over the years, the leaders had to develop the habit of adjusting programs to the people's interests. The CCP's organizational techniques obviously form only one explanation of their eventual success, which occurred from 1937 on; their identification with the anti-Japanese struggle obviously is the key factor. In sum, the means developed to achieve victory strongly affect the nature of relations between rulers and ruled after victory.

The other aim of nurturance having both intrinsic and instrumental value is the cultivation of egalitarian attitudes in the people. "Egalitarian" is used in the sense of minimizing status differentials among people in different positions, occupations, regions, etc. It is not used to refer to equalizing distribution of income or wealth. In traditional Chinese attitudes toward social behavior there is a contradiction between the ideal that "all men are brothers" and the actual existence of barriers that have impeded any approximation of the ideal. There are barriers between a clan or village and outsiders, among people from different regional areas, and, as an ancient maxim states, between "people who work with their minds and rule, and people who work with their hands and are ruled." Officials were scholars, "teachers of the people." They were classicists as well as bureaucrats. Thus the major class division was between scholar-officials and the rest of the people. Chinese leaders in contemporary China have themselves stated that the chief status differential today is between "mental aristocrats" and manual laborers. As a consequence of the old tension between the ideal and the fact, traditional Chinese utopias were often societies characterized by an absence of barriers such as family, sex, and race. Chinese Communist leaders have drawn strength from the claim that they are the first to work for the elimination of the tension by minimizing the barriers, and thus to progress toward the utopian state of "Grand Union" (*Ta T'ung*, a term Mao has used to refer to Communism itself). The significance of status alteration cannot be played down in China today. It is an important factor in the periodic manual labor on the farm required of officials and educators, and in the restructuring of the entire educational system beginning in 1966 to include labor. The technique used to break barriers is role switching. Officials become peasants, intellectuals become factory or farm workers, students serve as teachers, and soldiers instruct officers. Khrushchev attempted something like this in the Soviet Union in 1958, but his attempts to eliminate the difference between those who do "black work" (*chornaya rabota*) and others were aborted by his successors. Problems experienced by the Soviets in implementing the labor requirement indicate that the Chinese may not be as successful with the policy as they initially expected. Chinese egalitarianism insists that differences in occupation or in urban and rural areas should not cause significant differences in attitude. The challenge, then, is to attain the benefits of industrialization without recasting old inequalities in the new form of a division between managers and technicians, on one hand, and the rest of the people, on the other.

Mass participation by means of the mass line and egalitarianism has instrumental as well as intrinsic value. The instrumental function reveals once again the major difference in conceptions of the relation between man and society in China and in the United States. In China, the mass line and egalitarianism are regarded as desirable because they facilitate the governing process. They are perceived as aids to more efficient fosterage by the rulers. The closest American counterpart of the mass line is the election of representatives, but its purpose is to protect the people against their rulers by providing the legal recourse of removal from office of those who purport to convey the people's interest to the government but actually do not. The mass line, in contrast, is intended primarily to solidify the relation of officials and the people, engaging the people's cooperation and thereby rendering the officials' tasks easier to perform. Egalitarianism in America has to do primarily with the protection of equal political rights by means of the vote and impartial treatment before the law. Relatively speaking, the creation of optimal environmental conditions for realizing equality of opportunity has been stressed less than the establishment of controls for the protection of the citizen against infringement of his rights by his rulers. In contrast, the instrumental function of "equality" in China was spelled out in Mao's remarks to André Malraux in 1965: "Equality is not important in itself; it is important because it is natural to those who have not lost contact with the masses."[9] In other words, it facilitates governing. In addition, an American might rightly add, it facilitates repression of dissent because it is used as an excuse for not permitting intermediaries between officials and the people. An example of such an intermediary in the United States is the American Civil Liberties Union.

The Transferability of the Chinese Experience

Now that the general philosophical principles underlying ideas about the function and nature of education have been examined, the question of the transferability of China's recent educational experience to a culture in which very different philosophical assumptions exist can be examined more specifically. But first, the post-Cultural Revolution structure of the system will be discussed briefly.

The five major characteristics of the new schools at all levels are: (1) reduction in the number of years of required attendance; (2) changes in admissions opportunities or criteria to favor peasant and worker children and to prevent school success from being regarded primarily as a ladder to special privilege, (3) greater emphasis on practical

[9] André Malraux, *Anti-Memoirs* (New York: Bantam Books, 1970), p. 464.

application of material studied, (4) heavy politicizing of all courses, partly through textbook revision, and (5) changes in governing boards. It is now believed that the nation's manpower needs can best be satisfied with a total of nine years primary and middle-school education, causing school youths to enter the labor pool at the age of fifteen or sixteen, as opposed to seventeen or eighteen previously. Ideally rural areas have a seven-year combined primary and lower-middle school run by the production brigade and a two-year, upper-middle school run by the commune. In cities, the primary schools usually offer a five-year course, followed by a four-year, combined lower-upper middle school.

Manpower needs, with the desire to create a "new man" having an appropriate attitude toward manual labor, lie behind the increase in practical training at all levels. The grounds of some schools are used to grow crops. The schools may build their own tool shops or establish alliances with farms or factories. Rural schools have introduced more congruity between their academic teaching and the local production practices than have those in cities. The curriculum in a typical urban middle school consists of mathematics, languages, physics, chemistry, history, geography, physical education, general political education, farming-factory work, "revolutionary art and culture," and Mao's writings. There are thirty-four weeks of classes, eight weeks of vacation and military training, four weeks on a farm, four in a factory, and one week of review, criticism, and selection of model students and class sections. Universities have also reduced the number of years in their standard program (at Tsinghua University, for example, it is down from six to three years) and have instituted other programs of varying duration depending upon estimates of time needed to teach skills. At the primary and middle levels, increased educational opportunity for children of peasants is achieved by expanding the number of schools and instituting a flexible schedule of operation. Grading procedures that caused failures and dropouts in the past have also been revised. At the university level, increased opportunity is achieved by eliminating or reducing the importance of traditional entrance examinations and making entry depend not only on scholastic promise but also on correct family background and on a satisfactory recommendation from one's farm or factory work unit on the basis of a two- to three-year, postmiddle-school labor experience). But it is by no means certain that entrance examinations will be entirely abolished.

Teachers at all levels, especially at the university level, continue to be intensively reeducated; among other things, this helps eliminate their traditional prourban, antimanual-labor bias. Governing boards of universities are now extremely large, with local factory workers, Party figures, and students having a formal role. Teachers themselves have less to say than in the past. In conclusion, it should be remembered that the structure of schooling in China, especially at the university level, is still fluid.

Is it meaningful to speak of the transferability of educational guidelines from one country to another when their conceptions of human nature differ, as well as their political doctrines that influence ideas about the basic function of state-supported education? The answer is that the experience of one country may be suggestive for another, especially in those areas where a common economic issue (such as providing for the nation's manpower needs) demands immediate attention and places limits on the impingement into policy of psychological and political presuppositions. Normally, the most that the experience of one country can do for policy makers in another is to provide a stimulus to them to formulate more adequately their own educational problems as well as the variables to be considered. It also can stimulate them to do it sooner than they might otherwise have done. No detailed models can be offered for imitation. Philosophical presuppositions remain and set limits on the transferability of content. Thus, in America, the focus on each individual's natural right to happiness and the satisfaction of his unique interests as the vehicle to achieve happiness will continue to act as a barrier to any attempt by educational officials to copy beyond a certain point the manipulative practices concerning the student's destiny in another society.

Many of the Chinese approaches are inapplicable to the United States because this country has already passed through the developmental stages that the Chinese are still facing. If anything, China could learn from the United States. For example, beginning in the late nineteenth century and the early part of the twentieth, vocational subjects were included in the regular curriculum of American schools, and there were calls from many quarters to change the arts and letters character of the curriculum in primary and secondary schools. One of the first stimuli was a Russian system of technical education presented at the Philadelphia Centennial Exposition of 1876. An early model program was the Manual Training School established in St. Louis in the 1880s by Calvin M. Woodward, in which the three-year secondary program was to be divided equally between mental and manual training. "Put the whole boy in school," urged Woodward.[10] The efforts of supporters were officially rewarded in 1917 by the Smith-Hughes Act, which provided federal aid to vocational education. The positive aspect of the trend was the inclusion of manual training in all the schools. The negative aspect, opposed by John Dewey and others, was the gradual emergence of certain strictly vocational institutions which split from regular schools along economic class lines. In the United States, at any rate, the departure from the conventional gentleman's education in the genteel arts was precipitated by businessmen as well as by workers and farmers. Among other things, businessmen wanted trade training freed from union control of apprenticeship programs.

But all three groups complained that existing schools were not preparing students for the kind of jobs they would be taking in a modernizing agricultural and industrial sector. In 1908, "Uncle Henry" Wallace, editor of *Wallace's Farmer*, wrote: "It is hard for many a middle-aged farmer to get a clear idea of what is meant by protein, carbohydrates, nitrogen-free extract, etc. Now, these terms are no harder than many which the pupils learn and which are of no earthly use to them in their everyday lives."[11] The movement toward curriculum reform was encouraged by capitalists in America and Communists in China, but in both cases similar economic changes were causative factors. There was an ethical consideration in the American practices for which there is a counterpart in contemporary China. This was the desire to terminate the traditional class division between "cultural" education and "trade" training. John Dewey's Laboratory School in Chicago was designed as a mirror image of society at large, and students were introduced to the full range of adult occupations. They constructed model farms in the classroom, played grocery store, visited workshops, and so forth. A major difference between the approaches to ending the division of types of education is that in China today children actually become farmers or work in shops, rather than temporarily pretending to change roles. The same desire to modify traditional status distinctions perpetuated by dissimilar educational opportunities led to the general acceptance in the United States by 1910 of the principle of universalized primary and some secondary education. Massachusetts was the first state to pass a law requiring school attendance, in 1852.

[10] Calvin M. Woodward, *The Manual Training School*, p. 239, cited by Lawrence A. Cremin, *The Transformation of the School* (New York: Random House, Vintage Books, 1964), p. 28.

[11] Henry Wallace, editorial in *Wallace's Farmer*, December 18, 1908, p. 1564, cited by Cremin, p. 44.

Mississippi was the last state to pass such a law, in 1918. Of course, this does not mean that the problem of educational equality is solved, as the statistics concerning dropouts and the dubious nature of college entrance criteria attest.

Similarly, scientific habits of problem solving were also required by the developing technology in America, and changes in the curricula were designed to provide them. As in China today, there was a fundamental shift away from exclusive use of written texts and rote memorization to the integration of practical exercises with theory. During the 1880s, Francis W. Parker was in charge of the Cook County Normal School in Chicago where much of the seminal work along this line was done in the lower school affiliated with it. Science began with nature study, mathematics was combined with work in the manual-training rooms and laboratories, and geography began with a study of local topography.[12] Dewey's methods for teaching students "how to think" and the ways of experimental inquiry emanated from the Columbia University Teachers College. In contemporary China, the vocabulary in which the desired changes are discussed has changed, but most of the fundamental aims of the teaching techniques have not. "Studying a problem dialectically" means studying it objectively rather than relying on some traditional analysis, uncovering the "contradictions" means isolating the key variables, and "combining theory and practice" means checking the actual results in a test situation with what the written text says should be the result and then revising procedures if there is a discrepancy.

In contrast to what has just been said, there remain several areas in which a highly developed country like the United States or the Soviet Union can still gain inspiration from the Chinese on formulating general answers to educational problems. One is more vigorously realigning educational programs to the nation's manpower needs. An example of inadequate preparation in the United States was the glut on the market of teachers-college graduates that developed around 1971. Both the United States and the USSR face major problems in the supply of skilled blue-collar workers and foreman-level personnel in factories. The Soviets have issued a number of decrees, most recently in June 1972, to schools to include more practical training so that graduates can meet the society's manpower needs. The United States cannot exercise the control over the student's destiny that the Chinese

---

[12] Cremin, pp. 131-33.

rulers enjoy. But Americans can learn devices used in African countries and already used in ROTC programs in the United States, namely, the "tied bourse," in which the student contracts to study a given subject and to accept a certain type of job upon graduation in exchange for state payment of his educational costs.

There is a spirit of experimentation that the Chinese leaders hope will be contagious. They have dared to toy with the sacredness of existing durations of educational programs from primary school through university. And they have shown that many of the nation's manpower needs can be met by people trained in shorter programs. The most dramatic program, and the one with the most obvious embryonic parallel in the United States, is the barefoot-doctor program. The students in this program receive up to a year of training and then provide treatment of uncomplicated ailments and basic diagnosis in geographical areas previously receiving minimal medical services. The embryonic American counterpart is the use of veterans with paramedical training as doctors' aides in some states.

In the long run, there is reason for some optimism about the ability of the United States to adjust curriculum requirements and student attitudes to manpower needs. Because of the educational ferment of the past hundred years, American schools and colleges already have some experience in integrating practical training in school programs. Thus, given the urgency of its own manpower needs plus the stimulation of examples from a country like China, American educators will find it easier to accept necessary changes like work-study, precollege work experience, the shortened academic program, and other departures from a strict and lengthy liberal-arts approach than they otherwise would.

The most important influence of Chinese educational theory on Americans could be a reexamination of the reluctance to combine academic and moral education. In tandem, there would have to be some movement toward adopting a more social and less atomistic view of human beings. Americans have been too imbued with the idea first formulated by Francis Bacon that "knowledge is power," an idea that gradually led into the idea of progress. The formula is that knowledge ensures power, which ensures happiness for the greatest number. If there ever was a value consensus within the past hundred years in the United States it was in the desirability of increasing scientific knowledge and the industrial growth that this knowledge makes possible.

It was assumed that both will lead to happiness. There is no longer any consensus about progress, but American schools go on as if scientific knowledge by itself is sufficient.

This paper argues for the recombination of academic and moral education wherever possible in order to achieve some value consensus, and this means making the teaching of values explicit, rather than implicit, as "progress" usually was. One could start with values such as survival, environmental protection, equal opportunity, and cooperation as well as competition. Interested citizens, school-board figures, and others with political clout would have some expectation of avoiding major opposition if these values were taught explicitly. Preschool children are already taught far more explicitly than older children that sharing is a virtue. In any case, it should be noted that to speak of the desirability of achieving value consensus through the educational system is not to say one seeks total value consensus, and says nothing about how dissent by teachers or students using the materials would be dealt with. However, the social costs of not having some consensus are too serious to let the status quo continue. At any rate, there are already implicit values in the curriculum and structure of the schools. For example, mathematics story problems often refer to calculating interest and dividends. Competition for grades and admissions-promotion criteria are also implicitly value-ridden.

The phrase used above was "*re*combination of academic and moral education" to achieve consensus. The practice was obviously found in the days of the Massachusetts Bay Colony. A recent historian has written that John Winthrop "would have been amazed at the cool assumption of later Americans that political order could be maintained without such tight moral unity."[13] Horace Mann hoped that the schools could introduce a "public philosophy" leading to some sense of community. His values included the standard nineteenth-century ones of progress, capitalism, and liberal Protestantism. The battle for the recombination was fought most vigorously in the twentieth century by George S. Counts, who wrote in the 1930s: "If Progressive Education is to be genuinely progressive, it must . . . face squarely and courageously every social issue, come to grips with life in all its stark reality, establish an organic relation witht the community, develop a realistic and comprehensive theory of welfare,

[13] Kenyon, p. 587.

fashion a compelling and challenging vision of human destiny, and become less frightened than it is today of the bogies of 'imposition' and 'indoctrination.' "[14] And one of the last, truly eloquent cries for such change was in an article Walter Lippmann wrote for *Commonweal* over thirty years ago entitled "Education Without Culture":

> There is no common faith [in the modern school], no common body of knowledge, no common moral and intellectual discipline. Yet the graduates of these modern schools are expected to govern themselves. They are expected to have a social conscience. They are expected to arrive by discussion at common purposes. When one realizes that they have no common culture, is it astounding that they have no common purpose? That they worship false gods? That only in war do they unite? That in the fierce struggle for existence they are tearing Western society to pieces?[15]

The most favorable conditions for applying the inspiring ideas of one society to another occur if the beginnings of similar ideas can already be found in the other society. Thus, the fact that stirrings of interest in the recombination of academic and value material have already recently appeared in the United States makes it more plausible to speak of China as a stimulus for more seriously reexamining the desirability of combining the two without using China as a model of the value content. In an article that originally appeared in *Harper's Magazine*, John Fisher wrote that the professor will be expected to be a moralist, and "in like fashion, our engineering students will learn not only how to build dams and highways, but where not to build them. Unless they understand that it is immoral to flood the Grand Canyon or destroy the Everglades with a jetport, they will never pass the final exam."[16] Paul Goodman wrote, "Whether or not it draws on new scientific research, technology is a branch of moral philosophy, not of science. It aims at prudent goods for the commonweal and to provide efficient means for these goods . . . scientists and inventors and other workmen are responsible for the uses of the work they do, and ought to be competent to judge these uses and have a say in deciding them."[17] The positive side of training students for adjustment to life as a guide-

[14] George S. Counts, *Dare the Schools Build a New Social Order?* (New York: John Day Co., 1932), pp. 9-10.

[15] Walter Lippmann, "Education Without Culture," *Commonweal* 33 (1940-41), 323, cited by Cremin, p. 326.

[16] John Fischer, " 'Survival U.': Prospectus for a Really Relevant University," *The Environmental Handbook* (New York: Ballantine Books, 1970), pp. 139-40.

[17] Paul Goodman, "Can Technology Be Humane?", *New York Review of Books*, November 20, 1969, pp. 28-32.

line for twentieth-century American education was the diminishing of the aristocratic nature of previous educational content and its successes in preparing people more adequately to meet real-life situations in which they had to apply theoretical knowledge. But, as Lawrence Cremin correctly stated, its defect was to train students to adjust to life as it is, rather than to have visions of what it might better be, and to think about how to go about realizing those visions.

It is commonplace for thoughtful Americans to note that their country faces urgent problems concerning its cities, industrial growth, race relations, and the nature of the military establishment. It is not commonplace to observe that before these problems can be accurately identified or solved by the nation as a whole there must be some moral unity or value consensus. The consensus is necessary to secure agreement with all possible haste on what the problems are.

The concept of man in America will continue to prevent the most manipulative characteristics of Chinese education from having any applicability in the United States. This is the assumption that individuals bring their own unique, self-generating interests to the groups to which they belong. It is coupled with the claim that each person is of equal worth and has an equal right to happiness. Therefore, when possible, everyone should be given the opportunity to develop his special capacities or interests. This is the assumption that commits leading American and British educationalists to variations on the idea of the child-centered school, in which the individual child rather than the content of the subject matter is the primary focus. Speaking in 1930, the president of the Association for the Advancement of Progressive Education said, "We do endorse by common consent, the obvious hypothesis that the child rather than what he studies should be the center of all educational effort. . . ."[18] Once more, in the form of open classrooms and the Summerhill approach, this style is in vogue. There is a confusion in the writings of Dewey as to what the policy implications of the stress on the individual should be, and this has also been reflected in the practices of most educators. Should the student's interests determine almost everything he studies—a romantic glorification of "the latent creativity in each individual," of "individual expression," and a dislike of structure? Or, should educators build on the student's special interests as a means of more effectively direct-

[18] Burton P. Fowler, "President's Message," *Progressive Education* 7 (February 1930), 159, cited by Cremin, p. 258.

ing him to study materials chosen by others? The latter interpretation is consistent with state intervention in order to bring about more congruence between programs and the nation's manpower needs. The unresolved confusion has been mirrored in periodic policy shifts. But the focus on the individual will continue to be a healthy barrier to efforts to carry state manipulation of the student's educational life beyond a certain limit.

The Chinese educational experience is most meaningful to developing agricultural countries like Tanzania or Sierra Leone, or their Asian counterparts that share modernization goals and some vague egalitarian ideas with the Chinese. The Chinese experience has demonstrated that if one wishes both to modernize and to minimize status differentials one must alter the kind of schools that now favor the offspring of an urban privileged sector at the primary and secondary levels. Such schools do not teach the skills needed by a modernizing economy. State funds are drained in the process of producing graduates with unusable skills who swell the number of the urban jobless. Until state funds are directed to increasing educational opportunity in rural areas and developing new agricultural skills, conditions in the countryside will continue to be undesirable for rural parents and their children. Country people need to be involved in curriculum design. Among other things, the city bias of educators must be reoriented. The liberal-arts curriculum must be supplemented by studies which are related to local production practices. Work-study programs help universalize education, because the money earned by the students can be used to maintain the schools, saving the state the financial burden. A massive campaign of political indoctrination among teachers and parents is essential, along with structural changes, in order to help reduce prejudices against rural life. The attack must be against both the forms of schooling and human attitudes.

Cultural differences between China and other developing countries make the importation of the details of the Chinese model dangerous and absurd. Two examples can be cited. First, as Robert Eno has shown, family and tribal units are regarded as keys to Tanzanian educational "self-reliance" and are not subject to the kind of tampering that has occurred in China. Second, some countries may have such a dearth of upper-level skills that they prefer to funnel whatever state funds are available into secondary schools even though it impedes the growth of local primary schools. The Chinese do not have such a shortage at that level, and pressures to realize the egalitarian ideal demand universal primary-school education.

Conclusion

Philosophical assumptions about man play a significant role in determining ideas about the desirable nature and function of education in China and America. In the former society, this is most evident in the fusion of academic and moral education that derives from the state's obligation to foster the growth of the student's social nature. In the United States, it is reflected in the notion that the individual student's unique interests should be protected from excessive manipulation by educational officials, because each person has a natural right to happiness that is achieved when he is able to satisfy his personal interests, except when so doing would injure others.

Different philosophical assumptions about man and society, as well as different stages of development, make the Chinese educational experience less meaningful to the United States than it can be to developing countries in Africa and Asia. China does not provide a detailed model for imitation. But the Chinese stimulate all countries to think through more carefully their own educational problems in terms of variables that the Chinese have found significant, and to do so more rapidly.

Law and Penology:
Systems of Reform and Correction

VICTOR H. LI

It is not difficult to describe the Chinese attitudes and approaches toward reform and correction, but it is very difficult to find a satisfactory way to relate the Chinese experience to the West's. This difficulty is due in part to the understandable emotion attached to terms such as "thought reform" and "thought control." American society has fixed ideas about the institutions and techniques which should be employed to control and correct deviant behavior. Many of these ideas range from idealistic to naive to plain incorrect. For example, the very use of the terms "criminal law" and "penology" evokes images of prisons, probation officers, parole boards, and the like, focusing one's attention on the courts and the formal criminal process. This attention is misdirected for the study of American society and makes no sense at all for the study of China. It is often implied that the American penal system is actually engaged in the reform of deviants. Whatever this system might do in the way of deterring potential offenders, punishing deviants, or isolating dangerous persons from the rest of society, there is almost nothing done to help a person reform.

The entire field of comparative legal studies needs to be reformulated into broader and less Western-oriented terms. Instead of the traditional approach of "comparing" particular legal institutions and principles, one might ask: What are the desired norms of behavior for various segments of society? What persons or institutions determine these norms? By what process are these determinations made, and on what rationales are they based? After the determination is made, how are the norms characterized and articulated? How much discretionary power is granted to lower levels to supplement, amend, interpret, or adapt these norms to local conditions? Finally, how are the norms communicated to the various segments of society? What means are used to influence the public to adhere to these norms? What is done when a person fails to adhere? These questions are framed without reference to a particular society, theory of law, or preexisting set of legal institutions and practices.

While all of these questions form a unified whole, this paper will deal primarily with the last three. First, these questions will be applied to the American system—in part to start with something familiar and in part to lay the foundation for comparisons with the Chinese approach. The Chinese attempt to handle the same three questions will be described, and then the possibility of transferring useful ideas from one system to the other will be considered.

The Western Model of Criminal Law and Penology

There is no question that the United States is a society based on law. Its larger law libraries boast of housing hundreds of thousands of books, each describing in excruciating detail what one can and cannot do in particular circumstances.

To have so many laws is not unlike having too few laws or even no laws at all. In either case, the layman has great difficulty learning the rules which purport to govern his conduct. That is, because of the sheer volume of material, he probably cannot find the precise law applicable to his case. Even if he does find an apparently appropriate law, he cannot be sure that there are not still other laws which are equally applicable or which alter the meaning of the law he has in hand. Obviously, even if he finds all the applicable laws, he cannot be sure that he properly understands their meaning. Finally, even if he understands their meaning, there is no assurance that he will have the opportunity or the legal standing to put his knowledge to use. It is clear that if a layman could deal adequately with the legal system, this country would not need its 400,000 lawyers (with another 100,000 in law school). And if the market is any indication of one's usefulness, the high income of the legal specialists accurately reflects the vital role they play in American society.

One possible, though impractical, solution to the problem of the layman's ignorance of the law is to undertake an active program of public education about law. This is not being done, except perhaps for areas such as traffic regulation or drug abuse. Two leading legal educators have written:

> Law schools . . . are focused almost entirely upon the training of professionals in the law. But, as this report seeks to stress throughout, the law is everybody's business. Not the least of the factors contributing to the contemporary crisis in respect for and enforcement of the law is the almost complete lack of understanding about the legal process among the public at large, and its younger members in particular. Nowhere in the United States is there an effective program for legal education of the citizenry—a most dangerous condition for a democratic society that looks to its people to make its own laws, and in large part relies upon voluntary compliance with those laws.[1]

Instead of instituting an educational program, the United States has adopted a much simpler and cleaner solution: it has defined the problem out of existence by creating the legal fiction that "everyone knows the law" and that "ignorance of the law is no excuse." If these statements were taken literally it would prove most troublesome and unworkable. Fortunately, they are not.

To begin with, many of the substantive provisions of the criminal law are in fact known by most people. It is not necessary to cite chapter and verse of the criminal code to know that one should not hit another person, or throw a rock through a window, or take money from a cash register, even if one feels like doing so. All this is part of a person's general knowledge, whether it is derived from childhood socialization or from watching detective programs on television.

At the same time, there are clearly many areas where general knowledge and beliefs are not congruent with the provisions of the criminal law. These include matters involving private and public morality (e.g., obscenity, sexual practices, use of some drugs, and some "political" offenses), as well as matters on which the law itself is complex or unclear (e.g., disorderly conduct, insanity, and conspiracy). In addition, moving away from conventional criminal law and into areas where the government's use of police power is backed by criminal sanctions (e.g., health and sanitation regulations and the

---

[1] Thomas Ehrlich and Bayless Manning, *Programs in Law at the University of Hawaii: A Report to the President of the University* (Honolulu, December 1970), pp. 12-13.

regulation of labor and business practices), the layman's knowledge of the law becomes more and more tenuous. This is especially true when no criminal sanction is involved but a citizen is trying to force the state to take or desist from taking a particular action (e.g., a change in zoning ordinances, greater or lesser welfare benefits). As the legal fiction that everyone knows and therefore can presumably use the law becomes more fictitious, the legal system becomes less viable and less able to govern conduct.

A second technique is also used to soften the provisions of the criminal law in cases where a literal application would lead to an "unjust" result. These cases include situations in which a person is truly and understandably ignorant of the law, the law itself is unclear, or the legislators had contemplated a different set of circumstances at the time they enacted the law, even though there is now a technical violation of the legal prohibitions. In such cases, various officials are granted a wide range of discretionary power concerning how to apply the law, and even whether or not to apply it. For example, if two persons get into a heated argument on the street, a policeman may ignore them entirely, he may tell them to break it up and go home, or he may charge them with a range of offenses, including disorderly conduct, assault and battery, disturbing the peace, and interference with an officer in the performance of his duty. At the police station, the two persons might be sent home, booked for some or all of these offenses and sent home, or booked and locked up. The public prosecutor then might choose to drop all or some of the charges, or might bargain with the offenders to plead guilty to some of them in return for dropping others and recommending a light sentence. The judge may accept or reject these recommendations, and if the offender is found guilty, may impose a relatively heavy sentence or may suspend the sentence entirely. Depending on the nature of the case, probation officers and parole boards have similar latitude. How each of these officials chooses to act depends on the character of the official and the offender, but also on a judgment by the official concerning what would be a "correct" disposition of the case, given the overall circumstances.

This liberal use of discretionary power adds a human element to an otherwise mechanical process and also provides the flexibility necessary to adapt rigid, formal rules to diverse, concrete situations. At the same time, it causes some serious problems. In many areas, including the criminal process, little is known about the extent and manner in which discretionary power is exercised, and consequently there is little control over its application. For example, how often does a policeman decide not to take formal action against an apparent offender? On what basis is this decision made? How does the prosecutor decide what cases to prosecute and what charges to bring? How does the plea-bargaining process, which disposes of some 80 percent of the cases reaching the courts, function? Is the system of discretionary justice, however desirable it may be, so pervasive and uncontrolled that the legal system in practice bears only slight relation to the formal legal system on the books?

Given this situation, however oversimplified here, how does this society, particularly through its legal system, attempt to govern conduct? Much of this work is handled through the childhood socialization processes during which a child learns what is "right" and "wrong." Beyond that, however, American society basically leaves people alone. That is, there exists an informal and continuous process of socialization wherein a person interacts with the people around him, and tries to make his behavior conform to their expectations, or, at least, tries to minimize conflict and unpleasantness with them. Aside from this generalized application of peer pressure, there is not a deliberate and structured attempt to inculcate values or to shape the conduct of adults. (For obvious reasons, religion and commercial advertising are not considered here.)

The overall effect of this system is that, however society operates in practice, in theory the state tends not to enter into or interfere with the ordinary activities of individuals. Clearly, this is an oversimplification since the state may enter into some areas but not others. It is not possible to draw clear lines between complete "interference" and total "noninterference." Nevertheless, the range of permissible behavior is, on the whole, quite wide. Minor deviations from the accepted norms are ignored, tolerated, or controlled and corrected through some informal means when the state is not a direct participant. Moreover, all of this is highly prized in the United States and is often described as a major aspect of democracy and freedom.

This freedom, however, has a price, although very likely a worthwhile price. When an adult begins to deviate from "proper" conduct, no systematic and effective effort is made to correct him. As the transgressions become more serious, still little is done—whether out of an affirmative philosophical conviction that noninterference is desirable, an institutional inability to cope with a problem of this magnitude, or a basic indifference to the well-being of others so long as their actions do not directly affect oneself.

In any case, at some point the transgressions become so serious that the state intervenes. Then the roof falls in, as the entire majesty of the law is visited upon the malfeasant. Put another way, up to a certain point a person is free to do as he wishes; he gets little encouragement or help to correct his conduct, even though his actions are undesirable and grow progressively worse. Finally, this person commits a "crime." While the exercise of discretionary power by an official provides some leeway for the case, basically the offender has fallen off the edge of a cliff where the state and society had left him too much alone and he loses much of his control over his own fate.

Note that the story basically ends here. If charges against the offender are dropped, he is returned to the top of the cliff. But having been returned to his original situation and given virtually no guidance or assistance, it usually is only a matter of time before he falls off again.

If charges are not dropped, the offender is moved through a legal process with which he is almost entirely unfamiliar and which he usually cannot afford financially. Should he be exonerated, he is returned to the top of the cliff as before, though this time possibly with a social stigma that makes him less able to reform. Should he be convicted and sent to prison, the situation becomes practically hopeless. The statistics on recidivism show that virtually no one is reformed as a result of this treatment. Indeed, some have suggested that jails and prisons are a kind of graduate school for criminals where their original values are reinforced and their professional skills are sharpened. Upon release, the offender carries a social stigma, generally has learned no socially useful skills, and usually returns to the milieu where he first developed his deviant tendencies. In a sense, this person is now beyond the pale, and never really gets returned to society.

The Chinese Model of Criminal Law and Penology

Like the West, China relies heavily on law, although very likely most Western as well as Chinese observers would not describe the situation in these terms. There are only a few items in the Chinese system that were proposed and passed by some legislature, that are formally designated "laws," or that resemble laws as they exist in the West. Nevertheless, using the questions posed at the beginning of this paper, there are many items which, in the sense of the term used here, could be called "laws." They are found not merely in law books, but, more importantly, in mass-communications organs such as the *People's Daily*. They are not usually labelled "law" and are not phrased in legal terminology. Yet they define in greater or lesser detail what is permissible conduct, provide means for ensuring that the desired norms of behavior will be followed, and describe the consequences of noncompliance. This is law. These laws have played a major role in bringing about the great changes, both in institutions and in attitudes, that have taken place in China since 1949.

The Western and Chinese legal systems differ, however, in that the West uses the legal fiction that everyone knows the law, while China tries to make this fiction a reality.[2] This is accomplished in part by making the normative rules of conduct readily accessible to the public, and in part by keeping the rules simple and free of technicalities so the layman can understand and apply them. Most important, the Chinese have undertaken a vigorous and thorough program of public legal education. With the exception of young children, everyone is a member of one or more "small groups" which are composed of about twenty persons who are closely affiliated through their employment, place of residence, or other ties. In addition to other activities, these groups engage in a number of hours of "study" each week; a substantial portion of the study sessions deal with matters falling under the rubric of law. Several hours a week times fifty-two weeks a year times twenty-three years, plus the hours spent in continuous, intensive study during campaigns and similar times, yield a great deal of specific knowledge about the law. Moreover, an effort is made to apply the general principles examined to the actual living and working conditions of the members of the group. This application of theory to practice not only enables the discussants to understand better the general principles, but also helps to explain ambiguities, fill in gaps, and provide an opportunity for the introduction of local initiatives and variations.

[2] For a more thorough discussion of the development and functioning of the Chinese legal system, see Victor H. Li, "The Role of Law in Communist China," *China Quarterly*, no. 44 (October-December 1970), pp. 66-111; see also Stanley B. Lubman, "Form and Function in the Chinese Criminal Process," *Columbia Law Review* 69 (April 1969), 535-75.

A second major difference between the Western and Chinese legal systems is that the small groups not only educate the public about law, but also play an important role in legal enforcement. They are extremely effective in bringing to light any member's deviations or incipient deviations from the accepted norms of thinking or behavior. Groups are formed of persons with close ties who must spend considerable time together. Thus, as a person's thinking begins to deviate, this is quickly observed by other members of the group during the course of study sessions or other activities. Similarly, one who steals would be unable to enjoy his newly found riches since the people around him would know or suspect how he had acquired them.

The discovery of deviations and crime is only one step in the enforcement and correction process. If a person truly loves his neighbor or truly is his brother's keeper, then he has a moral and social duty to correct his brother's shortcomings. If truly no man is an island and the actions of each person directly affect the lives of all others, then the "group," however defined, has a real and direct stake in controlling the actions of its members. This is entirely contrary to the Western approach of legally, though possibly not morally, discouraging the intrusion by one person into the lives of others, except when something very serious is involved. In place of the "officious intermeddler" rule in most Western tort law and the consequent unwillingness of bystanders to go to the aid of a person in trouble, the Chinese (and, indeed, all the socialist countries and a few others as well) impose on the citizenry a legal duty to go to the rescue of a person in distress. Similarly, comments and criticisms made about another's life-style or work-style are regarded, in the ideal case, as proper exercises of a social duty to one's fellow man, not as invasions of privacy or as meddling in the affairs of another. No legal limitations are imposed on "standing" to raise a complaint or to sue, and there are no "victimless crimes" since these acts directly harm all of society.

The process of enforcement and correction begins with the first efforts at studying new laws. During the course of study, a person learns both the specific provisions of the law and also their rationales. Presumably, doubts or questions one may have are raised and are argued out within the group. This process not only clears up most of the ambiguities, but also produces a common understanding among all members of the group as to the meaning of the rules. There will still be areas where, by design or by inability to do better, the group will be unable to figure out what conduct is desired of its members.

These areas, however, are relatively small. They tend to concern changes in policy, and hence by definition tend to involve a degree of uncertainty until all the changes are completed. In these areas, the group must tread carefully, and probably ought to seek further clarification and instruction. In any case, all members of the group are in the same predicament, and hence within the group there is little problem of lack of notice or of the imposition of an unknown standard.

At this point, a person understands the meaning of the rules and accepts the underlying rationale. He then slowly internalizes the norms of behavior prescribed by these rules. If doubt or misunderstanding arises, additional study is carried out which may clear up these questions or which may produce a new common understanding.

There is no enforcement problem for those who have internalized the norms. Others who have not done so might still adhere to these norms in order to avoid the unpleasant consequences which result from their violation. Such persons would not present much of an enforcement problem, although the group must be watchful for violations and must be sure that the enforcement and deterrent system is functioning properly.

Finally, there are persons who, for a variety of reasons, violate the desired norms. The handling of these persons shows another major difference between the Western and Chinese approaches to correction and reform.

Most people do not commit serious crimes without warning. Such actions are a part and perhaps the culmination of an entire pattern of dissatisfaction, unhappiness, or confusion. This pattern is manifested in many ways and grows gradually, with minor problems becoming increasingly serious. The Chinese, through the small groups, treat these symptoms of unhappiness and possible deviation as soon as they appear. The effort is to solve problems before they get entirely out of control, somewhat like treating a physical disease.

As a person begins to express improper thoughts or deviant tendencies, others will try to "help" him. This takes the form of criticizing the incorrect actions and explaining what would be correct. It also involves discovering and curing the root causes of the problem. For example, a person might be sloppy in his work and consequently damage production. He is criticized for his carelessness, but also he is given additional technical training to improve his skills. Moreover, other aspects of his life are examined to find the root causes of his difficulties. Perhaps an unhappy marriage is adversely affecting his work; if so, the factory group must find means of "helping" his family life.

If the offender does not respond, the group increases pressure. Criticisms grow harsher and longer. More and more persons join in as the scope of the criticisms increases. At some point, the employer and the neighborhood apparatus formally take part. Finally, the threat of criminal sanction is made; the public security or some other state enforcement agency becomes involved; and then the criminal process is invoked.[3]

This gradual process differs considerably from falling off the edge of the cliff. The principal effort is to stop the decline as early and as quickly as possible. Since problems attacked early are much more easily resolved, this effort is successful in many cases. At the same time, an attempt is made to return the offender to the good graces of society. This is possible, partly because problems are attacked before the offender has strayed too far or caused too much damage. In addition, a rationale for the cause of the deviance is given which allows everyone to accept the idea of nearly complete reintegration. Wrong thinking and misinterpretation of facts are due to a combination of subjective factors within the person (e.g., capitalist tendencies) and external factors that exist in society (e.g., poverty and unequal distribution). One ramification of this approach is that no offender should be blamed for all his actions, since some portion of the offense might be traceable to external factors. If care is taken in one's phrasing, it is possible to condemn an act without condemning the inner man. Consequently, in dealing with offenders, even serious ones, there is no need to begin with a bias against their basic characters or to regard the offenders as basically incapable of being reformed. This is an oversimplification, of course, since there are biases against the basic character of persons having bad class backgrounds. Nevertheless, it still means that the Chinese accept much more readily the possibility of reform and of perfectibility.

A second ramification is that some external factors must be corrected. Society in general and the offender's peer group in particular must take active steps to rehabilitate him. Merely returning the offender to

[3] On the formal criminal process, see Jerome A. Cohen, *The Criminal Process in the People's Republic of China, 1949-1963: An Introduction* (Cambridge: Harvard University Press, 1968). For a discussion of group study, see A. Doak Barnett, *Communist China: The Early Years, 1949-55* (New York: Frederick A. Praeger, 1964), pp. 89-103.

his original circumstances after meting out criticism or punishment would be quite improper. The group must alter the undesirable external conditions, and must continually "help" and supervise the offender so that he does not begin to deviate again.

Most important of all, the Chinese appear to accept as a given that, when confronted with a clear distinction between good and evil, most people will choose the good. Hence, there is no great surprise at and no great resistance to the idea that most people are completely reformable. An offender can analyze why and where he went astray, state that he now recognizes his past errors, and promise to sin no more. While he will continue to be supervised, the group can accept with relative ease what he says and allow him to rejoin it as a full-fledged member.

This discussion of the Chinese system of correction and reform does not include a description of the handling of serious criminal offenders. That subject has been dealt with in considerable detail elsewhere.[4] Suffice it to be said that the handling of serious criminals differs in degree but not in kind from the handling of minor offenders. Serious criminal offenders constitute only the barest tip of the correction and reform iceberg. The great bulk of the work in this area concerns minor offenders of the type described above. It may well be true, if one does not take things *too* literally, that there is basically no crime in China. Attacking problems at an early stage and across a wide range works. Moreover, it would require quite an unusual person who could resist the social pressures which are systematically applied to him as his deviations increase. This is especially true since discovery of deviations is nearly certain and escape from "help" and supervision is nearly impossible.

Thought Reform and the American Penal System

"Thought reform" has a bad connotation and usually reminds people of brainwashing and 1984. It should be noted, however, that American society is thoroughly familiar with thought reform both in concept and in method. The childhood socialization process is an obvious example. First-year law school (and perhaps many other educational

[4] Allyn and Adele Rickett, *Prisoners of Liberation* (New York: Cameron Associates, 1957); André Bonnichorne, *Law in Communist China* (The Hague: International Commission of Jurists, 1956); and Harriet Mills, "Thought Reform: Ideological Remoulding in China," *Atlantic Monthly*, December 1959.

situations) and advertisements are two other equally striking though less obvious analogies.

The Chinese use the term "thought reform" to describe an approach to dealing with behavior. It is not limited to deviant behavior. Instead, the basic question is how do you get people to behave in a particular way when either they disagree with you or they have been ignorant of your wishes. All the problems of communication, internalization, and supervision which were previously discussed apply here.

Given the shambles of the American penal system and the relatively healthy state of the Chinese system (at least in its ideal form), the question arises whether there are concepts and methods developed in China that can be applied in the United States. On the whole, the answer is no. Thought reform will work only in China.

The problems that arise are both practical and philosophical. On the practical side, there does not appear to be a willingness to devote sufficient human and material resources to improving the United States penal system. That being the case, the Chinese approach, which requires a massive input of resources, cannot be used. Is there the will to spend thousands of hours in study sessions so that "small groups" can help formulate local norms and communicate these norms to all members? Is there the will to spend more thousands of hours to implement the system, to criticize deviant conduct, and to supervise offenders? And is there the will to invest the tremendous amount of money that is needed to "correct the external conditions" which were part of the causes for deviations in the first place and which thereafter contribute to recidivism? Of course, the practical and the philosophical considerations are not separable. Resources are not expended in this way in part because philosophical and political priorities are different in the United States.

There also seems to be doubt whether criminals are reformable, and hence there is an unwillingness to spend large resources in this area. Perhaps this attitude is due to the fact that Americans think of "correction and reform" not as it applies to early and minor offenders, but only in relation to serious offenders who might well be unsalvageable. Even the Chinese do not claim that everyone can be reformed. This attitude may also be traceable to certain strands of the Judeo-Christian tradition which contain the notion of "original sin" and have little faith in the intrinsic goodness and ability of man. In any case, it is considered dangerous when there are no external standards or law to restrain and channel man's "natural" urges. Thus, when a person is placed under the control of his small group, it may be an invitation to arbitrariness and localized tyranny. The Chinese view the same situation as a fine application of the concept of the mass line. The difference lies in whether one believes that an "unbridled" small group will tend to act properly or improperly most of the time.

Finally, on both practical and philosophical grounds, it is probably felt that the Chinese system entails the loss of too much privacy and freedom. The line between loving one's neighbor and busybodying is quite thin at times. And even if the collective life is preferred over individualism, it would still require considerable time to learn the techniques of properly loving one's neighbors.

Throughout this paper, the Chinese system has been discussed in its ideal state with little mention of how it works in practice. There are not enough data for a thorough exploration of this question, although the author's prejudices are that the ideal and the practical do not differ greatly in this area. Some questions can be raised, however, which suggest that thought reform may not be working well even in China, so why import it here.

The opportunity for reintegration into society is a vital aspect of the system of reform. Without this, all incentives to reform are negative in character. In the years immediately following 1949, the Chinese could tell deviants that they were products of the old society and that this accounted for much of their evil behavior. They were then told that this was a new society and, if they reformed, they could have a full share in building the new China.

Twenty-three years later, it becomes increasingly difficult to say that errors are due to external conditions rather than to subjective factors. Hence the bulk of the blame is due to some flaw in the character of the offender. At the same time, as the revolution stabilizes, it becomes harder to correct the external conditions. Consequently, an offender is quite likely to be returned after criticism or punishment to much the same conditions that contributed to producing his earlier deviant tendencies. Moreover, as revolutionary ardor cools and the situation becomes more settled, less effort may be devoted to the thought-reform process. The result could be that the systems of correction and reform will become more perfunctory and therefore more coercive and less effective.

Leaders and Masses*

RICHARD M. PFEFFER

The Chinese Communists (CC) under the leadership of Mao Tse-tung developed the basic methods, values, and goals necessary to make bureaucrats and political leaders reasonably responsive and accountable before they actually established complex and vast bureaucratic hierarchies. This early development in the 1930s and 1940s is attributable in no small part to the CC's dual commitment to vanguard leadership and to meaningful mass participation. This dual commitment required the CC to confront at the outset the issue of how the vanguard is to relate to the masses of people over time. The particular patterns of relations they created tended simultaneously to encourage responsiveness and accountability on the part of leaders to the people and to encourage participation and active support on the part of the masses for the revolutionary movement.

The CC created these patterns because they were engaged in a protracted people's war against both the Kuomintang and imperialism and because they believed in the kind of society implicit in these patterns. The CC won primarily because they succeeded in developing leaders and institutions that enabled them to learn from and to serve the masses and, thereby, to mobilize them.

Such leaders and institutions provide a most effective check on bureaucratic rule. They also may be more effective in achieving many

* The author examined this subject at greater length in his "Serving the People and Continuing the Revolution," *China Quarterly* (October-December 1972), pp. 620-53.

ideals of democracy and good government than American-type institutions, which have produced a static, privatized system of democratic elitism. With the development of large-scale bureaucracies in China after 1949, however, Maoist values and methods frequently were overshadowed by more conventional approaches to industrialization and governance. During and in the wake of the Cultural Revolution (CR) Maoist institutions and ideals, developed in the Yenan (1937-45) and final civil war (1945-49) periods, have been revived and adapted to China's society of the 1970s.

Before Liberation

China's crises in the twentieth century generated in Chinese leaders a recognition of the need for an organized vanguard party to lead and educate the backward masses. Sun Yat-sen, Chiang Kai-shek, and Mao Tse-tung all supported the idea of a tutelage period during which the vanguard is to organize in a sustained manner the attack on China's deep-seated socioeconomic problems and to raise the consciousness of the people, enabling them eventually to displace their tutors. The CC, personified by Mao, went far beyond others in their commitment to mass participation, egalitarianism, and class struggle as the means for achieving the collective good. In the eyes of the Communists, China could be saved and the collective interests of the people well served only by dismantling the exploiting classes of China and by ensuring that the new leaders remained intimately identified with the masses.

Various means were devised to accomplish this identification. Local leaders, for example, frequently were recruited from the impoverished masses. Leaders at all levels shared in the common self-sacrifice of war and revolution, eschewing bourgeois and semifeudal lifestyles and engaging in manual labor side by side with peasants and workers. Radically decentralized organization facilitated the development of basic-level institutions in which members of local communities were encouraged collectively to influence issues and personnel most critical to their existence. Ideological and rectification campaigns were carried out to shape and consolidate the value consensus and personnel required for such a decentralized revolutionary movement to cohere and progress.

One of the constant themes of these campaigns was that the CC had to serve the real needs of the people. But if the existence of the vanguard is justified by the backwardness of the masses, that same back-wardness means the masses at times will not understand their present needs and frequently will not understand the relationship between immediate needs and future development. Who, then, is to decide the needs of the masses? In such cases the vanguard must enlighten the masses. This, though, raises several archetypal problems. First, how is the vanguard to achieve mass acceptance of its views? Second, who is to enlighten the vanguard itself, which after all still carries within it self-interests and constraining values and habits of the old society? And, finally, how, if the vanguard is to play so determinative a role in the revolutionary process, is the consciousness of the masses to be consistently raised so as to guard against the vanguard's being trans-formed into another ruling class and to facilitate its being phased out of its tutelage role?

The Chinese Communists' continuing "solutions" to these problems lie in substantial part in the Maoist quality of the ongoing relation-ship established between vanguard and masses. Education and influ-ence in the relationship is a two-way street. Prolonged imbalances in the relationship produce either commandism, on the one hand, where-by the vanguard gets out of touch with mass needs and tolerances, dictates what the masses should do and thereby discourages mean-ingful mass participation, active support and growth, or tailism, on the other, whereby the immediate, limited consciousness of the masses narrowly determines vanguard decisions and future development.

A dialectical interaction between leaders and masses characterized practical politics at the grass roots level. The quality of the relation-ship was epitomized by a kind of mass-based community control, which, as class struggle intensified in the last half of the 1940s, in-creasingly came to mean something approaching class control by the poor-and-lower-middle-peasant majority of each rural community in the liberated zones.

Mass-based community control meant many things. In the first place it meant that new feelings of community were created on the local level, by which the enemies and the people were redefined and new concepts of justice were formulated and practiced. With the sense of new community, feelings of cooperation, of resisting and struggling together were enhanced. Community control meant that Party, govern-ment, and military cadres generally worked among the people, sharing a more-or-less common experience and language. It meant that the local leaders, at least, were close to the people, able to learn from the masses as well as to teach them. The management of local affairs no longer was remote from the masses.

As part of mass-based community control a variety of mass meeting formats was developed and spread in which evil landlords and scoundrels were assaulted verbally and physically and made to confess their crimes. In these same meetings poor peasants for the first time confronted their oppressors, spoke of their bitterness, and developed their own sense of collective class consciousness.

Mass meetings were held not simply to rid the community of traditional exploitation but in addition as psycho-administrative devices to ensure, for example, the effectiveness of self-regulating tax collection systems in border region areas. Mass meetings also were held to ensure that cadres, especially Party members, would be made to confront the constituencies they were supposed to lead and serve. In that confrontation the masses could be educated by the cadres, while the cadres, in turn, were educated regarding the needs, hopes, tolerances, and capacities of the masses. Through these open-door rectification meetings the masses had the opportunity to actively participate in shaping the perceptions and behavior of the local leadership and in putting pressure on the cadres to be politically responsive. These mass meetings were community-based trials, involving public criticism and public self-criticism, through which local leaders had to pass.

Stemming from such participation was a growing consensus and attachment to many of the principles and goals of the revolutionary movement. From such widespread and intense commitment emerged a sense of principled government. Men worked and saw their work in terms of contributing to the revolution. Working for themselves by working for the movement was something from which the masses of men and their leaders took great satisfaction.

The sense of community and patterns of behavior that were created in the liberated zones of China extended to nearly all areas of life. Striking is the extent to which the CC were able to apply their concerns and methods to warfare, to administration, to production, to education, and to politics. The mass line, for example, was not limited in its application to political institutions but was applied as well to economic, educational, and even military institutions. In the 1940s the CC consolidated their highly integrated model of revolutionary governance and development and applied it across the board. The movement, relatively speaking, was at one in theory and practice.

1949-65

But the question in 1949, once the CC were victorious, once they had to deal directly with domestic and international problems as the effective government of a nation-state, was whether they would be sufficiently self-motivated, sufficiently self-confident, and sufficiently agreed on the priority to be given in practice to the Maoist revolutionary elements of the movement's tradition to maintain the egalitarian, participatory, collectivist, and responsive revolutionary elan, style, and content. Would they be able to sustain what was not simply a romantic and revolutionary struggle but also a good government? Or, seemingly without the imposed necessity of having to win a people's war, would they lose this virtue?

In retrospect it is clear that the apparent need to centralize rule in order to manage and guide the national unit, combined with the imperatives of hierarchy and specialization seemingly implicit in the mastering and spreading of modern technology, led in the 1950s to the disintegration of the revolutionary movement and to the dominance of nonrevolutionary rule between 1949 and 1965. The integrated Maoist model for revolutionary governance and development, successful before the movement seriously sought to industrialize and to govern all China, was rejected as a comprehensive model thereafter. Instead, in the early 1950s the CC, feeling perhaps somewhat out of their depth as they had in the 1920s, once again adopted a Soviet model. That model of rule and industrialization stressed specialization, hierarchical and stratified relationships, centralized bureaucratic methods, individuated material incentives, and conventional technological development. After 1949, the dominance of the Soviet bureaucratic model was somewhat offset, but not replaced, by the Maoist style of revolutionary development, salient during the high tide of socialization in 1955-56 and the Great Leap Forward.

The alternation between the Soviet model and the Maoist model gave Chinese politics a dualistic quality. But the growing bureaucratic institutions for achieving generally agreed-upon goals were highly antithetical to Maoist campaigns and concerns. The two Chinese models—the dominant one tied to Soviet style industrialization and rule and the other to the Chinese revolutionary tradition—however complementary they may have been as a complex strategy for revolutionary development, remained disintegrated. As time went by, various groups within the elites increasingly attached themselves to one or the other, making the struggle in the last half of the 1960s for transformation of the system through reintegration essential, if not inevitable.

An earlier attempt at reintegration during the Great Leap Forward had failed. As a result of the economic disruptions of the three hard years of 1959-61, the dominant group in the Party leadership came to feel that more stringent efforts at bureaucratic coordination and "rationalization" were required once again. In the early 1960s hierarchical decision making was reemphasized; middle-level bureaucracies were expanded; and generally the gap between administration and the masses was restored.

The Party, thus, came to preside over the implementation of a rule and development strategy that, on the one hand, seemed to be dictated by certain technological imperatives of the industrialization process and, on the other, seemed likely to thwart realization of the movement's ultimate revolutionary values, of which the Party itself was supposed to be the organizational embodiment and guardian. It was hoped in vain that the Party somehow could keep "politics in command," that it could preserve the end goals of the revolutionary movement and make governance and industrialization serve those goals. But it could not.

This failure of the bureaucratized Party explains the "reversion" in recent years to the Maoist tradition of community control and mass participation. What impelled the Chinese leadership in the 1940s and what has impelled the Maoist leadership during and since the CR is necessity. In the 1940s the narrow need was to win the war of national liberation and then the civil war. In the 1960s and 1970s the need has been to achieve industrialization without sacrificing the revolutionary goals of egalitarianism, collectivism, and participation.

To achieve these goals one cannot, following the Soviet model, rely almost exclusively upon bureaucratic and political elites. For elites, Mao has believed since the 1930s, tend to become self-serving, as power in class society inevitably tends to corrupt powerholders. Maoists, then, must rely in substantial part upon the masses to "educate the educators." But, if Maoists cannot rely exclusively on elites to continue the revolution until its final goals are realized, neither can they assume the masses will remain revolutionary. If revolutionary elites at some point after victory tend to become ruling elites, revolutionary masses at some point tend to become ruled masses, and the revolutionary movement turns into nonrevolutionary rule.

These tendencies cannot be overcome by formulas or technical gimmicks. Coping with them appears to require, particularly after a revolutionary movement has come to power, brilliant and assertive leadership, a continuing high degree of conscious commitment to final goals, and the driving force of mass participation. This trialectic at its core requires revolutionary politics—the building of new and shifting coalitions among the relatively deprived classes and groups in the society in support of continuing the revolution. These coalitions must be mobilized through persuasion, by convincing the masses that their collective interests are best served by continuing the revolution. For the revolution to be continued, in short, the masses of people must be convinced its continuance will serve them. And the most effective way to convince them is for the continuing revolution in fact to serve the people.

The CR and Its Institutional Aftermath

The reason that many of the institutions flowing from the CR are reminiscent of the 1940s does not lie in lingering romanticism, carried by fond memories of the "good old days." The reason is that the essential necessity for these institutions remains the same, although the specific content has changed. The essential necessity is to convince the masses that their interests are best served through their support for continuing the revolution. Because these institutions were successful in the 1940s in coping with this problem and because today they again appear at least more likely than any other methods to achieve success, the institutional aftermath of the CR bears marked resemblances to the 1940s. The CR represents the return to the integrated Maoist model of revolutionary governance and development.

As such, one of the major thrusts of the CR has been to pave the way for increased decentralization. The CR and the continuing rectification movements associated with it can be seen as necessary preludes to radical decentralization—necessary in the sense that personnel and ideologies first had to be rectified if radical decentralization was not to lead either to intense localism led by entrenched local elites or to the reestablishment of elaborate control bureaucracies. Given this sort of decentralization, the revival of various forms of mass participation and community control may be creating a more responsive political system. The extensive bureaucracies, particularly the one previously associated with the civilian wing of the Party, may well not be resurrected. Or at the least, such bureaucracies, if they are resurrected, are likely to be substantially offset by a system of mass-based community control, as well as by other mechanisms for enhancing the accountability and responsiveness of administrative and political leaders.

Community control in China today, of course, is relative, not absolute. The rectified national leadership continues to play a vital role in determining and coordinating national policy and in formulating the broad guidelines for community development. But within these limits the transformation appears to have been substantial. The scope of community control has been broadened and vigorous attempts have been made to promote the mass line approach to decision making, particularly at the basic level.

Effectively incorporating the mass line approach into the decision-making process, though, is easier said than done. While it may be relatively easy to incorporate patterned mass participation and supervision into basic-level decision making in order to enforce some direct responsiveness and accountability on the part of local cadres to their constituent masses, it is much more difficult to enforce such responsibility on cadres at higher levels. There, artifice of some sort is required as a functional approximation of the kind of daily contact and familiarity basic-level cadres and the masses enjoy with each other. If the cadres above the local level are not made to appreciate conditions at the grass roots and are not kept amenable to collective mass influence, then the significance of the mass line will be severely curtailed.

Similarly, persuading the masses that continuing the revolution is in their collective interest requires great effort. If members of the masses are to be persuaded to sacrifice certain immediate interests for the collective, they must come to believe that through participation in collective decision making they are benefiting materially, as well as psychologically, in significant areas like education, old age security, and health.

What institutions, then, have been revived or created through the CR to deal with problems of accountability and responsiveness in China's vanguard system? Are, for example, various output institutions made to service the needs of the people? If so, how? Are the masses encouraged to participate in shaping community development? In what ways? Are basic-level cadres institutionally made to confront their constituents? Are higher level cadres made more empathetic to the problems of the masses? Do the masses have an opportunity for inputs into provincial and central governing organs?

The open-door rectification process, the transformation of China's educational system, the establishment of May 7 cadre schools, and the extension of direct class representation in China's revolutionary committees all seem to suggest that the CC are trying to build greater responsiveness and accountability into the system. Through the creative application of the Maoist core elements of community control and mass participation, the Maoists are trying to enlist mass support for continuing the revolution.

Open-door Rectification: One vital way in which the masses have directly participated in the CR and its aftermath has been in the rectification and rebuilding of basic-level Party and government committees. Although the forms of mass participation have varied and its intensity and frequency appear by 1971 to have been sharply reduced as the new committees were set up, the complex reality of mass participation in rectification can hardly be denied.

Since 1968, the Chinese press and radio repeatedly have referred to the anxieties and hesitations connected with mass participation and to the conflict engendered between "left" and "right" factions over the extent to which rectification should be carried out through mass criticism. The very mention of these problems suggests that mass participation has not been a mere formality. Further, the critical importance of open-door rectification has been asserted and reasserted in no uncertain terms. In Maoists' eyes there is no way to resolve basic political contradictions and to assure the continuation of the revolution other than through continuing or repeated open-door rectifications of basic-level units:

> Practice proves that it is the revolutionary masses who are most concerned about the rectification of the Party and also understand best the situation of the Party organization and Party members of their own units. Only by carrying out the open-door rectification, by relying on the masses, can we prevent the work of Party rectification from "taking the old road and restoring the old order," and can we better purify the Party organizations organizationally and ideologically and build every Party branch into a strong fighting bulwark armed with the Thought of Mao Tse-tung.

In terms of increasing accountability and responsiveness the practice of open-door rectification serves many related functions. First, it gives the masses an opportunity for and a sense of meaningful participation, mobilizing them to judge the conduct of Communists and cadres. Second, such trials by the masses undoubtedly make leaders more sensitive to their constituencies. And, third, the process facilitates exposing and weeding out those within the Party who cannot pass mass examination and provoking and revealing through struggle new activists among the masses, who then can be recruited into the Party. Open-door rectification helps the Party to be informed of mass feelings and to be practical at the grass roots level. It stimulates the masses to be active and responsible and provokes all to heightened consciousness.

The Educational System: One of the main purposes of the CR was to transform China's educational system. The educational goals of the CR include: (1) greatly increasing the enrollment in schools of children of the poor and lower-middle peasants and workers; (2) making education serve the concrete needs of the masses; (3) reducing, if not eliminating, the technocratic and cultural elites' status and hierarchical control of education, and preventing their revival; and (4) "putting politics in command of education," which means inculcating in those connected with the educational system Maoist revolutionary values, methods, and goals as the highest standards for judging all other theories and practices. Significant steps to achieve these goals have been taken in schools at all levels in the last few years.

In the case of rural primary schools, sometime in the fall of 1968 remaining state-run units were placed under the control of production brigades. This renewed emphasis on local community control of education by the masses who are most directly affected by it is predicated on community self-reliance in supporting local education. Self-reliance, in turn, provides the community with the leverage necessary to influence local education. With community control, for example, teachers, like other members of the brigade community, are increasingly being paid on the basis of workpoints rather than being paid wages by the state. Their performances as teaching members of the brigade are evaluated by other members. Their share of distributions depends on the overall performance of the brigade in production as well as on the evaluation of their work in public meetings by fellow brigade members. In this setting, issues such as the quality of education and teacher promotions can become matters in which the poor-and-lower-middle-peasant majority of the community plays a major decision-making role.

The step of tying the material welfare of teachers directly to the brigade in which they teach also contributes to the process of reeducating teachers by reducing the gulf between teachers and commune members. Instead of being cadres paid by the state, they are made accessible to mass supervision and are better integrated with the masses and with productive labor. Moreover, as a result of mass-based community control, the content of rural education appears to have shifted more toward directly serving the needs of peasants. These schools, in addition to inculcating a minimal level of general intelligence training and a large amount of political socialization, largely function as community vocational-training centers.

The same practical service orientation also seems applicable to higher education. In implementing this transformation, teams of workers, peasants, and members of the People's Liberation Army (PLA) have acted as guides in the struggle, criticism, and transformation process and in the actual shaping of the content and form of education.

Chinese documents and visits by foreigners to various Chinese universities confirm that students enrolled since 1970 have indeed mostly been children of workers, peasants, and PLA members who generally have had two years or more of practical experience. Visits confirm, too, that older, veteran workers and poor and lower-middle peasants with abundant practical experience but only limited formal education also are being enrolled, though to date only in very small numbers. Finally, visits confirm that university and college students in general have been recommended for admission by fellow members of their production units, thereby giving the masses of their work community who know most immediately their character and talents a direct say in who goes on to higher education. It further appears that while at college most such students study disciplines related to the needs of their work units of origin, to which most graduates are expected to return in order to help improve production and management.

Consequently, graduates of institutions of higher education no longer will be "three-gate cadres"—cadres who passed from the gate of privileged family, through the gate of school, and thence through the gate of employment in technical, intellectual, or managerial work relatively untouched by the hard realities of life for the vast majority of China's less privileged millions. Thus, the quality of one of the major recruitment pools for members of the upper bureaucracy will be significantly changed.

Many aspects of the ongoing transformation in education can be seen in the case of Kiangsi Communist Labor University (KCLU). KCLU is an agricultural university established during the Great Leap Forward and explicitly founded upon Maoist premises that education should serve proletarian politics and should be combined with productive labor. At the university today half the students' time is devoted to productive labor. The school has 132 campuses and approximately 50,000 students, ranging from the main campus of about 1,000 students situated in the countryside outside Nanchang, to quite small campuses of 100-plus students situated in many of the eighty-nine counties of Kiangsi. The university runs more than 390 cultivated farms, tree nurseries, and animal-husbandry farms, and about 250 factories throughout Kiangsi. Its curriculum is divided basically into four departments: agriculture, forestry, animal husbandry and veterinary medicine, and farm machinery.

Of the 1,000 students on the main campus, about 300 are the children of workers, while another 60 percent are children of poor and lower-middle peasants. The percentage of children from peasant families is said to be still higher at branch campuses, suggesting that these may be located in more remote rural areas.

Each of the branch campuses is under the jurisdiction of the revolutionary committee of the county in which it is located. The main educational task of each branch is to serve the concrete needs of these counties, while the primary purpose of the main campus is to train teachers for assignment to various branch campuses. Thus, the orientation of KCLU as a whole is toward recruiting students from worker and peasant families and toward serving local needs in the counties of Kiangsi Province.

May 7 Cadre Schools: If through transforming the educational system and open-door rectification it is possible to institutionalize a reasonable degree of responsiveness and accountability on the part of basic-level cadres and teachers to the masses of their local community, it is much more difficult to institutionalize the same quality of direct relationship for higher-level bureaucrats. Several mechanisms, including the setting up of May 7 cadre schools and the practice of direct representation by members of the masses in important government bodies, have been experimented with in an effort to cope with this problem.

The May 7 cadre schools have been set up nationwide since October 1968 by territorial and functional administrative units. They are permanent facilities located in the countryside to which administrative cadres from all levels of government and Party above the production-unit level are being sent by rotation for ideological revolutionization. It is expected that all such cadres will have spent at least six months on rotation in a May 7 school by the mid-1970s. After that, cadre rotation for reeducation in these schools is expected to recommence and to continue indefinitely.

The schools serve as partial, functional substitutes for the direct and continuing involvement with the masses that only basic-level cadres can experience. Through them, higher-level cadres are effectively required to simulate this experience. By contrast, cadre schools before the CR, assertedly influenced by the Liu line on cadre training, are said to have been much more separated from the masses and from the "three great revolutionary struggles" than today's schools. In pre-CR schools the cadres reputedly wore cadres' clothing, ate cadres' food, and spoke cadres' language. Such cadres, at best, carried out a kind of divorced self-cultivation, considering their mistakes and failings almost exclusively behind closed doors. They became accustomed to thinking of themselves as leaders, not as commoners; to living relatively comfortable, rather than arduous, lives; and to restoring as a mark of their status the traditional and bourgeois disdain for manual labor and for the countryside. They came, in short, to approximate a new ruling class, complete with its own self-justifying world outlook and lines.

The May 7 cadre schools, predicated on the view that one must take society itself as the great school for learning Marxism-Leninism, for learning about class struggle, and for understanding and learning to apply creatively Mao's Thought, combine manual labor, ideological study, and mass work in an atmosphere pervaded by a spirit of self-reliance, self-sacrifice, hard work, and "revolutionary mass criticism." Taking part in manual labor is seen as a necessary but not a sufficient condition for bringing cadres back to the reality of mass life and for their ideological transformation. The setting directly confronts the cadre with the objective struggle for production and class struggle, thereby sharpening the reflected struggle within him.

In the confrontation, interconnections between various elements of the bourgeois-revisionist world view are brought out. The view of manual labor as demeaning and as punishment, and the belief that officials are "one grade higher than other people," or, alternatively, the view that temporarily doing manual labor can be useful for career advancement (getting a "plate of gold" through manual labor) are challenged. From their experiences at May 7 cadre schools many cadres are reported to have realized, for example, that they had despised manual labor largely because they subconsciously believed that as cadres they were superior to ordinary peasants. On the other hand, many cadres discouraged by their treatment during the CR are also reported to have understood that being a cadre is no more burdensome than being a peasant and that the real obligation of all is to serve the people and the revolution.

The aim of the material alteration in the cadres' lives at these schools is to promote a subjective change in cadres' world outlook, to revolutionize their ideology and behavior. The purpose is to create new leaders who do not place themselves above the masses and who can intuitively understand the problems of the masses.

Although it would be naive to expect complete or permanent transformation of cadres' values through the May 7 school experience, anyone who has visited these schools and conversed with cadres presently attending, and with others who have attended, cannot but be profoundly impressed by the respect and sense of pride with which cadres uniformly discuss the impact of the school experience. The fact that cadres encountered in China, all of whom had previously attended the May 7 cadre schools, mingled easily and unabashedly with workers and peasant may, perhaps, provide some circumstantial evidence of the utility of the schools.

Direct Class Representation: But even if the May 7 cadre schools are reasonably successful in revolutionizing many cadres, that cannot ensure that the practical understanding and collective interests of the masses will be effectively represented once the cadres have reimbedded themselves in China's bureaucracies. Consequently the CC are trying in other ways to increase the likelihood of such representation. One way is by having peasant and worker classes represented in governing committees by other peasants and workers, often by model members of each class.

Revolutionary committees, for example, have been established at all levels of government since 1967 upon the understanding that they should include substantial numbers of mass representatives. These committees appear in fact to have included such representatives, especially at the local level, to a degree hardly appreciated by Western analysts.

The primary observed characteristic of the process of setting up revolutionary committees has been the increasing dominance of the PLA in these committees. Commentators have noted that, as of December 1968, twenty of the twenty-nine provincial-level revolutionary committee chairmen were active military men and nine were revolutionary cadres, while none were mass representatives. From such facts commentators have concluded that the role of the masses was downgraded as the CR waned.

By contrast, very little has been made of the fact that of the then estimated total of 216 members of provincial-level revolutionary committees the composition of the 85 percent whose backgrounds were known was surprisingly equally divided among the military, the cadres, and the masses. These statistics assume greater importance when one realizes that they deal with the highest levels of provincial and regional government. The masses in fact are less well represented relative to the PLA in the chairmanships of provincial revolutionary committees than they are in the standing committees of these committees. Similarly, the masses appear to be less well represented in the standing committees than in the provincial revolutionary committees as a whole.

This is part of an understandable pattern: the lower one goes in the hierarchy, the more likely the masses are to be represented by delegates who themselves are workers or peasants.

The lower one goes in the hierarchy, the easier it is for governing committees to involve mass representatives and the more sense it makes for the masses to have a direct say in what, at the most basic level, amounts to their local community. This seemingly patterned increase in the proportion of members of the masses who act as representatives of the masses in formal governmental units as one goes down toward the local community may well be one manner in which China's prevailing balance between centralization and decentralization is formally institutionalized.

Substantially represented at the pinnacle of the Chinese political system, with approximately one-quarter of the Central Committee of the CCP composed of model workers and peasants chosen to represent the masses, the masses seem likely to get a decent hearing in the Central Committee, where matters are most centralized. With much greater numerical representation at the base of the hierarchy, the masses seem likely to have a very influential voice in local community affairs.

So, if it is true that the role of the masses has been reduced from its "destructive" highpoint in the CR, it seems also true that, at least to the extent one can take their numbers as significant, the role of the masses in government organs has increased measurably as compared with most periods between the early 1950s and the CR. Unless one expected China to be governed by Red Guards, it is the increase rather than the decrease in the potential role of the masses that should be noted.

Adapting China's Developmental Experience

These are a number of institutionalized ways in which political leaders and bureaucrats in China are encouraged to be responsive and accountable to their immediate constituents and to the Chinese people as a whole. It is tempting to think that some of China's innovative institutions, such as the May 7 cadre school, might be successfully transplanted to other developing countries or advanced industrial countries like the United States. But this is the same technocratic fallacy that spawned theories of counterinsurgency which hold that counterrevolutionaries can utilize the techniques of revolutionaries to win the hearts and minds of the native population. Institutionalizing accountability and responsiveness to the people, like winning hearts and minds, is not merely a matter of technique, as Americans should by now recognize.

The reason that Chinese-type institutions cannot be adapted to most other societies is not, as some undoubtedly will argue, primarily because China is more authoritarian, or its citizens more indoctrinated or better organized than those of other societies; nor is it because China is less industrialized than, say, advanced industrial societies. Rather, it is primarily because the Chinese people are committed to achieving revolutionary ideals that have not yet been embraced by the majority of peoples in most developing countries and are hardly even discussed any more by people in advanced industrial societies. Much of China's developmental experience could in fact be adapted by trial and error for use elsewhere. But it could be meaningfully adapted for use only in societies committed to values, life-styles, and goals consonant with China's.

It is the profound commitment on the part of vanguard and masses alike in China to social justice, to egalitarianism, to the supremacy of the collective good, and to meaningful mass participation that enables Chinese institutions to achieve what successes they do at reasonable cost. The continuing vitality of this commitment makes the institutions described in this paper more than mere formalities.

Whether such institutions could be adopted by any but revolutionary societies is a moot question. That they could not be adopted in the United States as presently constituted, however, is beyond question.

In China, for example, there is an unparalleled sense of the public interest and a related deep commitment to serving the people. This conscious commitment makes sacrifices, such as those involved in attending the May 7 cadre school, worthwhile to most cadres. In the United States, by contrast, except in times of crisis the public interest is defined as the product of interest-group liberalism. "The people" are fractured into pluralist interests, and the government is controlled by private interests that dominate the public interest, as federal-housing scandals, the recent rise in milk prices, and numerous other phenomena make all too clear.

In China the attachment to extending egalitarianism in theory and practice provides the basis for infusing cadres with a sense that they are not better than peasants. In the United States even the call for egalitarianism is seen as threatening. Economic equality is still opposed as "creeping socialism." Across the board, we have settled for equality of opportunity—which is to say gross inequality in practice —and rejected even the ideal of full equality.

In China, difficult as it may be for Americans to believe, mass participation in basic-level politics is sustained and intimate. In America we have accepted the inevitability of elite domination of our system and again have settled for formalisms like biannual elections and the narrow competition that exists between elites although we know they are inadequate substitutes for meaningful mass participation and elite accountability.

This sense of settling and loss of ideals for governance has led to such cynicism and apathy in America that corruption in government no longer angers or even interests us. In this context, adopting Chinese-type institutions, which grew out of the CC's revolution against social injustice, privatism, and static elitism, would be tragic-comic.

America has much to learn from China, but it does not wish to learn. America is in need of radical change, but the reigning aphorism of the day is the conservative "politics is the art of the possible." In our anxiety to preserve the status quo, we have imprisoned hope and striven to forget, as Max Weber has said, "that man would not have attained the possible unless time and again he had reached out for the impossible." This is the first lesson we can relearn from China's developmental experience. After this lesson it will not be simply a matter of learning but a struggle for power.

The Family

MARTIN KING WHYTE

In the political turmoil of the decades before 1949, some commentators argued that Communism could not triumph in China because the loyalties which Marxist-Leninist regimes require were incompatible with the strong family orientations embedded in the Confucian tradition. The triumph of Communism did not result in the refutation and abandonment of this line of argument. Some commentators felt that the price of this triumph had to be the destruction of the Chinese family. The original incompatibility argument was maintained, but Communism and not the family was seen as the victor.

A generation later, the available evidence suggests that these early arguments were oversimplifications on a number of counts. First, they overestimated the scope of the Chinese Communist attack on the family. The Chinese Communists did launch vigorous attacks on many aspects of the Chinese family, but they never seriously contemplated abolishing the family as an institution, as many of their Soviet predecessors had in the 1920s. Radical reform was the order of the day after 1949, and in most cases these efforts accelerated changes that were already well underway as a result of economic change and Western influence. Second, the incompatibility argument neglected the flexibility of the family as an institution, its ability to adapt and accommodate itself to changing political and economic structures without breaking down. Finally, the early arguments did not foresee that the changes would yield a new family system which the regime would sustain and nourish. The following pages present a general picture of the official policies toward the family, of the changes which have occurred, and of the combinations of new and old found in contemporary family patterns in China.

As in most discussions of contemporary Chinese social life, some caveats are in order. As in pre-1949 China, the "ideal family" is more easily portrayed than the actual behavior of people. In the virtual absence of demographic, legal, and other statistics, and of detailed sociological and anthropological field studies, the evidence which sustains the following analysis is a hodgepodge of the official press, travellers' accounts, contemporary literature, refugee interviews, and occasional captured documents.[1] The gaps are large. Crude estimates and impressions will have to serve in some cases until more evidence becomes available.

After 1949, China's new rulers made vigorous efforts to change the traditional Chinese family, which they saw as unsuited to the future socialist society. The most direct aspect of these efforts was the promulgation on May 1, 1950, of the Marriage Law of the People's Republic of China, and the attempt in the ensuing years, using political campaigns, trained propaganda teams, women's associations, and local cadres to persuade and pressure the populace to change their family behavior to accord with the new law. But many other events of these years—land reform, collectivization of agriculture, and expansion of education—also affected the Chinese family in complex and sometimes contradictory ways. The changes occurred at an uneven pace, with variations particularly between rural and urban areas. (Developments in minority areas are complex and poorly reported and will not be discussed here.) Perhaps the best way to get some grasp of these developments is to examine several important aspects of the Chinese family.

Age of Marriage

The 1950 law specified minimum marriage ages of eighteen for females

[1] The best summaries of family change, particularly for the 1950s, are Ch'ing-k'un Yang, *The Chinese Family in the Communist Revolution* (Cambridge: MIT Press, 1959); M.J. Meijer, *Marriage Law and Policy in the Chinese People's Republic* (Hong Kong: Hong Kong University Press, 1971). See also William J. Goode, *World Revolution and Family Patterns* (New York: The Free Press, 1963), chap. 6; Jan Myrdal *Report from a Chinese Village* (New York: The New American Library, Signet Books, 1965); and W.R. Geddes, *Peasant Life in Communist China*, Society for Applied Anthropology, monograph no. 6 (Ithaca, N.Y., 1963).

and twenty for males. Since the *average* age at marriage before 1949 seems to have been in the seventeen to twenty range, with instances of child betrothals, this law represented an attempt to encourage marriage at later ages. The 1931 Kuomintang Civil Code specified minimum marriage ages of sixteen and eighteen. The 1950 law has remained unchanged, but in recent years official propaganda has encouraged even later marriage ages, generally about twenty-five for females and thirty for males. Considerations of population limitation, health, and educational and occupational commitment all seem to play a role in this stress on delayed marriage. The local marriage-registration officials are supposed to check household registration and other documents to make sure that applicants have passed the minima. In recent years they have been expected to try to dissuade couples not far beyond the minima from registering. The popular press and women's association cadres have tried to persuade the public that there are good reasons for delaying marriage and to counter the many attitudes that encourage early marriage, such as the desire to continue the family line, the fear that the best partners will be gone, and the fear that late childbearing is more dangerous. These measures, with other changes such as increasing access to education, seem to be having some effect, but popular attitudes are still not in total accord with official ideals. Urban residents, students pursuing advanced education, and political activists seem to be most responsive to the calls for delayed marriage. Refugee interviews with former peasants suggest that rural residents are marrying somewhat later than before 1949, but still relatively close to the eighteen to twenty minima. The gradual rise in rural living standards, in fact, may promote earlier marriage, since poverty and economic insecurity were formerly major reasons why China's poor peasants had to delay marriage. One can speculate that marriages below the ages of eighteen and twenty have declined sharply, but even this trend depends upon the vigilance of local cadres and marriage-registration officials. In the period of low popular morale after the failure of the Great Leap Forward, when presumably such vigilance was low, in one brigade in Fukien Province eighteen girls with an average age of fourteen were sold into marriage.[2] In sum, the apparent trend is toward later marriage ages, a trend underway before 1949, but not approaching universal compliance with the ideal twenty-five to thirty range.

[2] C.S. Chen, ed., *Rural People's Communes in Lien-chiang* (Stanford: Hoover Institution Press, 1969), p. 203.

Freedom of Marriage

Traditionally most marriages were arranged by parents, often with the help of go-betweens, and in many cases without the couple's having met before the ceremony. The 1950 marriage law states that marriage is to be by free choice of both partners, and no third party may interfere. In the early campaigns to implement the marriage law, energetic efforts were made to explain and justify free marriage choice, which already was being followed increasingly in urban areas and among the educated. In marriage-registration procedures, couples were asked whether they were marrying of their own free will, and those who would admit to parentally imposed arrangements were supposed to be refused registration. A stage of investigation was allowed to check evidence of parental interference. There was some opposition to this aspect of marriage reform by parents concerned with their loss of influence over marriage choices. Subsequently, officials clearly indicated their desire was to end totally arranged marriages, rather than to terminate all parental influence in marriage decisions. Thus seeking parental advice and even help in locating a mate is not forbidden so long as the young couple has the decisive voice in whether to marry. In fact, parents who do not try to dissuade their children from early or bad marriages (e.g., with political outcasts) are to be criticized.

One problem which occurs in China as in other societies in transition from arranged to free-choice marriage is that opportunities for meeting and courting the opposite sex are somewhat limited. No "dating culture" has emerged in China, and both traditional values and revolutionary asceticism are hostile to its emergence. Particularly in the schools, where the dating culture flourishes in American society, strong official pressures discourage youths from getting romantically involved. In this situation, with free marriage choice urged, but with limited opportunities for getting to know potential spouses, modified forms of marriage arrangement arise. Marriage arrangers continue to exist, either in the form of local figures who customarily provide introductions, or simply of parents, relatives, and friends. In some locations, officials have recognized the need to provide youth with help in finding mates and, in an effort to take business away from traditional marriage arrangers, have encouraged cadres of the local production unit, the women's association, and the Communist Youth League to arrange introductions to youths in other units. Political authorities can also play negative roles in marriage decisions. Party and Youth

League members are expected to report their developing romantic interests to these organizations. If they want to marry someone from the former wealthy classes or someone with a questionable personal history, they will be strongly discouraged, although not absolutely forbidden, from doing so.

Not only is the young couple supposed to have the major say in marriage decisions, but the exaction of money and gifts in connection with marriage is prohibited. Here, too, popular opposition and confusion led to some qualifying and back-tracking. The relevant provision in the marriage law is meant to prohibit marriage entered into primarily because of possible economic benefits to one side, generally the bride's family. Gifts exchanged as part of the celebration of a marriage entered into by free choice are not prohibited, although they should be modest ones, in keeping with the official emphasis on frugality. Thus token bride prices are still permitted in China. Some localities have tried to take these gifts out of the realm of family-to-family transactions by instituting modest wedding gifts such as socks, towels, and the works of Chairman Mao from the commune, factory, or Youth League unit. In sum, blind marriages are probably relatively rare in China today, occurring in backward areas where the marriage law is not vigorously enforced as in the rural Fukien brigade mentioned previously. But arranged and approved marriages continue to coexist with free marriages, as they do to some extent in other societies where free marriage choice is valued.

Monogamy, Divorce, and Remarriage

In traditional China, divorce was strongly discouraged and apparently rare for the upper classes, although probably not so uncommon among the poor. For wealthy males, concubinage provided a way to take secondary wives if the first was not satisfactory, but women were allowed no such privilege. Men were encouraged to remarry after the death of a spouse, but women were strongly discouraged, although again this applied more to the upper classes than to the lower. The 1950 marriage law specified that polygamy was prohibited, that divorce would be allowed upon request of the couple or, after mediation and possible litigation, upon the request of one party, and that it was illegal to interfere with remarriages. Since concubines were not very common, existing only among the dethroned wealthy classes, the provisions in regard to polygamy caused relatively few problems, although there continue to be occasional reports of individuals covertly taking secondary wives. But the provisions regarding divorce generated considerable opposition. Many women tried to use the new law to get out of unhappy forced marriages in which their husbands and in-laws wanted to hold them. More generally, rising divorce was viewed as evidence of the undermining of sexual morality and of the family, as it often is in other societies. (In fact, the relationship between a particular divorce rate or change in that rate and the "health" of the family system—as distinct from individual family units—is by no means clear. Many preindustrial societies, such as Tokugawa Japan, combine high divorce rates with strong and relatively stable family systems.)

Some local cadres and propagandists actively encouraged divorces, intent on gaining support for local social change from those liberated from forced marriages. Other local cadres, afraid of losing power over their own wives, refused to push this part of the marriage law or even actively resisted demands for divorce. With the implementation of the marriage law, divorce cases did increase rapidly (from 186,167 cases in 1950 to 409,500 in 1951, and to 398,243 cases in the first half of 1952), but the Chinese press continued to report instances of suicides, beatings, and murders arising from marital disputes.[3] The new divorce provisions seem to have fulfilled a great popular need while simultaneously giving rise to great popular anxiety.

Whether as a result of this resistance or of the fact that the 1950 law had already largely fulfilled its purpose of freeing many women from unhappy marriages, by the mid-1950s the official position toward divorce had gradually changed. This did not take the form of new legal obstacles to divorce, as in the Stalinist divorce freeze in the Soviet Union in the 1930s, but of active dissuasion. Registration officials, mediation committees, and local courts pressed for reconciliation to prevent rash divorces and generally allowed divorce only as a final resort. Visitors to China confirm the nature of these pressures; they report that a relatively small percentage of divorce applications now leads to actual divorces.[4] The number of divorce cases reached a high of 1.1 million in 1953, and then began a decline to 510,000 in 1956,

[3] Goode, p. 317.
[4] Felix Greene, *Awakened China* (Garden City, N.Y.: Doubleday & Co., 1961), pp. 195-207.

the last year for which there are figures.[5] (All of these figures represent divorce actions brought to court and thus probably omit divorces by mutual consent, for which only registration is necessary.) After an initial wave of divorces, then, the rate began to subside. More recent events should have had a contradictory effect upon divorce. Later marriage should encourage marital stability, while the growing occupational equality of women and the assignment of spouses to jobs in different locations may encourage divorce. There is little information available about the remarriage of widows, but since the prohibitions were the strongest in the wealthy classes displaced by post-1949 changes, it can be supposed that this provision has been more easily accepted by the Chinese.

Husband-Wife Relations and the Role of Women

In traditional China the father-son tie and not the husband-wife tie was the dominant link in the family system, in terms of obligations and loyalties. Because of patrilineal descent, arranged marriage, and patrilocal residence, the wife's initial position in her new home was weak. Close husband-wife ties might develop over time, but public displays of conjugal affection were frowned upon, and in household disputes the husband was expected to side with his parents against his wife. Women were seen primarily as performers of domestic tasks, although necessity forced many of them from poor classes to work outside the home, particularly in parts of south China. As in other aspects, family change and demands for women's rights had already developed before 1949, particularly in urban areas. After the Communist victory, this trend was accelerated. Now the primary bond in the family is supposed to be between the husband and wife, rather than the father and son. One symbolic contribution to this shift has been the popularization of a new, more intimate, form of address between spouses, *ai jen* (literally, lover). This term is used reciprocally, indicating the newly desired equality between spouses, an equality which has been given more than symbolic substance by granting women inheritance, divorce, and other rights. Although the conjugal tie is supposed to be closer than in the traditional family system, it is not supposed to have the exclusiveness and possessiveness that often characterize this relationship in the West. Neither partner is supposed to interfere with the

[5] Meijer, p. 113.

other's active involvement in outside activities, even though there is less time for home duties, or to protest job assignments entailing prolonged separation. These prolonged separations, of course, appear stranger to a conjugal-minded Westerner than to the Chinese, for whom family separations were common, at least for males, long before 1949. Such separations are not necessarily accepted with equanimity, however, and refugee interviews give evidence that people often try to use personal connections to get spouses transferred to work near them.

The clearest change in the status of women is their increasing employment outside the home. Women who are solely housewives are found in China, as well as many who are involved in part-time rather than full-time jobs, but nonetheless the exodus from the home has been impressive. Formal barriers to the education of women and to the variety of occupations have fallen, although informal barriers remain. Women are still not equally represented in the Communist Party, in educational institutions (particularly at higher levels), and in posts of local leadership. One of the major obstacles to greater equality is that state-supplied facilities for the care of young children and for domestic work are not sufficient to relieve all families of these burdens, and among much of the population this kind of work is still seen as more appropriate to women than men. In spite of repeated efforts to encourage the equal sharing of domestic tasks, in much of the population (again, particularly in rural areas) women are under the "double bind" of economic and domestic work, while men have more time after work to participate in political and cultural activities. The regime has not been totally consistent on the issue of the role of women. At some times since 1949, women have been urged not to shirk or be dissatisfied with domestic burdens, and publicity has been given to model housekeepers; at other times, this emphasis on the domestic roles of women has been branded a political deviation. Clearly, substantial changes have taken place both in closer husband-wife ties and in increased status of women within and outside the home, although popular practices have not fully caught up with official ideals.

Household Composition and the Role of the Aged

The traditional ideal was to assemble a household of many generations in one compound, with sons and grandsons marrying and continuing to live in the parental home. It is well known, however, that the average household in China never looked much like this ideal, with rarely more than three generations under one roof, and with an average family of only around six members. But the ideal remained a compelling force, and when fortune struck the most humble individual, the drive to build up a large family began. Within any large household, members of the oldest generation, particularly the males, were supposed to have almost absolute authority over the lives of other household members. After 1949 a variety of efforts, particularly the land-reform campaign, served to change both the traditional ideal and the reality. The confiscation of landlord land and other properties and, after 1955, the collectivization of agriculture and industry, made it difficult and not so advantageous economically or politically to accumulate a large family unit. The allotment of private plots in rural communes to households may, in fact, encourage family division, although plot-allotment procedures seem to differ from place to place.

The forces behind the large-family ideal have clearly been reduced, but a number of features of Chinese society keep the nuclear-family household from completely sweeping the field. According to travellers' reports the three-generation family is still found in urban areas and is fairly common in rural areas. Most of these seem to be three-generation stem families (an older couple living with one married child, generally a son) rather than the traditionally favored joint families (an older couple with several married sons). The continued viability of this stem form is due not only to traditional attitudes, but to such matters as housing shortages, uneven child-care facilities, and inadequate welfare for the aged. There was publicity given to homes for the aged set up in the countryside around 1958, but it is clear now that these homes were the exception rather than the rule, generally for old people without relatives to rely upon. Most of the rural aged live with a married child or rotate from one child's home to another and provide baby-sitting and household help in exchange for a home and security. The duty of the young to support their aged parents was sanctified in article 13 of the 1950 marriage law. The rural aged do not depend totally on their relatives for security, however. They may also receive partial support from the welfare funds set aside by rural production units.

In rural China the household, whether of two or three generations, is not just a place for members to eat and sleep, but an economic production unit (though reduced by collectivization) with a private plot, animals, fruit trees, and a household head coordinating family economic activities. In some locations it still seems common for the commune to pay the wages earned by all family members to the household head rather than to each individual, although the head has no legal right to such financial control. A major difference from former times is that, in the case of a three-generation household, it is increasingly the second-generation male who is the household head, rather than the male in the oldest generation.[6] The aged in rural China, then, continue to live for the most part in minimally extended family units where they play important roles in child care and household work, but have reduced authority.

In the city the nuclear arrangement is no doubt more dominant, but three-generation households, generally also of the stem type, still occur. Housing shortages and the need for child care and for domestic help—not family economic enterprises—are the factors creating this form of urban family structure. Contrary to the impression of some recent visitors, not all work units have adequate facilities to care for the children of their employees, and grandparents or other relatives help when needed. Retirement pensions are available but not generally ample for the urban aged to live comfortably without part-time work or help from their families, and there is a critical shortage of urban housing.

The few large patriarchal households of the past appear to exist no longer, but they have not been completely replaced by the nuclear household and separate residence. Both official policies and shortages in facilities continue to give China's aged a valued, if not so authoritative, role in the family. If health standards improve and the life span increases more rapidly than the supply of housing and nurseries, this valued role may be even more highly emphasized in the future.

Relations with Extended Kin

In pre-1949 China, families belonged to larger kinship units, generally termed clans, and loyalty, material aid, and ritual activities were oriented toward this unit and its members. Favoritism toward fellow clan members and intense rivalries with other clans were common, particularly in southeastern China, where single-clan villages are nu-

[6] Inferred from Myrdal, pp. 70-76; Geddes, pp. 62-65.

merous. The clan as the guardian and supporter of Confucian family traditions was a particular target of post-1949 family reforms, although not a word on the topic is contained in the 1950 marriage law. Land reform in the late 1940s and early 1950s resulted in the confiscation of clan corporate properties and ancestral temples. The land was redistributed, while the buildings were converted into such facilities as schools and offices. In the mass struggle meetings which climaxed the land-reform campaign, poor peasants who were not kin were urged to support one another in attacking wealthy kin. Wealthy villagers who had dominated the clan organizations were attacked and in some cases beaten and killed. Those who remained became more or less permanent social pariahs, to be supervised and periodically criticized in subsequent years. At the same time, new political and economic organizations were introduced in rural areas which used class rather than kinship criteria in selecting members and leaders. All of this represented an effort to bring about a major reorientation from kinship to class loyalties. To the extent that the state and the family systems were incompatible, the contest was more between state and clan allegiances than between the state and individual family loyalties. The attack on the clans seems to have been fairly successful. Without corporate property, ritual centers, effective leaders, or freedom to organize, Chinese clans have lost most of their former power.

Underneath the new political and economic structure, however, clan and extended kinship favoritism and rivalries continue to exist in rural China. Organizational changes in the countryside have not entailed the relocation of local populations, and most people live where they did before, with neighbors who are often close relatives. The rural communes and their subordinate divisions, brigades, and teams, for the most part conform to the natural village and neighborhood lines and thus tend to support, rather than cut across, preexisting kinship cleavages. Refugee interviews support the idea of continued rivalry and favoritism occurring in work assignments, cadre selection, and work-point allocation. Even the national model Tachai Agricultural Brigade is not immune, for a neighboring brigade dominated by Wangs envied and tried to cause trouble for the Tachai Brigade, which is dominated by Kuos.[7] Even though clans and clan elders no longer play a key structural role in Chinese society, the allegiances remain

[7] Klaus Mehnert, *China Returns* (New York: E. P. Dutton & Co., 1972), p. 58.

and continue to affect the operation of the new organizations. The continuation of these allegiances is due not only to survival of traditional attitudes, but to the way in which new organizations reinforce traditional cleavages.

Kin ties are of less importance in urban organizations. One of the explanations often given for the uneven economic progress before 1949 was the inefficiency of economic enterprises, which often chose employees on the basis of personal ties rather than skills. Since 1949 vigorous efforts have been made to establish new recruitment and training procedures which would rule out such favoritism. In cities, instances of using connections to get jobs or to provide for relatives still exist, but recruitment procedures based upon skills, education, and political criteria seem to be well established. One major exception revealed through refugee interviews and Red Guard materials is that, at least prior to the Cultural Revolution, highly placed cadres were often able to arrange privileged jobs for their wives. There were also some special schools for the children of high-ranking cadres, which have since been disbanded. Nonetheless, the socialization of economic enterprises and the establishment of state and Party channels for job allocation in urban areas have resulted in a major decline in nepotism and other particularistic practices.

Kinship Ritual

Traditional family rituals conflicted with the ideas of the Chinese Communists both because of the expenses involved, which were seen as wasted resources, and because they tended to bolster clan loyalties and traditional religious views. The new elite has consistently advocated simplifying and economizing on weddings and funerals and has introduced new political holidays to replace traditional ones. The confiscation of clan temples during land reform largely eliminated public worship of clan ancestors, but household ancestral tablets remained for those, particularly in the older generation, who wished to honor immediate ancestors. In the "destroy the four old and establish the four new" stage of the Cultural Revolution in 1966, Red Guards in many areas tried to confiscate and destroy remaining household ancestral tablets and replace them with pictures and quotations of Mao Tse-tung. It is not yet clear how widespread such occurrences were and whether household ancestral tablets are gone, never to return.

Efforts have also been made to consolidate and reduce the area allotted to graves in order to free more land for agriculture, in spite of the violence this does to traditional ideas of "wind and water" geomancy. Secular, simplified weddings have been devised, with pledges of loyalty to the state and to Mao Tse-tung, speeches by local cadres, and refreshments. While meetings and entertainment are provided on new holidays, such as May 1 and October 1, the people have been urged to devote themselves to working especially hard on some traditional holidays. What seems to have occurred is that the most important traditional holidays continue to be celebrated, although in modified form, while the new holidays have been accepted as well. And in spite of the new emphasis on frugality, there is evidence in refugee interviews and in the captured documents from Fukien Province that, in some rural areas at least, the desire to hold more costly weddings and other celebrations is still being satisfied. Again the evidence on family ritual suggests marked change, but not complete success.

Parent-Child Relations

The 1950 marriage law states that parents have the duty to rear and educate their children, and children have the duty to care for and assist their parents. The traditionally emphasized absolute power of the older generation and absolute obedience of the younger generation are supposed to be replaced by concern and care in both directions. Parents and children alike are also supposed to put the demands of the state and local work units ahead of personal and family interests. In other words, the family is expected to be increasingly open to outside demands. The most extreme displays of this new emphasis have often shocked outsiders accustomed to the traditions of filial piety and family loyalty. Children do sometimes publicly denounce prominent parents during political campaigns, and "family Mao Tse-tung's thought study classes" have been set up in which children criticize the backwardness and selfishness of their parents. Some parents do urge their children to go off to distant places to settle as peasants, rather than to stay at home and try to find high prestige jobs. But these highly publicized examples probably exaggerate the extent to which the regime has aggravated or politicized parent-child relations. Family study classes seem to be the model to emulate rather than the general rule, and parents who urge their children to leave for the countryside are widely publicized precisely because parents have been reluctant to do so in the past. The vast majority of youths are never called upon to denounce their parents, and even those who do are often denouncing the ideas of former bad classes in the abstract, while continuing to live harmoniously with their parents. Parents critical of the regime are generally guarded in the comments they make around young children, however, for fear their criticisms will be carelessly revealed to outsiders. Perhaps because of the general danger of family relations' being upset by the intrusion of politics into the home, many husbands and wives are reluctant to discuss with family members political problems and issues at their workplaces, and the status of the home as an apolitical haven is jealously guarded. Travellers' reports and refugee interviews convey the impression of generally warm and supportive parent-child relations in spite of pressures and tensions. The continuing decline of patriarchal family authority seems to make it possible for fathers, in particular, to have closer and more nurturant (but less authoritative) relations with their children than was formerly the rule.

Parental authority is not dead in China. Parents continue to play the dominant role in early child-rearing and discipline. Even after children enter nurseries and schools, the vast majority live with their families, spend many of their free hours in family activities, and continue to receive substantial parental training and discipline. In rural areas, where the youth help with domestic tasks and work on the private plot, learning needed agricultural skills from family members, the importance of parents as both models and disciplinarians remains particularly strong. With the increasing availability of extrafamilial, agricultural-training institutions and agronomists, this importance of parents in imparting skills can be expected to decline in the future.

The regime is not trying to eliminate parental authority. From time to time propaganda is even launched urging youths to be more diligent in working at home and respectful toward their parents. The official attitude seems to be that youths should obey their parents when there is no conflict with higher demands, but should oppose, criticize, and persuade them in the event of such conflict. Since distinctions are never made this neatly in social relations, some tension between parental and state authority continues, as when parents try to keep their children at home or urge them to work more on the private plot and less on the commune's land. But this is a tension rather than an incompatibility, since most parents adapt their behavior to outside demands in order to maintain close ties to their children and to avoid placing obstacles in the way of their children's fitting into the new society.

The Pattern of Family Change

What conclusions can be drawn from this survey of family change? First, it seems obvious that marked change has taken place in Chinese family ideals and, more slowly and unevenly, in behavior. Some changes have been slow or uneven, not simply because of the backwardness or resistance of some of the people, but because of the complex effects of various other institutional changes since 1949. Family change has been less rapid in rural than in urban areas not solely because of peasant ignorance and superstition but to some extent because rural institutions are still based partly upon kinship units. It is also clearer now that post-1949 changes were not designed to destroy the family as an institution, but rather to replace traditional family norms with new ones seen as more compatible with an industrializing socialist society. Finally, a point which needs some amplification, the emerging family form is not radically new but in many respects is not too dissimilar from family systems in the West.

William J. Goode has examined family changes that have taken place in America, Western Europe, Arabic Islam, sub-Saharan Africa, India, China, and Japan. He concluded that the wide range of changes taking place, from varying starting points and at different rates, tends to be in the direction of what he calls the conjugal family. Its primary characteristic is that a wide range of in-laws and blood relatives are excluded from the everyday affairs of the nuclear family unit. From this main characteristic follow a number of other important features of the conjugal family:

1. The couple cannot count on a large number of kinfolk for help, just as these cannot call on the couple for services.

2. Neither couple nor kinfolk have many rights with respect to one another; thus their reciprocal obligations are few.

3. Necessarily, then, they have few moral (or other) controls over one another.

4. Kinfolk do not choose the couple's residence location—which is, therefore, "neolocal," and reinforces the couple's independence. . . .

5. The couple's choice of one another as mate was dependent on them, not based on the rights or interests of kin; in turn marital adjustment is primarily between husband and wife.

6. When this system emerges, the age at marriage will change; but theory does not permit a prediction of its direction—youngsters must be old enough to take care of themselves.

7. Fertility is based on the needs of the couple, and may be high (frontier) or low (urban industry).

8. The system is omnilineal; neither kin line has great weight.

9. The small nuclear unit is the chief place where the emotional input-output balance of the individual spouses must be maintained, since there is nowhere else to go.

10. Consequently, the divorce rate will be high—though again, we cannot predict whether it will fall or rise when such a system emerges.

11. Remarriage, after the death of one's spouse or after divorce, is highly probable.[8]

There are discrepancies in details, but the fit with the family changes occurring in China is obvious. The decline in the power of clans and extended kin, the increased importance of the husband-wife tie, the delayed marriage and increased divorce rate (although with a subsequent decline), the acceptance of widows' remarrying, and so forth, clearly fit in with trends found in other societies. Some of the changes in the Chinese family, such as the openness to external demands and the high rate of employment of women, are not specified in the conjugal ideal type, and other changes are still in process, including the shift to neolocal residence and the changing role of the aged, and the fit with the Goode's conjugal family type is less clear. But on major points, at least, the Chinese family seems to be moving in a familiar direction. This does not mean that families in China will some day be exactly like those in America or Western Europe, only that the direction of change is toward increasing similarity.

What is distinctive about the changes in the Chinese family is not so much their direction, but their acceleration, and this in turn rests upon the methods by which these changes have occurred. The changes toward the conjugal family in most societies occur in a glacial fashion, as education gradually expands, as new extrafamilial employment opportunities develop, as bureaucratic forms of organization and hiring become more dominant, and as ideas of equality and individual fulfillment slowly win favor among the educated urban classes and begin to trickle down to other parts of the population. (Some societies, of course, may already have family systems not far different from the conjugal ideal type before these kinds of changes occur. Some scholars argue that America was one such society and that an existing almost-

[8] William J. Goode, "Industrialization and Family Change," in *Industrialization and Society*, eds. Bert F. Hoselitz and Wilbert E. Moore (Paris: Mouton, 1963), pp. 240-41; idem, *World Revolution and Family Patterns*, pp. 7-10.

conjugal family form facilitated subsequent industrialization.) In China all of these changes have occurred, but faster, and they have been backed by pressures not generally present in other countries.

Some of the added forces for change are shared with the Soviet Union and other Communist countries. Land reform and socialist transformation, state control over the mass media and most employment opportunities, state enforcement of population and marriage registration, and the attacks on former elite classes all tend to give the Party and state increasing influence over family behavior and customs. To these elements are added distinctive Chinese Communist change efforts. Trained propagandists and organizers proselytize and pressure in family-related mass campaigns, where models of the new family morality are praised and studied, while practitioners of feudal patterns are criticized and isolated. Urban residents are formed into residents' committees and small groups, with group leaders and activists to observe and pressure their neighbors to resolve family disputes, adopt birth-control practices, and send their children to the countryside. Small discussion groups in schools, factories, and other work units hold regular political study sessions where official norms are dissected and where deviants are subjected to the mobilized negative opinions of other group members. Thus the sources of family change in other societies are reinforced by the impressive political and social control apparatus evolved by the Chinese Communists. While substantial residues of traditional patterns remain and change in the family system is by no means easy or automatic, the changes that have occurred have been both broad and relatively rapid.

What can other societies learn from this experience? Goode's evidence leads to the conclusion that most industrially developed societies already have family systems not unlike that toward which China is moving, although the pattern and pace of change may have been different. In developing societies, trends toward the conjugal family are generally underway, as they were in pre-1949 China, although often at a snail's pace.[9] Family sociologists debate the details and the logic, but the consensus is that some approximation of the conjugal family form is more suitable to industrialized societies, whether communist or capitalist, than many of the traditional family forms that preindustrial societies possess. For developing societies with traditionally

[9] The best summaries are Marion J. Levy, Jr., *The Family Revolution in Modern China* (Cambridge: Harvard University Press, 1949); Olga Lang, *Chinese Family and Society* (New Haven: Yale University Press, 1946).

different family forms, then, some movement in a "conjugal" direction seems likely, and indeed unavoidable, if other institutional changes of a "modernization" type are encouraged.

But are the methods and pace of family change in China desirable in other developing societies? They may not even be possible. The post-1949 changes in China depended on the impressive political apparatus developed during the years of struggle for power, a general popular mandate for change, a systematic plan for the restructuring of the social order, and a compelling ideology to support and justify change. Elites in developing societies who do not possess such powerful political resources will generally find it difficult if not impossible to bring about such rapid and extensive change, in the family or elsewhere, and may have to content themselves with a longer journey.

The Treatment of Minorities

HENRY G. SCHWARZ

When the average American thinks of the Chinese, his only image is of the Han people. According to the Chinese census, however, 6 percent of the population is non-Han, which places the size of China's minorities around 48 million, more than all of the minorities in the United States.

The neglect of China's minorities and of the challenge that they pose is understandable. Unlike the situation in the United States and India, for example, most minorities in China do not reside among the dominant ethnic groups in the major centers of commerce and industry or in the densely populated rural regions. To be sure, prior to 1949, many Manchus and Moslems did live in the larger cities and, as a result of Communist policies, their numbers and those of other minorities in eastern Chinese cities have increased considerably during the past twenty years.

Even today, however, most minorities live in the border regions and in relatively inaccessible portions of several provinces of eastern China, i.e., the core-Han area.

Prior to 1949, not only did relatively few foreigners stray into China's minority regions, but the Chinese themselves tended to travel little. When they did, they stayed within the Han region. The only significant exceptions were the few Chinese "missionaries" like Chang Ch'ien and Hsüan Tsang; the slightly more numerous Chinese officials posted in minority areas; the members of occasional military expeditions which suppressed some rebellions in border regions, such as Tso Tsung-t'ang in the 1870s, or reasserted Chinese political claims, such as the campaigns into Tibet in 1910 and into Mongolia in 1919; and ethnographers such as Fei Hsiao-t'ung who studied the minority groups (in Fei's case, Yunnan).

The Historical Experience

China, from the very beginning of its dynastic existence, had been obliged to take cognizance of the various non-Han peoples living around it. Man's largest creation, the Great Wall, is massive evidence of the perennial Chinese concern with the so-called barbarians. The Hsiung-nu, against whom the wall had originally been constructed, were at one time so powerful that they were treated as equals by the Chinese.[1] But the wars that broke out in the period 133 to 119 B.C. greatly reduced the strength of the Hsiung-nu. In later history the Chinese officially recognized several other non-Chinese groups as their equals or superiors, and China paid tribute or submitted to them. The Tibetans, Uighurs, Mongols, and Manchus come readily to mind. When China was strong politically and militarily, Chinese control extended beyond the core-Han area. During the Han, T'ang, and Ch'ing dynasties Chinese settlers, mostly demobilized soldiers and convicts, helped protect the dynasty from external attacks and spread Chinese civilization to vast regions.

The reverse process also occurred at various times in history. Starting in the 630s, more than a million Eastern Turks settled in the Ordos Bend, which at that time was within the control of the T'ang dynasty. Their military leaders were integrated into the Chinese armies, and the sons of Turkish noblemen were induced to live at the imperial capital of Ch'angan, in modern-day Honan Province. The ultimate intent was sinification, and quite a number of "barbarians" were so successfully assimilated that they were accepted as Chinese by the court and promoted to the higher ranks of officialdom. Perhaps the clearest example is the famous An Lu-shan rebellion in 757. The main leaders of the rebellion had originally been non-Chinese. An Lu-shan's mother was Turkish and his father was perhaps Sogdian; Shih Ssu-ming was Turkish. Both had risen to high positions in the Chinese hierarchy, the former to military governor and the latter to general. The rebellion was eventually put down with the aid of Uighur cavalry

[1] Wolfram Eberhard, *A History of China* (Berkeley: University of California Press, 1971), pp. 75 ff.

who fought to save the T'ang dynasty. If these events sound strange 1,200 years later, it is well to remember that both the rebels and the rescuers considered themselves Chinese—proof that sinification worked.

Sinification, however, did not mean integration, let alone equality. As a rule, only some members of the upper classes of some non-Han societies were permitted to enter the Chinese scholar-official elite. Everybody else, sinified or not, was kept at arm's length. This included large numbers of traders residing and visiting in China's major cities. Arabs in the South and Central Asians in the West and North were obliged to live and conduct their businesses in segregated quarters. It must be said, however, that Chinese merchants were also assigned to special sections in the cities, so that it cannot be determined with certainty whether foreign merchants were segregated primarily because they were foreign or because they were merchants, but probably their foreign origin was as important as their occupation. Even in high T'ang when China's ruling elite was enamored with all things foreign, a basic ethnocentric bias against the non-Han persisted and prevented any minorities except some upper-class persons from entering the mainstream of Chinese state and society.

This ethnocentric bias caused the Han to see themselves at the center of civilization with various barbarians ranged hierarchically below them. Basically, however, because other ethnic groups—with difficulty—could become part of the Chinese civilization, the Han possessed a cultural view of the world. The definition of "China" remained basically unaffected by political and military reverses. As mentioned earlier, the Han were willing to accommodate themselves to equal treaties and to military occupation. But such setbacks had little effect on a self-image that was fundamentally cultural. Since the cultural achievements of the non-Han were considered slight, the Han saw little need for integrating those relatively few non-Han who lived within the domain of cultural China but who retained their own culture. It is not surprising, therefore, that in the entire history of dynastic China, one finds almost no evidence of an explicit minorities policy. The two exceptions, interestingly enough, were made not by Chinese but by the Mongols and Manchus, the two non-Han peoples who managed to conquer all of China.

The Mongol's nationality policy was, of course, designed by a minority to protect itself and other minorities against the Han majority. Because the Mongols held the upper hand militarily, their policy discriminated against the Chinese. It divided the population of Qubilai's domain into four major groups: (1) Mongols, who were subdivided into the oldest Mongol tribes, White Tatars, Black Tatars, and Wild Tatars; (2) Central Asian allies, like the Naimans, Uighurs, and Tanguts; (3) North Chinese; and (4) South Chinese. The last group had virtually no rights. Its members were forbidden to bear arms and to intermarry with members of the other groups. The first two groups monopolized the state and the economy, with the Mongols in charge of the government machinery and the Central Asians dominating all commerce. By today's standards, the Mongols' nationalities policy was hardly more than an adjunct to a policy of military occupation.

The Manchus' nationalities policy similarly sought to preserve their control of political and military policy acquired through conquest. Although in sheer numbers, the Han held most governmental posts during the Manchu reign (1644-1911), the highest positions within the court in Peking were the exclusive preserve of the Manchus. The Manchus discriminated against the Han by forcing them to wear a pigtail and by forbidding them to intermarry with Manchus and to migrate into Manchuria. The latter prohibition was partially lifted toward the end of the dynasty. On the other hand, the Manchus did not create a hierarchical order of classes, as the Mongols had done. Instead, the Manchus gave lip service to the idea of five theoretically equal *tsu* (nationalities), namely the Manchus, Han, Mongols, Tibetans, and Moslems. Little of the theory found its way into practice. All non-Han, except of course the Manchus, were governed through colonial offices in Peking and through native traditional rulers. No thought was given to integrating non-Han into the mainstream of Ch'ing state and society. To put it bluntly, the idea of the unity of the five *tsu* meant in practice segregation and inequality.

Little changed during the Republican period. The several constitutional compacts between 1912 and 1946 ritually reiterated the principle of equality before the law for all nationalities.[2] Not until 1946 did there seem to be a serious attempt at a national policy toward minorities. The Kuomintang's constitution of that year promised aid for local self-government, education, culture, water conservation, and much more. It also stipulated a fair share for the minorities of the seats in the National Assembly and the Legislative Yüan. Although these

[2] For a summary of constitutional provisions for minorities during that period, see Henry G. Schwarz, *Chinese Policies Towards Minorities: An Essay and Documents*, Western Washington State College, Program in East Asian Studies, Occasional Paper No. 2 (Bellingham, Wash., 1971), pp. 46-48.

promises looked good, they were never implemented.

In the first place, time had clearly run out for the Kuomintang in mainland China. When this constitution was promulgated, Chiang Kai-shek was deeply engrossed in the war with the Communists, and even with the best of intentions, he could not have spared the time, manpower, and resources to put the Kuomintang's nationalities policy into practice.

Second, Chiang's intentions are open to question. His constitutional promises were made in the eighteenth year of his party's twenty-one years of rule on the mainland. Moreover, their implementation was entrusted to the Mongolian and Tibetan Affairs Committee, which China's eminent political scientist Ch'ien Tuan-sheng characterized at the time as the "lineal but emaciated descendant of the . . . Li-fan Yüan." Professor Ch'ien said that the sole function of this body was "to supervise the governments in Mongolia and Tibet. . . . In doing little, it has done badly. . . . If [it] is competent at all, it can at least make a study of the multifarious and complex problems of Tibet and Mongolia. But the [committee] does not seem to be gifted with that foresight."[3]

Ch'ien's description of the committee as a mere descendant of the Ch'ing dynasty's colonial office was apt in light of Chiang Kai-shek's own views on the minority problem. In *China's Destiny*, he slightly modified the old Manchu cliché of the five *tsu* by declaring that they all belonged now to the Chinese nation. Chiang never spelled out his views on the minority problem, but perhaps they were similar to those of the historian Li Tung-fang who wrote in Chungking in 1945, and hence with obvious Kuomintang approval, that there were no real differences between Han and non-Han because all the minorities had come originally from the Han. It is not surprising, therefore, that cynics have said that the real authors of the Kuomintang's constitutional promises of 1946 were the Communists because they had, by virtue of their own attractive policies and actions, induced the Kuomintang to follow suit.

The Formative Period

From its founding in 1921 through the early 1930s, the Chinese Communist Party (CCP) did not enunciate a minorities policy. During

[3] Ch'ien Tuan-sheng, *The Government and Politics of China*, (Cambridge: Harvard University Press, 1950), p. 219.

the Communist-Kuomintang alliance in Canton and during the first stage of the Northern Expedition, all CCP efforts seem to have been directed to political goals lying entirely within the Han core area of China. But the bloody destruction of the alliance in 1927 decimated the Communist Party and drastically changed its policies and strategies. As an indirect and incidental consequence of the tragic events of that year, the Communists gradually turned their attention to the question of minorities.

Many Communists who survived the Kuomintang holocaust fled into the mountains of southern China, especially the southern rims of Hunan and Kiangsi. There they recuperated, regrouped their forces, and rethought their future strategies. Almost four years after their escape into the mountains, the Communists issued their first policy statement on minorities. The constitution of the Chinese Soviet Republic promised all minorities the right to secede from China and pledged that the Communists would assist the minorities to overthrow their rulers and to develop their cultures and languages.[4] Since the various Communist base areas in southern China had few minorities or none at all, this first official statement on minorities might appear as an empty promise. It is true that the promised right to secession was never fulfilled. When a few years later the CCP Central Committee arrived in northern China and worked among appreciable numbers of Mongols and Moslems, they quietly dropped all mention of this promise and gradually replaced it with an insistence on China's territorial integrity. The CCP eventually did redeem its pledges to overthrow the traditional minority leaders and to cultivate the cultures of minority peoples.

These promises—especially the one of the right of secession—should be placed within the national political context of the time. The Communists were, of course, determined to overthrow the Kuomintang and they used every possible means to reach that goal. One such means was to sow discord between the Kuomintang and the minorities by making promises which the Communists knew the Kuomintang was unwilling or unable to make and, in the case of secession, the Communists themselves later proved equally unwilling to grant.

Soon after the Communists started their several Long Marches from the South to the North in the early 1930s, they learned to appreciate

[4] Schwarz, p. 49.

the importance of minorities. On several occasions, timely and successful negotiations with certain tribes enabled Communist forces to shake
off pursuing government troops. After these various encounters with
minorities, the Communist leadership probably concluded that the
importance of the minorities transcended their small share of the total
population. In addition, the Communists recruited minority peoples
into the Party during the Long Marches who subsequently played
major roles in the liberation of their areas after 1949.

This appreciation was deepened when the war against Japan broke
out in 1937. The Japanese had succeeded in obtaining allies among
the Mongols, whom they organized into military units and sent
against Communist and other Chinese forces. Two of the Communist
base areas had some Mongol communities, and it was, therefore, essential for the Communists to keep their loyalty. The result was the
gradual evolution during the war of a comprehensive nationalities
policy which in its essentials has remained in force to this day. Minorities were given the right to govern themselves at the village level.
They were given preferential treatment in elections, and minority-
affairs committees were established at various levels of government.
Their arts, religions, languages, and literatures received official encouragement, temples were built and refurbished, and special schools
for minorities were opened. This series of policies culminated in 1947
when the first large autonomous area was established in Inner Mongolia.

The Hopeful 1950s

The particular circumstances which brought the Communists in close
contact with some minorities before 1949 undoubtedly constituted
one important reason for the further evolution of minorities policies
after 1949. Specifically, strategic considerations continued to impel
the Communists to pay close attention to minorities. The Western
half of the country, where most minorities live, became extremely
important for China's economic development. Oil, lead, tungsten,
uranium, and many other important minerals are located there. Minority areas, especially those in the West, took on added political and
military strategic importance as relations with India and the Soviet
Union worsened. These factors, combined with poor transportation
links to core China, historically strained relations between Han and

non-Han, and in some areas continued close links between minorities in China with people living in neighboring countries no longer friendly, were the primary forces behind China's active and extensive concern with its minorities.

The Soviet model shaped China's treatment of its minorities to a lesser degree than is usually thought. Certainly, both countries have designated many autonomous areas and have pursued similar cultural policies toward their minorities. One cannot deny that the Chinese imitated specific Soviet administrative and cultural policies. The basic reasons for this similarity, however, are not so much political and ideological affinity as they are somewhat similar circumstances—geographical, political, cultural—of minorities relative to the governing elites of the two countries. The Chinese Communists, in short, would have treated their minorities quite differently from the Soviets, had any one of the factors mentioned earlier differed greatly from the Soviet experience.

China's policies toward minorities have been applied in two broad fields, the administrative and the cultural. Some fifty-four groups have so far been designated as minorities, most of them during the first half of the 1950s. Thirty-six minorities have been given some ninety-eight autonomous areas at the provincial, intermediate, and county levels. An autonomous area is usually named after a single minority, such as the Nukiang Lisu Autonomous Chou in Yunnan. With a few exceptions, this designation merely means that there is a predominant minority in the area. Sixteen areas, where no single minority clearly predominates, are named after two or more minorities, like the Haihsi Mongol-Tibetan-Kazakh Autonomous Chou in Tsinghai. Three autonomous counties have such a complex ethnic-linguistic composition that they have been designated *kotsu* (various minorities) areas.

The state constitution of 1954 specified the following administrative rights of minority areas: proportional representation in congresses and governments, management of finances, organization of public security forces, and the formulation of statutes governing the exercise of autonomy. All of these rights, however, are subordinate to national programs, laws, regulations, and organizations. Moreover, these severely curtailed rights are exercised by a government structure which, in turn, is wholly subject to the Party, where any special consideration for minorities is categorically denied.

The cultural policies toward minorities consist of the creation or modification of written languages; the preservation and use of native traditions, customs, and religious beliefs; and the use of native languages in official business such as governmental meetings and court proceedings.

The leadership applied its minorities policies slowly and cautiously. It began by sending relief teams into minority areas in the early 1950s, giving food, medical aid, and political education. At the same time, it eased the tax burden and reversed the price structure, making local produce more expensive and manufactured goods cheaper. Most significantly, the leadership also ordered the Academy of Sciences to undertake extensive research of the languages, customs, and habits as well as the geological and other natural features of minority areas.

These measures supposedly produced quick results. As early as 1951, Chou En-lai reported sharp increases in the number of hospitals, schools, and students among minorities. These figures continued to rise sharply throughout the 1950s. It is impossible to determine exactly how much progress these figures really represented, but the leadership probably did its best during most of that decade to improve the life of most minorities and did succeed in several instances.

Yet the probable rise in living standards became less and less the criterion by which minorities and the leadership measured the success of the minorities policies. As in the past, the relationship between the Han and non-Han claimed attention toward the end of the 1950s. By 1957, it had become so urgent that discussions of material improvement received only secondary attention. Instead, officials increasingly condemned ta-Han chu-yi (Han chauvinism) which manifested itself in such practices as the Han peremptorily taking over leadership positions in minority areas instead of working through local minority officials, in discriminating against minorities in the hiring and promotion of personnel, and in the allocation of resources. Chief blame was placed upon an admittedly widespread attitude among the Han that they were more advanced in all fields of human endeavor.

This official denunciation of Han chauvinism was remarkable for two reasons. It was the first time in modern Chinese history that a Chinese government actively denounced a practice as old as Chinese history. Second, the leadership turned against Han chauvinism at a time when some minorities resisted the reimposition of central control. The Communists meted out cruel retribution against rebels in

some cases, but in others they were exceedingly patient and conciliatory.

The leadership's conciliatory policy toward minorities in the early
1950s, like its relative neglect of them later, can be fully understood
only in the context of China's national conditions and policies. Internal conditions were good in the early 1950s. Extensive land reform
had been carried out without a major setback in its timetable. The
economy was being rapidly rebuilt and expanded, and the rampant
inflation was brought under control. External conditions were equally
good. The war in Korea was stalemated away from China's frontiers,
and no other threat was in the offing. The Soviet Union began to aid
China with loans, technicians, and machinery and may have raised
expectations in Peking for much increased aid in the future. In this
context, occasional resistance and continued friction were seen in Peking as relatively minor disturbances. The leadership needed harmony
to get the raw materials, essential for the success of the First Five Year
Plan, which were located in the minority areas. It thought that harmony could best be obtained by blaming Han chauvinism for these disturbances and by actively implementing a policy of some administrative
and cultural autonomy.

By 1957, however, the leadership's optimism began to flag. The
limitation of space permits listing only a few of the major factors
accounting for this crucial change. The First Five Year Plan had succeeded in purely material terms, but some leaders, primarily Mao Tse-
tung, had noted as early as 1955 many imbalances and tensions in
the society. The single-minded concentration on heavy industry had
been obtained at a price that at least some leaders considered excessive.
Specifically, the rapid growth in heavy industry had been underwrit-
ten largely by maximum agricultural exploitation and by aid from the
Soviet Union. But it became increasingly unlikely that Soviet aid
would grow sharply to sustain further rapid industrialization during
the Second Five Year Plan. Nor did it appear that much more could
be squeezed out of agriculture in the immediate future. By the mid-
1950s, agricultural increases began to level off and barely kept pace
with population increases.

Yet China had little choice but to expand agricultural production.
In the early 1950s, the minority areas had been exempted from the
series of agricultural reorganization schemes. Moreover, the vast
herding lands remained largely untouched by the plough. The leadership removed this exemption around 1957 and thus inevitably soured

its reasonably good relations with the minorities. Unfortunately, this change in policy came at a time when several years of massive migrations of Han into minority areas had already led to a rising tide of mutual recrimination and discrimination. The short-lived Hundred Flowers period of relatively free criticism unleashed an avalanche of sharp attacks by minorities against virtually everything Chinese, including the CCP itself.

The leadership was thus caught between the necessity of greatly increasing agricultural production and the desire to respond to the minorities' denunciation of Han chauvinism. The solution, if that is the proper word for it, was the forceful and often forcible conversion of grazing lands into farm land and the simultaneous shift of official opprobrium from Han chauvinism to local nationalism. Officials, both Han and non-Han, in minority areas were fired and several pillars of the policy of regional autonomy were obliterated.

The Integrative Period

Since 1958, the official policy has been *gleichschaltung* of the minorities to the Chinese in several fields. First, when the rural communes were unveiled in August 1958, they were ordered established everywhere in China, including most minority areas. Second, the leadership now claimed that the Han were more advanced in all fields, a claim which only a short time earlier the same leadership had denounced as Han chauvinism. Third, earlier concessions such as the exemption from the national marriage law were withdrawn. Fourth, the cultural policy was changed in two important respects. Courses in the Chinese language and instruction in subjects using Chinese had been introduced in higher grades or had been absent altogether, but they were now introduced in the lower grades of most minority schools. In literature, minorities had been permitted to use native forms and to place their subject matter, although increasingly socialist in nature, in native settings. By the end of the 1950s, native forms had almost disappeared and content had become virtually indistinguishable from contemporaneous publications in the Han region.

At the same time, Han migration into minority areas has continued. In the virtual absence of firm statistics, a reasonable guess would be 3 to 5 million additional Han migrants since the early 1960s. They have come from all walks of life. Many of them are farmers sent to Tsinghai, Sinkiang, and Inner Mongolia to convert pastures into fields. Others are workers to man new factories set up in minority areas. Still others are engaged in land reclamation. Finally, Han migrants have come to dominate most major administrative centers where they are in charge of Party, government, economic, and cultural institutions.

Tibet and Sinkiang provide the most dramatic examples of the worsening relations between Han and non-Han. Of all the minority areas, Tibet had enjoyed the highest degree of autonomy during much of the 1950s, and this autonomy was guaranteed in a unique agreement between Peking and the theocratic government of the Dalai Lama, who had considered Tibet an independent country. Yet, in 1959 Tibet became the worst oppressed minority area when the Chinese army ruthlessly suppressed demonstrations in Lhasa on behalf of the Dalai Lama, who then fled to India. For several years, many Tibetans, especially those in the eastern part of the region, continued to resist the army through guerrilla warfare. Although the causes for this quick and spectacular reversal of fortunes are extremely complex and far from fully known, it appears that they had much to do with Peking's growing uneasiness about the international situation in the late 1950s. The leadership had convinced itself that the Tibetan local government was conspiring with certain foreign powers against China. Another important cause of the Tibetan debacle was Peking's growing impatience with what it considered deliberately slow reform measures by the Dalai Lama's regime.

The situation in Sinkiang was rather different. Sinkiang was never an ethnic or cultural unit, and no responsible person there considered Sinkiang an independent country. Still, some minorities, notably the Kazakhs, had sought autonomy shortly before the Communist takeover. After 1949, the Chinese army had to be called out several times to crush rebellions in various parts of the region. When relations with the Soviet Union grew strained at the end of the 1950s, Peking's position in Sinkiang became precarious. Several minorities, including the Kazakhs, Kirghiz, Uzbek, and Tajik, live on both sides of the border. Moreover, since at least the 1930s, Soviet influence was pervasive throughout Sinkiang. As late as 1955, Soviet troops were stationed there, several so-called joint-stock companies were in fact run by and for the benefit of the Soviet economy, and Soviet mobile stores continued to supply the population with consumer goods. When the minorities began to resist Peking's attempt at *gleichschaltung*, the Soviets, so the Chinese claim, encouraged the minorities. At any rate, it is known that in 1961 and 1962, several hundred thousand minorities fled across the border. The Soviet Union also began to beam radio programs toward Sinkiang that were conducted in languages spoken on both sides of the border and aimed at fomenting further unrest in Sinkiang.

The latest and clearest example of a harsher policy toward minorities was the dismemberment of the oldest autonomous area, Inner Mongolia. Sometime during the Cultural Revolution, that region's size was cut in half and its territories awarded to the primarily ethnic Han provinces of Kansu, Heilungkiang, Kirin, Liaoning, and Hopeh, and the Ningsia Hui Autonomous Region.[5] The action may have been in retaliation against renewed sentiments for Mongol independence. The Maoist group made this charge during the height of the Cultural Revolution, but it is not convincing. Closer to the truth is the speculation that the Chinese leadership became increasingly worried about its border security as relations with the Soviet Union and its client state Mongolia plummeted. It is entirely possible that by assigning the western and northern portions of Inner Mongolia to ethnically Han provinces (and, more to the point, to wholly Han military commands), China's border security may have been psychologically if not materially improved.

As the leadership hardened its policy toward minorities, it also began to say and do less about them. There have been quite a few reports from various minority areas since 1958 and occasional statements concerning all minorities. The latter, however, have been platitudinous and perfunctory. Perhaps the best illustration of the declining attention to minorities is a comparison between the state constitution of 1954 and the one drafted in 1970. The former devoted eight articles and a section of its preamble to minorities, the latter only one article.[6]

There can be little doubt that various changes in China's domestic and international situation have deeply affected the shift in the treatment of minorities. But it would be a mistake to assume, as some have done, that such changes have been the most important factors. Of equal importance are the changes within the minorities themselves, particularly in individuals. Given the great diversity among the fifty-

---

[5] *Chung-hua jen-min kung-ho-kuo ti-t'u* (Map of the People's Republic of China), 6th ed., December 1971.

[6] Schwarz, pp. 82-84; "Revised Draft of the 'Constitution of the People's Republic of China,'" *Issues and Studies* 7 (December 1970), pp. 89-93.

four officially recognized minorities and the virtual impossibility of accurately gauging such subtle psychological phenomena as personal attitudes and motivations, it would be hazardous to generalize. Nevertheless, there is some information about changes within the more numerous minorities such as the Uighurs, Mongols, and Tibetans that may serve as the basis for some provisional observations.

It may be assumed that most people who held privileged positions before 1949 and lost them were least friendly to the new regime. Odd as it may seem, however, earlier antagonisms often gave way to cooperation. Among the many possible reasons for this change were age and children. Most men mellow with age, especially in a new state where their children grow up with adequate health care and schooling and advance in the society. Serfs, slaves, and others who had been disadvantaged before 1949 were naturally among the most enthusiastic followers of the Chinese Communists as the latter raised their social and political positions.

Most significant, however, was the growing segment of the minority population that had no personal recollection of life before 1949. Like youth elsewhere, young members of minority groups turned their backs on their parents. They may also have sensed that, regardless of their own feelings at the moment, the path to success no longer lay in a separate minority culture but in the larger context of China. They felt, for example, little attachment to traditional literary forms while they knew that a firm command of Chinese was an absolute prerequisite for advancement. As they became proficient in Chinese, these young people gained more access to the mainstream of Chinese informational media which, in turn, molded them into Chinese citizens.

If these observations have any merit at all, they help one to understand better the changes in the treatment of minorities during the past decade. The elimination of earlier privileges and exemptions can be seen not only as a reaction to changes in the political and diplomatic position of China but as a consequence of voluntary sinification on the part of an increasing number of minorities. As astute students of China's history, the leaders must know that in the short span of two decades, they have accomplished more in the treatment of minorities than any dynasty had. But they probably know also that in one crucial aspect they must do better than the best leaders of Han and T'ang and lead the way toward full integration and equality.

Does the Chinese treatment of minorities have any lessons for the United States? The answer must be in the negative. China's minorities are wholly different from any of America's present-day minorities. Nor were the Indians of the nineteenth century and their treatment by the dominant whites comparable to the situation in China today. China has had relations with its minorities for many centuries and, in some major cases, for over two millenia. No minority, not even those who were able to conquer parts or all of China, ever doubted China's position as the cultural and civilizational center of the world. At one time or another, China had physical possession of every minority area now lying within the People's Republic of China, and from the mideighteenth century until 1949, all Chinese governments either had or claimed to have sovereignty over all present-day minorities in China. In other words, the Communist leadership's problem has never been the conquest of an open frontier but the full integration of minorities who had always been under China's civilizational if not political influence.

The Chinese Mirror

FREDERIC WAKEMAN, JR.

Once, during his long eighteenth-century reign, Louis XV asked a favorite minister how to improve the affairs of his realm. "Sire," he was told, "you must innoculate the French with the public spirit of the Chinese." At that time Confucian China seemed to embody many of the positive values which Europeans felt they lacked. As François Quesnay expressed it, the country was "the most beautiful in the world, the most densely populated, and the most flourishing kingdom known."[1]

First of all China was a physiocratic utopia. Because Confucianists recognized agriculture as the economic foundation of the state, they ranked farmers far above artisans or merchants, encouraged only a limited degree of domestic commerce, and kept China in a state of autarky by prohibiting foreign trade in mercantile frivolities. Second, China's enlightened despotism was based on virtue. "The legislators of China," wrote Montesquieu, "confounded their religion, laws, manners and customs; all these were morality, all these were virtue. The precepts relating to these four points were what they called rites; and it was in the exact observance of these that the Chinese government triumphed."[2] To François Quesnay, therefore, the Chinese emperor contrasted sharply with European sovereigns whose lack of concern

[1] François Quesnay, *Despotism in China*, trans. Lewis A. Maverick (San Antonio: Paul Anderson, 1946), p. 165.
[2] Montesquieu, *The Spirit of the Laws*, trans. Thomas Nugent (New York: Hafner Publishing Co., 1949), p. 301.

for virtue made them unwilling to accept criticism from their subjects. Third, China was a meritocracy. A man's rank was determined by his capability, which was not measured in terms of martial skill or technological expertise, but rather by the degree of his learning. In this empire of mandarins, scholars remonstrated with the monarch, the humblest peasant could receive a public education, and the most illustrious family in the kingdom was descended from Confucius. Finally, the Chinese were rational humanists, worshipping a deistic *t'ien* (heaven) without idolatry, placing man at the center of a perfectly ordered universe. Such a perfect natural religion, argued Leibnitz, should be taught to the rest of the world.

These Enlightenment characteristics of Confucian China had been derived from the writings of Jesuit fathers serving the emperor in Peking. Although their descriptions were based on social realities such as the examination system, the Jesuits sometimes represented Confucian ideals more accurately than existing conditions. But the Chinese were not foisting an illusion upon gullible Europeans. Both sides had an interest in this ideal projection, since the *philosophes* had universal aspirations of their own. If there had been no China, Voltaire would have been forced to invent one. China was often conceived to suit the observer, becoming a pawn in European political debates. When Lord Chesterfield extolled the Chinese civil service system during the 1630s, he was really protesting the corrupt patronage of Walpole; and when Voltaire insisted in his essay *On Confucius* that China was fortunately spared superstition, he was actually attacking the power of the church. On the other hand, Montesquieu's claim that Chinese despotism was arbitrary and capricious was intended to show that only institutions, not rites or norms, could check tyranny.

Criticism overcame praise when some European values altered during the French Revolution and the Industrial Revolution. China's former virtues appeared to become defects. Then, too, the Europeans' perspective of China shifted from the mannered court of Peking to the busy trading port of Canton. The meritocracy now seemed to be composed either of corrupt customs officials or of effeminate literati who spent all their time memorizing irrelevant classics. Enlightened emperors appeared to be oriental despots, applying barbaric tortures to kowtowing sycophants. Portraits of deistic humanists like Confucius or Chu Hsi were supplanted by images of Chinese joss houses and opium-smoking coolies. All that China had offered the West seemed to have been simple inventions like gunpowder, the compass, or paper.

In short, the universality of Chinese civilization was regarded as hopelessly particularistic, doomed to obscurantism until Westerners could bring it enlightenment.

The technological superiority of foreign military power slowly forced China to acknowledge this judgment as well. At first its officials attributed England's victory in the Opium War (1839-42) to better weapons which could be imported to defend the universal *Tao* (Way) of civilization. Even when further defeats shook China's assumption of civilized superiority, the Chinese scholars were loath to relinquish their culture's claim to the leadership of mankind. Westernized scholars like the translator Wang T'ao realized that the Chinese world order was shattered, but still maintained their belief that China could forge a new and peaceful *Tao* for the warring states of Europe. That same sense of mission suffused the utopianism of K'ang Yu-wei, the philosopher who led the unsuccessful reform movement of 1898. K'ang's unitary vision of a future global community reserved the Chinese their place in a new universal scheme of world history, in which mankind together overcame the failings of any particular race. "Do [Greeks, Indians, and Frenchmen] progress?—then I progress with them; do they retrogress?—then I retrogress with them," he insisted, proposing China's responsibility to humanity.[3]

But at the same time Germans, Japanese, and Englishmen were, in the words of the day, carving up China like a ripe melon. The imperialist scramble for concessions belied K'ang's faith in world harmony and made doctrines like Social Darwinism much more current among the Chinese. Even so, the Confucian aspiration for universality lingered on until the eve of the 1911 revolution. Technocrats were already replacing humanists, and military skills counted for more than classical literacy, but some imperial bureaucrats argued to the very end that the eternal substance (*t'i*) of Chinese civilization could be preserved with Western techniques (*yung*).

When Confucian political values were finally abandoned, there was still not an absolute break with the past. Traditional attitudes toward man and nature continued to shape the actual forms which Social Darwinism, liberalism, and radical criticism took in China during the early 1900s. But to contemporary iconoclasts, the past was being rejected altogether. The virtue which Montesquieu had ambivalently ad-

---

[3] K'ang Yu-wei, *Ta-t'ung shu* (The Book of Great Harmony), pp. 3-4, cited by Kung-chuan Hsiao, "In and out of Utopia: K'ang Yu-wei's Social Thought," *Chung Chi Journal* 7 (May 1968), 102.

mired was now seen to be an ideological mask for the patriarchal tyranny of family and monarchy—self-supporting atavisms that trammeled the individual and weakened the nation. As a concept of universal struggle and national competition replaced the former ideal of harmony and world civilization, radical intellectuals searched for new values to combat the "tyranny of Confucian superstition." Two of these—democracy and science—had, by the middle of World War I, become fundamental postulates for many Chinese intellectuals. Personified by Ch'en Tu-hsiu in his journal *New Youth*, "Mr. Democracy and Mr. Science" were related to an "all-pervasive, eternal and inevitable" structure of natural law. Man-made law (religion and ethics), on the other hand, was partial and temporary. "Therefore, the future evolution and progress of mankind must be based on the budding science of today; we must seek gradually to improve man-made laws so that they conform with the results of natural laws. Only when this is done can life and the universe be in perfect union."[4] China had somehow fallen out of step with the scientific laws of nature. The rise of the West was accounted for by its discovery of those laws. Now that the Chinese were conscious of the discrepancy between their traditional culture and universal principles like science or democracy, they could replace their irrational Confucian ethics with a rationally determined social system that would restore China to its place in the world.

But would that be sufficient to recover cultural esteem? China had once defined the *Tao* of civilization; now it had to live by someone else's rules. Ch'en Tu-hsiu seems to have adopted the West's scientism without much difficulty, but other members of his generation were troubled by the choice between personal attachment to their "irrational" past and a presumably universal world view which was partly a Western invention. Some tried to give China a special claim of its own to this new universality by seeking prototypes of science and democracy in their own past. Other traditionalistic thinkers broke sharply with the iconoclasts by insisting that China possessed a unique national essence which had to be preserved if the culture was to survive at all. In either case, uneasiness with Western values may explain why some Chinese intellectuals turned sharply away from science and democracy after World War I.

This was not, however, the sole reason for the reaction against posi-

[4] Ch'en Tu-hsiu, *Hsin ch'ing-nien* (New Youth), 2, no. 5 (1917), 1, cited by D.W.Y. Kwok, *Scientism in Chinese Thought, 1900-1950* (New Haven: Yale University Press, 1965), pp. 76-77.

tivism and liberalism after 1920. The brutality of the European war contradicted the sunny optimism of scientism. Man's conquest of nature and belief in material progress seemed to have been twisted into an obsession with inhuman machines and selfish gain. Searching for spiritual values, Chinese of a more conservative bent rejected Western materialism in favor of Asian idealism. During the 1920s philosophers like Liang Sou-ming insisted that members of the May Fourth Movement of 1919 had adopted materialism so avidly that China's humanist legacy of spiritualism and harmoniousness with nature had been overlooked. Not only that; May Fourth thinkers had been too eager to emulate the West, and so failed to realize that Asian idealism was better suited than European materialism to save mankind from itself.

World War II reinforced the opinion that scientific materialism had destroyed the nineteenth-century political world. "A new world," argued Lin Yutang in his widely read Modern Library edition of *The Wisdom of China and India*, "must be forged out of the elements of Anglo-Saxon, Russian and Oriental cultures."[5] Traditional China's neglect of systematic and scientific speculation had once been thought a major disadvantage. Now it seemed a positive virtue. Mysticism and spiritualism even likened Confucian civilization to the more advanced elements of Western culture, creating a new claim to universality for the Chinese. "The nineteenth-century shallow rationalism naively believed that the question 'What is a blade of grass?' could be answered adequately by considering the blade of grass as a purely mechanical phenomenon. The contemporary scientific attitude is that it cannot. Since Walt Whitman asked that question with his profound mysticism, no one has been able to answer it, and no scientist will presume to answer it today. And let us remember, in that mysticism and distrust of the mechanistic view of the universe, Walt Whitman is Chinese."[6]

Partly because popular writers like Lin Yutang depicted China in this way to English-language readers, and partly because Westerners themselves questioned scientism after World War I, a new image of the Chinese was gradually formed. Quesnay had admired the Chinese for their utilitarianism. They were, he said, "actuated by a desire for

[5] Lin Yutang, ed., *The Wisdom of China and India* (New York: Random House, 1942), p. 567.
[6] Ibid., pp. 567-68.

gain. . . . Their principal study turns in the direction of the more useful sciences."[7] But by the 1920s precisely the opposite quality appealed to philosophizers like J.W.T. Mason. For them the Chinese were spiritual aesthetes, careless of gain and admirably heedless of utility. "Even in her vices," Mason wrote in an uncalculated insult, "China shows a delicacy of aesthetic discernment which the western world is incompetent to follow. The frequent coarseness of utilitarian methods of accomplishment causes western vice to take coarse forms, while the delicacy of the Chinese aesthetic life results in vice evolving in keeping with its environment. One may compare the stimulus of opium smoking in China with the frequently gross consequences of alcoholic intoxication in the West."[8]

Republican liberalism was another fatality of World War I and of the rise of warlordism in China. Ch'en Tu-hsiu's "Mr. Democracy" gave way to the Chinese Communist Party which Ch'en helped found. The war itself, as Li Ta-chao proclaimed in November 1918, represented not the victory of Wilsonian democracy, but rather the triumph of Bolshevism in Russia. "The victory over German militarism does not belong to the Allied nations. . . . It is the victory of humanitarianism, of pacificism. . . . It is the victory of Bolshevism."[9] According to Li (who strongly influenced Mao Tse-tung), the Bolshevik Revolution signaled a new historical era in which the world's most backward areas—Russia and Asia—would take a leading role. This did not restore to China its role as a static model for the West, but it did satisfy universalist yearnings by dividing the world into two conflicting social systems, one of which was validly occupied by the Chinese. Through the dialectic of world history, what had been seen as backwardness now promised progress—the latter becoming a new universal principle which inspired Chinese Marxists to believe that the future was ultimately theirs.

This analysis is not meant to imply that Marxists owed their success in China solely to an antidemocratic, antiscientific public mood. In spite of the nondemocratic definition of freedom in classical Marxism, democracy remained a fundamental ideal for Chinese Communists, whether it was embodied in Mao's "New Democracy" of the 1940s, or

[7] Quesnay, p. 190.

[8] J.W.T. Mason, *The Creative East* (London: John Murray, 1928), p. 65.

[9] Li Ta-chao, *Li Ta-chao hsüan-chi* (Selected Works of Li Ta-chao), p. 113, cited by Ssu-yü Teng and John K. Fairbank, eds., *China's Response to the West* (New York: Atheneum, 1965), p. 246.

in the egalitarianism of the Cultural Revolution. Scientism, too, remained an article of faith, especially since part of Marxism's appeal was its claim to scientific materialism. In that sense, more of Engels than of Marx was absorbed by Chinese Communist leaders, who believed along with Mao Tse-tung that "the history of science furnishes man with proof of the material nature of the world and of the fact that it is governed by laws and helps man to see the futility of the illusions of religion and idealism and to arrive at materialist conclusions."[10]

But the scientific claims of what has often been called vulgar Marxism posed other problems for the Chinese. Was their case compatible with Karl Marx's historical predictions? Did faith in the universality of Marxism mean proving China's correspondence with the iron laws of historical materialism? The Chinese Revolution, won in the countryside with a peasant army, did not at first seem to tally with the canonical Marxist notion of revolution. Nor, after the establishment of the People's Republic, did the transformation of the means of production always coincide with Lenin's industrial prescription for socialism. Besides, China's central place in the world was not guaranteed by merely illustrating Marxist verities. At least in Mao Tse-tung's view, China had to make a more positive and fundamental contribution of its own. Accordingly, his rise to power within the Communist Party was accompanied by the claim that he alone had been wise enough to adapt the abstract theory of Marxism to the real circumstances of the Chinese setting. Mao, in other words, had sinified Marxism.

Mao's sinification of Marxism established a broad Chinese claim to historical significance at two different levels. In a particular sense, the Chinese Revolution was held up as a model war of national liberation which other semicolonial and colonial areas of the world could emulate. At a theoretical level, Mao's adaptation of abstract principles to actual conditions was said to have further developed the original Marxian theory of practice. *Praxis* was obviously not a Chinese formulation alone; the relationship between theory and practice was imbedded in the very core of classical Marxism. Whether expressed as the contradiction between abstract laws and concrete circumstances, or as the dialectic between historical determinism and free will, theory and practice had to be combined if thinkers were to change—not just

[10] Mao Tse-tung, "Dialectical Materialism," cited by Stuart R. Schram, *The Political Thought of Mao Tse-tung*, rev. ed. (New York: Praeger, 1969), p. 124.

analyze—the world. Mao's formulation, however, was much less abstract. Theory as such, theory in the void, was useless scholasticism. Even scientific Marxism—in Mao's words—was nothing more than animal excrement if it was not used to make a revolution. Intellectuals, he told new members of the Party during the rectification campaign of 1940-42, lovingly stroke the arrow of theoretical Marxism, but they must not forget that the arrow is useless unless it finds a target.

By emphasizing the instrumentality of Marxism, Mao Tse-tung tried to create a revolutionary methodology with general applicability elsewhere. Because the Chinese Revolution had successfully brought the abstract and the concrete together in its own history, it deserved to be a model for the entire world. To be sure, such a claim would be rejected by the Soviet Union (where Maoism is not even accepted by intellectual dissidents), but it did become current in other parts of the West. Recently, for instance, an American historian wrote, "The Chinese revolution offers inspiration not only to those who would expel colonial oppressors. Nor is its message limited to new nations striving to overcome poverty, economic stagnation, and domination by the industrialized metropolitan powers. It addresses men and women everywhere who seek to create a society free from stifling oppression, arbitrary state power, and enslaving technology."[11]

Once again, it would seem, China has become a kind of mirror for the West, reflecting its projections in verso on a background of China's own creation. For some European Marxists, in fact, China has become as much of a pawn in theoretical debates as it was earlier for the *philosophes.* Structural Marxists like Louis Althusser have cited Mao's exemplary pragmatism to resolve some of the contradictions surrounding the problem of false consciousness, while neo-Hegelian Marxists use Chinese peasant consciousness to refute arguments that the workers' *embourgeoisement* makes revolution seem hopeless in the capitalist West. On the other hand, Marxist positivists can just as easily see Maoism as "the cult of backward countries . . . the cult of primitivism combined with the belief in the revival of mankind through its least developed segments."[12]

But China is not simply a blank screen for the images of others. The Cultural Revolution and a diplomatic détente have upset the precon-

[11] Mark Selden, *The Yenan Way in Revolutionary China* (Cambridge: Harvard University Press, 1971), p. viii.

[12] Lesek Kolakowski, "Intellectuals Against Intellect," *Daedalus* 101 (Summer 1972), 12.

ceptions of even the best informed observer. Visitors return from China daily, with perhaps more knowledge about conditions there than Enlightenment admirers possessed. Because there is an empirical reality behind the images, one must attempt to see how instructive China's principles of social organization, economic rationality, and political formation are for the rest of the world. But even though these principles may have practical relevance for the present, it is difficult to disassociate them from their national context. Indeed, it is the combination of a *soi-disant* universal Marxist system and a particularly tenacious political culture of its own that makes Maoist China of such great theoretical interest to social scientists.

The People's Republic, for instance, may adamantly reject its Confucian past but it is still deeply influenced by that old order. Four examples from what could easily be a long list of such influences immediately come to mind. First is the memory of the dynastic cycle, which has certainly inspired some of the Maoist fears of revolutionary retrogression and revisionism. The concern for the republic's mortality has been widely felt. Mao's own opponents at the Lushan Plenum in 1959 critically compared his rule with the despotic and short-lived Ch'in dynasty, while Marshal Lin Piao later illustrated the danger of capitalist revisionism with many examples drawn from the vicissitudes of imperial history.

A second disposition from the past is evident in the recurring Maoist emphasis on ideology rather than on technical expertise. Scholars have often related this bias to the Confucian elevation of the ethical generalist over the professional specialist. To be sure, historians are now arguing that there were many more bureaucratic specialists in imperial China than the usual image of the well-rounded literatus admits; but there certainly is a similarity between the Confucian ideal of sincerity of motive in public service, and the Maoist emphasis on the sincerity of proletarian consciousness in the cause of revolution.

Populism is another inherited element, despite significant differences between imperial and revolutionary versions. Confucian populism was mainly symbolic: emperors ruled for the sake of an abstract people whose revolts were simply omens of cosmic disorder. Modern populists took legitimacy away from heaven to bestow it upon the people, whose spontaneity—at least in Mao's thought—deserved the fullest trust. Both kinds of populism, however, placed enormous faith in the capacity of the masses, once aroused, to perform superhuman tasks.

A final example is the extraordinary moralism of Chinese Communism. Mao's faith in the capacity of exemplary revolutionary virtue to educate even the worst revisionist has meant that even in the bitterest conflict, the victor does not normally exact the ultimate toll. Mao has repeatedly said that one must not kill the patient to cure the illness. Like Confucianists, Chinese Communists believe in moral redemption through self-examination. And, like many imperial statesmen, Mao relies on norms as much as on institutions to regulate society.

These similarities between an ideally serene Confucian empire and revolutionary China are not actual historical continuities. High Ch'ing and the People's Republic are separated by a century of radical social change, so that one could as easily point to countervalues as to identities: the masses rather than the individual, antibureaucratism rather than bureaucratism, struggle rather than harmony, and so forth. What the traditional influences do suggest is really only a truism: particular cultural elements continue to shape the actual contours of the Maoist model. These national particularities do not necessarily prevent the model from being transplanted in whole or in part, especially since it is Mao's concrete method that constitutes the nonspecific universality of Chinese Marxism. However, the West cannot afford to ignore entirely the historicity of Chinese Communism, and it should resist the temptation once again to transform China into its mirror.

This essay began with a list of four of the characteristics which Enlightenment thinkers perceived in China. Although China is far from timeless and Westerners have abandoned many of their own universalist pretensions, some of these characteristics oddly persist in different guises even today. The physiocratic element, for example, has partly been resurrected by post-Rostowian economists who now perceive certain kinds of "underdevelopment" as a positive virtue. Given the growing gap between metropolitan economies and the Third World, the prevalence of diseconomies, and the regulated flow of global resources, it would seem that parts of the world have little hope of catching up with the heavily industrialized countries on the latter's terms. By trying to develop according to a capitalist or Soviet Russian model, agroeconomies may be condemning themselves to continual poverty and economic exploitation. With the benefit of this hindsight, China can now be seen to have made a correct choice by refusing to depend on capital investment alone. Its relative autarky thus appears an advantage, particularly since Coca Cola franchises and consumer goods can be likened to Quesnay's mercantile frivolities. Praise of China's efforts to unite countryside and city by deurbanizing also suggests the physiocratic image of China as a nation of industrious husbandmen, resisting the blandishments of international hucksters.

China is even sometimes viewed as the land of virtue, rather than of institutions or laws, although such an outlook is evidently less in reaction to Montesquieu than to Weberian sociology, which assumes growing political and economic rationalization throughout the world. Maoist China challenges the inevitability of that rationalization, whether as a form of growing allocative complexity (Eisenstadt) or as party bureaucratization (Michels). It accomplishes this—much as it did for Louis XV's minister—by repeated "innoculations of public spirit," or what sociologists would still call normative methods. However, given the tendency of socialist revolutionaries to become party bureaucrats, thereby creating Djilas's "new class" with a real interest in preserving allocative powers for itself, some decisive figure is needed at the top of society to inspire permanent revolution. In this context, Mao has occasionally been cast in the *deus ex machina* role of an enlightened despot by observers who share his abhorrence of selfish technocrats and self-seeking bureaucrats.

Meritocracy and humanism, the third and fourth characteristics of the Enlightenment image of China, have obviously altered dramatically. But, with a twist, they still reflect the projections of outsiders. The People's Republic certainly recognizes merit, but it attacks the elitist connotations of a meritocracy in which the successful are rewarded with high status. The attack on bourgeois authorities within the universities and the replacement of entrance examinations with certificates of proletarian merit during the Cultural Revolution were designed to prevent the emergence of such a meritocratic elite. Of course, so extreme an egalitarianism not only distinguishes Communist China from almost any other society one can imagine; it is also a sectarian quality which is usually overcome by the civil complications of governing a complex society. Furthermore, it requires a despotic leveling of the citizenry. To Western observers with a liberal intellectual temperament, this has been most visible in the attack on intellectual autonomy during the Cultural Revolution. But to other Westerners angered by the academic entrenchment of modern mandarins in their own countries, the same sort of leveling can obviously hold great appeal.

The same ambivalence affects Westerners' judgment of modern China's claim to humanism. If humanism is scholastically defined as the study of the humanities, the People's Republic evidently fails to qualify. But if the word encompasses a nonintellectual humanitarianism, then Maoism is probably more humanistic than any other form of statecraft. In fact, Confucianism's linkage of the individual's nature with kind is not so very far from Maoism's identification of mass man with the force of nature itself. Standing in the center of a constantly evolving universe, the Chinese people must wrest their livelihood from t'ien but that struggle likens them in Maoist imagery to cosmic tornados and tempests sweeping across the land. This is what some scholars have called Mao's voluntarism, his exuberant belief that men can overcome machines, that spirit prevails over matter, and that subject can sometimes determine object. Because such a voluntarism appeals to others who are alienated by technology, Maoist idealism is easily confused with an antimechanical primitivism. But Chinese Communism does not deny technology. Machines are still considered to be scientific instruments for man's socialist transformation. China is not a nation of Luddites.

The heuristic similarity between Enlightenment views of China and those of the West is not intended to suggest that the Chinese model is irrelevant elsewhere. Historicists can avoid the peril of crosscultural observation by grasping the humanist ideal of a thing studied for its own unique sake. But while historicism constitutes a valid approach, it can easily become too narrow, exiling the Chinese to a kingdom all their own where any claim to universality immediately loses respect. On the other hand, those who would like to abstract China from its historical context must constantly be aware of their own cultural assumptions and needs. This familiar appeal for self-awareness may sound avuncular, but the caveat deserves repeating because any effort to relate Chinese values to other modern societies poses a classic phenomenological problem. China and its observers see much of themselves in each other. The meeting point of their gazes creates an image as real as each particular society so that the Enlightenment's China genuinely existed. But to preserve the integrity of both subject and object, perceiver and perceived, the projections have to be tested constantly at both sources. Otherwise, each can easily become the mirror of the other's universal aspirations, and their particular reflections a willed distortion of the real.

Selected Bibliography

Barnett, A. Doak. *Cadres, Bureaucracy and Political Power in Communist China.* New York, Columbia University Press, 1967.

Donnithorne, Audrey. *China's Economic System.* New York, Praeger, 1967.

Hinton, William. *Fanshen: A Documentary of Revolution in a Chinese Village.* New York, Random House, 1968.

Horn, Joshua S. *Away with All Pests: An English Surgeon in People's China.* New York, Monthly Review Press, 1971.

Schram, Stuart. *Mao Tse-t'ung.* Baltimore, Penguin, 1966.

Schurmann, Franz. *Ideology and Organization in Communist China.* Berkeley, Center for Chinese Studies, University of California, 1968.

Schwartz, Benjamin. *Communism and China: Ideology in Flux.* Cambridge, Harvard University Press, 1968.

Selden, Mark. *The Yenan Way in Revolutionary China.* Cambridge, East Asian Series No. 62, Harvard University Press, 1971.

Solomon, Richard. *Mao's Revolution and the Chinese Political Culture.* University of California Press, 1971.

Vogel, Ezra. *Canton Under Communism: Programs and Politics in a Provincial Capital, 1949-1968.* Cambridge, East Asian Series No. 41, Harvard University Press, 1969.

Wheelwright, E. L. and Bruce McFarlane. *Chinese Road to Socialism: Economics of the Cultural Revolution.* New York, Monthly Review Press, 1970.

Whitson, William. *The Chinese High Command: A History of Communist Military Politics, 1927-71.* New York, Praeger, 1973.

Index